GLOBAL NORMS AND LOCAL COURTS

Global Norms and Local Courts

Translating 'the Rule of Law' in Bangladesh

TOBIAS BERGER

OXFORD
UNIVERSITY PRESS

OXFORD
UNIVERSITY PRESS

Great Clarendon Street, Oxford, OX2 6DP,
United Kingdom

Oxford University Press is a department of the University of Oxford. It furthers the University's objective of excellence in research, scholarship, and education by publishing worldwide. Oxford is a registered trade mark of Oxford University Press in the UK and in certain other countries

First Edition published in 2017

Published in the United States of America by Oxford University Press
198 Madison Avenue, New York, NY 10016, United States of America

British Library Cataloguing in Publication Data
Data available

Library of Congress Control Number: 2017941207

ISBN 978–0–19–880786–5

Acknowledgements

The ideas and arguments presented in this book developed in several different places and emerged out of many conversations; I would like to acknowledge some of the most important ones. Thomas Risse has taught me to pursue empirical research without getting trapped in disciplinary divides, falling into meta-theoretical trenches, or otherwise losing the ground under my feet. He has been an extraordinary supervisor for the thesis on which this book is based. So has Matthew Nelson, who has taught me how to ask big questions in small settings (like village courts); he has been an invaluable source of advice and inspiration for over a decade now. Shalini Randeria has been equally generous with both the amount of time and the depth of advice she has kindly offered; our long conversations in Berlin and Vienna have been essential for turning the thesis into a book.

The book initially started at the Berlin Graduate School for Transnational Studies, where I greatly benefited from discussions with Tanja Börzel, Markus Jachtenfuchs, Nico Krisch, and Michael Zürn, who all provided vital comments at the initial stages of the project. So did Anja Breljak, Anke Draude, Jana Hönke, Daniel Jacob, Matthias Kötter, Robert Lepenies, Jasmin Lorch, Kerstin Schulz, Stefan Skupien, Digdem Soyaltin, and Siddharth Tripathi. Important intellectual and moral support also came from the wider academic community in Berlin with the *Sonderforschungsbereich* 'Governance in Areas of Limited Statehood', the *Kolleg-Forschergruppe* 'the Transformative Power of Europe', and my colleagues at the Centre for Transnational Relations, Foreign, and Security Policy at the *Freie Universität* Berlin, especially Ingo Peters, Ursula Schröder, Anna Holzscheiter, Simon Koschut, and Matthias Ecker-Erhardt.

Many thanks also to Veronica Priefer for her enthusiastic support, Alexander Ziegler for his close reading of the empirical chapters, and Lena Rohrbach for her analytical clarity and precision. In and beyond Berlin, I also owe very special thanks to Carmen Brandt, Lisa Fink, and Franziska Korn for the many long and incisive exchanges about Bangladeshi politics, to Malte Frøslee Ibsen for wide-ranging discussions about (global) injustice, to Matteo Garavoglia for never growing tired of explaining Brussel's bureaucratic complexities to me, and to Saskia Schäfer for her unfailing intellectual support over all those years. Finally, I am deeply indebted to the Myxa Research Group and its members Alejandro Esguerra, Benjamin Faude, Lea Hartung, Nicole Helmerich, Alexander Kleibrink, Anne Koch, and Alexandros Tokhi. Without their ceaseless support, this would have been a very different book. Probably, it wouldn't have been a book at all.

In London, Enze Han, Jeff Howard, Rahul Rao, David Mosse, David Lewis, Leslie Vinjamuri, Katy Robinson, and Cosimo Zene all generously commented on various aspects of the project. Werner Menski carefully read and constructively commented on several individual chapters. So did Stephen Chan, who has been both a charitable reader and an extraordinary mentor for many years. In addition, Emanuel Adler, Jeff Checkel, and Elisabeth Shakman Hurd provided very helpful feedback on specific aspects of the book and its core arguments. Particular thanks go to Andrew Hurrell for helping me to think through my questions of norm translation also from historical and philosophical perspectives; his generous advice and encouragement have been invaluable for the project as a whole.

In terms of multidisciplinary dialogue, I greatly benefited from a brief stay at the Department for Law and Anthropology at the Max Planck Institute for Social Anthropology in Halle (Saale). I would like to thank Maria Sapignoli, Katrin Seidel, Brain Donahoe, Bertram Turner, and Kalindi Kokal for their time and enthusiasm as well as Keebet von Benda-Beckmann for an instructive discussion about the social lives of documents. Finally, I also owe special thanks to Marie-Claire Foblets, both for her invitation to spend some time at the Institute and her astute feedback on the overall argument of the book.

In the process of writing this book, I have incurred a number of institutional debts. The Fritz-Thyssen Foundation kindly provided both the initial PhD scholarship as well as a Completion Grant to write it up. The Collaborative Research Centre (*Sonderforschungsbereich*) 700 'Governance in Areas of Limited Statehood' paid for a conference trip to the ISA Annual Convention in New Orleans in 2015. The British Council funded a brief stint in Bangladesh for the CITICON Workshop organized by the University of Bath and the Bangladesh Institute for Development Studies. The significantly more prolonged previous field research trips have been generously supported by the German Academic Exchange Council (DAAD). The DAAD also funded a six-month-long research stay at SOAS. The Institute for the Human Sciences in Vienna awarded a junior visiting fellowship.

In Vienna, I would like to thank all fellows at the institute, and in particular Luiza Bialasiewicz, Andrew Brandel, Holly Case, Filipe Calvão, Claudie Fiorini, Adil Hasan Khan, Iva Lucic, Katherine Miller, Lipin Ram, Gunnar Folke Schuppert, Jyotirmaya Sharma, and Ezgi Yildiz for their helpful comments and overall support of the project. David Jenkins both patiently listened to and assiduously read various draft versions of my argument (more than once). Steven Lukes pushed the conceptual apparatus of this book and greatly enhanced my understanding of the philosophical pitfalls of analysing human rights in translation. The rector Shalini Randeria as well as the permanent fellows of the institute and its administrative staff have held it all together and thereby created a vibrant intellectual environment that allowed for many conversations across disciplinary divides, geographic boundaries, and specialized audiences. My heartfelt thanks to all of them.

My greatest debt is to the people who supported my field research in Bangladesh. As I promised confidentiality, not all of them can be named. Of the people that can be named, two in particular stand out: Sumaiya Khair at the Law Faculty of the University of Dhaka has been an outstanding intellectual host and I am deeply grateful for each and every one of our conversations; most of what I know about the law in Bangladesh, I have learned from her. Most of what I know about the rest of the country I have learned from Khorshed Alam, whose unbound passion for justice and social struggles in Bangladesh has been as inspiring as it has been insightful; he is terribly missed. In Bangladesh, I would also like to thank Asma and Alamgir Serajuddin, Ferduos Jahan, Mirza Hassan, Ridwanul Hoque, and Tunazina Iqbal Sahely for their warm patience with all my questions and queries. Finally, Shuaib Rahman, Mukaddesul Haque, and Puspita Hossain as well as Feroj Ahmed and his friends kindly introduced me to their cities, Dhaka and Khulna, and thereby greatly extended my horizon beyond rural Bangladesh, for which I am very grateful.

Many thanks also to Dominic Byatt and the production team at Oxford University Press as well as the anonymous reviewers of the initial manuscript for their very helpful and instructive comments and suggestions. Last but not least, I would like to extend my most heartfelt gratitude to my friends and family—and in particular my parents who have supported me through all the ups and downs that writing this book has unavoidably entailed. Needless to say, I am the only one to blame for the outcome.

Contents

List of Abbreviations

ADR	Alternative Dispute Resolution
AL	Awami League; political party in Bangladesh
AVCB	Activating the Village Courts in Bangladesh; project funded by EU and UNDP
BNP	Bangladesh National Party; political party in Bangladesh
CBO	Community-Based Organization
CEDAW	Convention on the Elimination of All Forms of Discrimination against Women
CRC	Convention on the Rights of the Child
EU	European Union
ICESCR	International Covenant on Economic, Social, and Cultural Rights
IR	International Relations
MFLO	Muslim Family Law Ordinance, 1961
MLAA	Madaripur Legal Aid Association; legal aid NGO and involved in AVCB
MLGRD	Ministry of Local Governance, Rural Development, and Cooperatives
NGO	Non-Governmental Organization
OVI	Objectively Verifiable Indicator
UN	United Nations
UNDP	United Nations Development Program
UNDP-AVCB	UNDP branch of the AVCB project
UP	Union Parishad; smallest administrative unit in Bangladesh

1

Introduction

Global Norms and Local Courts

The building looks familiar. It is long, one-storied, with a flat roof top, wooden doors and window seals, painted in deep blue, and thus starkly contrasting the bright yet fading paint of the concrete structure. A colonnade runs along its flank, making the building seem light and airy, somehow softening the boundary between the inside and the outside. It is a typical primary school as they exist all over rural Bangladesh. These schools are usually run by the state. Occasionally, they are built, equipped, or in some other ways supported by international donor agencies. This one is probably not, there are at least none of the typical signs international donors are inclined to leave behind. There is only the national flag, posted in the quad adjacent to the solid structure of the school. Both the flag and the compact structure it adorns visibly affirm the presence of the state in this village in southern Bangladesh.

It is an early Saturday evening in late 2012. About fifty people have gathered outside the school. At least thrice as many have assembled inside, awaiting the trial of three men from two neighbouring villages. A conflict over trespassing had escalated, leaving one person severely injured. This is a very complicated case. It involves not only several parties from different villages but also multiple interrelated conflicts. It also involves the state's enforcement agencies. A formal case has been filed with the police station and official investigations have been initiated. Now, the state's law-enforcement agencies need to be stopped, medical bills for the injured have to be covered, broken relationships must be restored, and different normative positions need to be reconciled.

The subsequent trial aims at taking on all these tasks. Respected members of the village community, local elected politicians, and recognized religious authorities appear before the court and give their opinion on the case before them. They do so by drawing on different sources of normative reasoning, including religious principles, customary values, and pragmatic considerations. They also rely on various forms of documentation like land titles, bank statements, payment slips, and medical records. They pass around documents, hear witnesses, exchange arguments, take breaks, start again. The trial lasts for hours. Different people move in and out of the classroom, where the key protagonists are assembled around a large table at the very front. The composition of this inner circle also fluctuates, with only a few key figures staying constant.

This is a non-state court in a state-run building. Just like the building, non-state courts like the one just sketched (and further discussed in Chapter 4) are very familiar in rural Bangladesh. They are called *shalish*. Neither recognized nor regulated by the state, *shalish* exist in various shapes and sizes. I have seen *shalish* with five and 150 people, negotiating anything from minor trespassing disputes to serious criminal offences. Many, though of course not all, of these *shalish* have taken place in buildings of the state like schools or local municipality complexes, especially if they trialled cases that were of concern to large segments of the respective village communities and therefore also needed to house a correspondingly large audience. It is thus no coincidence that non-state justice regularly operates through the physical structures of the state. Instead of inhabiting neatly separated legal universes, state and non-state law are intricately intertwined in rural Bangladesh. They are part of a larger legal landscape in which secular and religious law, customary principles, local conventions, and various transnational influences overlap and coincide. The transnational influences range from specific interpretations of Islamic law that are transported via diaspora communities in the Persian Gulf to the 'project law' that emanates from international donor agencies like the World Bank in highly aid-dependent countries like Bangladesh (Randeria 2003; Günter and Randeria 2001).

This persistent legal pluralism is an empirical reality not only in Bangladesh but anywhere in the world. Legal pluralism refers to a situation in which a multiplicity of normative and legal orders overlap and coincide within a given socio-political space (Benda-Beckmann 2002). And in most of the world, this legal pluralism exists in the absence of a state that would be strong enough to conclusively impose a unitary order on the plurality of normative and legal systems that exist within its territory. Such areas of limited statehood have been historically the rule rather than the exception; and they continue to be so in most of the world today (Risse 2013a). This persistence of legal pluralism in the absence of a fully controlling state therefore points to a much deeper *problematique* when it comes to the global diffusion of norms. These norms, and especially the ones that intend to delineate the contours of normatively desirable political order, like human rights or the rule of law, tacitly presume to operate against the backdrop of fully consolidated states. Yet if most states around the world are not consolidated in the ideal typical way Max Weber (1978) famously defined, and if they are not likely to converge on Weberian models in the future either, what happens to global norms when they enter these complex political landscapes in which the state is just one of many powerful actors?

1.1. GLOBAL NORMS AND LOCAL COURTS

Until recently, non-state courts like the *shalish* described at the outset have been largely absent from international donor initiatives aimed at strengthening the rule of law. Since the 'Rule of Law Revival' (Carothers 1998) in the late 1980s, international legal experts have understood this almost exclusively as the rule of state-backed law. Hence, the vast majority of rule of law programmes initiated over the past three decades has focused on the reform of constitutions and other laws, the introduction of new bureaucratic technologies, and the training of judges, lawyers, and prosecutors as well as members of state enforcement agencies. The scope of these legal interventions has, in fact, been so broad that Stephen Humphrey could reflect on his long-standing experience as an international rule of law expert by stating, rather laconically: 'It took me some time to admit that, if I was honest, I wasn't fully sure what "the rule of law" meant. It took me a little longer to realise that, in fact, few others were either' (Humphreys 2010, xiii). Nonetheless, most experts tacitly agreed upon two things. Firstly, that the rule of law was part of a liberal triad and as such intimately linked to adjacent concepts of democracy and human rights (Ehm 2010). Secondly, that the rule of law was a matter of the state.

This latter aspect has recently started to change. Significantly propelled by the World Bank's 'Justice for the Poor' project as well as a landmark study by various United Nations (UN) agencies on 'Informal Justice Mechanisms' (UNDP et al. 2013), non-state institutions have lately started to catch the attention of international donor agencies. Yet moving beyond the state is intricately difficult. Legal expertise is largely recruited from leading law schools in Europe and the United States, where state-centric understandings of law understandably prevail. Imagining law without a state thus proves to be an arduous task; and non-state justice institutions are consequently viewed with suspicion. On the one hand, there are some widely recognized advantages as non-state courts tend to be fast, efficient, and legitimate. Located usually within the vicinity of the people who use them, they are deeply embedded in local normative orders and therefore offer much needed alternatives to corrupt and inefficient state-backed legal systems. On the other hand, non-state courts are often criticized by national and international human rights agencies for their patriarchal biases, their non-conformity with international human rights standards, and their overall tendency to perpetuate power hierarchies. International donors are thus confronted with the challenging task of rescuing the seeming advantages of non-state courts from their perceived shortcomings (Berger 2017). Although there is disagreement about the exact strategies through which this can be done, a broad consensus exists on the need for context-sensitive programmes, based on a sustained empirical analysis of the specific conditions in which the respective courts operate. There is also an overall consensus to engage non-state institutions through what two leading experts of the World Bank, Deval Desai and Michael Woolcock (2015), have termed 'Experimental Justice Reform'. Their call for experimentation is as justified as it is telling; it shows how moving law beyond the state feels like treading onto uncharted territory.

Yet, in fact, this territory is not quite uncharted. As a concept, 'the rule of law' has been circulating internationally for at least two centuries. It was a central moral justification for the British Empire in the nineteenth century (den Otter 2007). It has figured prominently in the law and development discourses of the 1960s and 1970s (Trubek and Galanter 1974). And, since the late 1980s, there has been a revival that turned 'the rule of law' into one of the central concepts of international development cooperation today. Contemporary transnational rule of law dynamics thus unfold in significantly longer historical trajectories (Zürn et al. 2012b). Within these trajectories, questions about the relationship of state and non-state law have recurrently appeared. The latest turn of international donors is thus much less a discovery than a rediscovery. At the beginning of the twentieth century, the British colonial administration in the Indian Province of Bengal introduced so-called village courts as quasi-formal institutions that would devolve judicial powers to local authorities on the condition that they adhered to some basic procedural requirements. The aim of the introduction of these courts was to ease the burden on the formal judiciary by offering fast and legitimate local alternatives. Almost exactly one century later, the European Union (EU) and United Nations Development Program (UNDP) aim to 'activate' these village courts, based on a strikingly similar line of reasoning. The 'Activating the Village Courts in Bangladesh' (AVCB) project is the empirical focus for the following investigation of what happens when international agencies promote global norms like 'the rule of law' through local non-state institutions like the village courts.

The Village Courts in Bangladesh

It is a late morning in early 2012. About forty women have gathered in a village in southern Bangladesh. They are sitting on old cement bags that have been split open and transformed into blankets, covering the mud floor of the courtyard where the meeting takes place. The youngest participant is only a few months old, the oldest is in her sixties. Most of them belong to the minority Hindu community in Bangladesh. None of them is very affluent; their household incomes depend on subsistence farming, day labouring, or work in one of the small shops at the main road nearby. This morning they have come together to talk about ordinary conflicts that occur within their village community, and how to solve them. The meeting has been organized by Tapathi, the fieldworker of a local non-governmental organization (NGO).

Her NGO, in turn, has been commissioned by international donors to improve access to justice for poor and marginalized people through village courts in rural Bangladesh.

Tapathi is the only one standing. She presides over the meeting with a wooden stick in her hand, which she uses to occasionally point towards the flipchart next to her. The flipchart is placed on a blue plastic chair. It contains a good dozen pages explicating various aspects pertaining to village court proceedings. The pages contain a mixture of short sentences and carefully crafted illustrations that display different scenes, for example a dispute over cattle trespassing, a village court session, and two people embracing each other in a moment of reconciliation. At the top of every page is the logo of the Ministry of Local Governance, Rural Development and Cooperatives. It consists of a red circle with a golden map of Bangladesh inside and the name of the ministry written on the outside. At the bottom of the pages are the blue logos of the EU to the left and the UNDP to the right. In-between the two logos is the name of the project that is funded by both organizations—'Activating the Village Courts in Bangladesh'.

In a firm voice and endowed with the authority of both the stick and the flipchart, Tapathi introduces these village courts. They are recognized by the state and can trial minor civil and criminal cases, which include cases pertaining to land disputes, outstanding loan payments, trifling quarrels between different members of the community, or the destruction of crops by domestic animals. For such cases, people can initiate a village court. All they have to do is pay a nominal fee and file an application with a local elected politician, the Union Parishad chairman. For every village court case, each conflicting party nominates two representatives, and together with the chairman, the resulting five-member jury decides the case in the village court. By law, they are required to resolve cases within three weeks after the application to the village court has been filed. No lawyers are permitted at any point within a village court case. Although recognized by the state, the village courts therefore strongly resemble the *shalish*, the kind of highly popular non-state court with which this chapter opened. Throughout the courtyard meeting, Tapathi argues that the village courts would be superior to both state and *shalish* courts. Unlike the state courts, she argues, they do not require significant financial resources for lawyers, clerks, and other court fees. They are fast and accessible; and they resolve cases with the aim of restoring friendly relationships between the conflicting parties. In this regard, they are very similar to the *shalish* courts. Yet unlike the *shalish*, she continues, the village courts include representatives of the conflicting parties and thereby break the exclusive hold of local elites over processes of conflict resolution through non-state justice institutions.

Reality is of course more complex and Tapathi faces lots of questions from the audience. 'What happens if the accused party does not attend the village court trials?' 'What could I do if the chairman simply refuses to accept a case application?' 'And what kinds of punishment can village courts impose, and how?' People move in and out of the meeting. One woman asks about a conflict she has with her neighbours whose goat has repeatedly eaten their seedlings, thereby undermining their livelihood. Can the village courts address such a conflict? Yes, they can. Further questions are asked and vivid discussions ensue about dynamics of conflict resolutions, the intricate workings of state and non-state institutions, and questions of justice more generally. Courtyard meetings like the one just described happen at regular intervals throughout the country. They are part of a much larger orchestrated effort made by the EU and UNDP to activate hundreds of village courts in Bangladesh. It is the most comprehensive intervention of international donor agencies in non-state justice institutions anywhere in the world today (UNDP et al. 2013, 220); and it relies on more than 1,000 fieldworkers like Tapathi to bring the village courts to rural Bangladesh.

The work of people like Tapathi is indispensable. It results in two kinds of change; and it is these changes that are at the centre of this book. On the one hand, the introduction of village courts through local fieldworkers and court assistants changes the dynamics of conflict resolution in rural Bangladesh. It allows poor and marginalized people to access local elites they could not have otherwise accessed. This, in turn, significantly improves their standing in processes of conflict resolution, particularly when these conflicts unfold against parties more powerful than themselves. On the other hand, the fieldworker and court assistants also change the meaning of transnational liberal notions of 'the rule of law' that underpin the current introduction of village courts through international donor agencies. They therefore *translate* transnational norms about 'the rule of law' in ways that make sense to the people inhabiting the complex legal landscapes of conflict resolution in rural Bangladesh. These norm translations are the focus of the following chapters.

1.2. CENTRAL ARGUMENTS

This book analyses how and under which conditions transnational norms like 'the rule of law' are translated as they travel back and forth between different contexts. It advances three interrelated sets of arguments that unfold along theoretical, methodological, and empirical lines.

Theoretically, I argue that in processes of translation, two kinds of change occur. Firstly, the notion of translation captures the ways in which the content of norms is transformed as they travel from one context to another. These transformations are decisive. Only if travelling norms are transformed in ways that make sense to people in the receiving context can they also, secondly, alter the socio-political dynamics within that context. These dual changes have largely been neglected in the International Relations (IR) literature on the diffusion of norms and ideas as most studies on the effects of global norms on local contexts pursue one of two lines of argument. Either they attest to the power of global norms and investigate the conditions under which local contexts are gradually approximated to existing global scripts (Risse et al. 1999, 2013; Lutz and Sikkink 2000; Simmons 2009), or they highlight the resilience of local contexts vis-à-vis global norms and argue that the latter are either resisted or integrated into the former in processes of 'localization' (Acharya 2004, 2009).

The translation perspective that is developed in this book is located in-between these top-down and bottom-up approaches to processes of norm diffusion—and remedies shortcomings of both. On the one hand, top-down approaches have developed increasingly dynamic models of the ways in which norms are diffused globally and succeed in changing local contexts. However, these approaches continue to assume the static content of norms and therefore underestimate the extent to which their meaning changes in processes of diffusion (Krook and True 2012). On the other hand, localization approaches that focus on precisely these changes have failed to account for the ways in which the political realities of receiving contexts change in response to globally diffused norms and ideas. The notion of translation opens the conceptual space in which we can think about the interactions of global norms and local contexts without having to assume (a) that global norms are largely ineffective, or (b) that these effects necessarily make diverse sets of contexts converge on established global scripts.

Global scripts consist of a multiplicity of norms like, for example, 'democracy', 'the rule of law', and 'human rights' in the case of contemporary transnational liberalism. Each of these norms in turn consists of three interrelated elements, which need to be disaggregated for the analysis of norm translation. As I argue in the following chapters, norms consist of institutional reference points, normative aspirations, and specific sets of practices that ground both institutions and normative aspirations in the habitually taken-for-granted patterns of social and political life within a given context.[1] Although empirically intertwined, these elements can be analytically disentangled. In processes of translation, the various elements change; but they change to different degrees. Norm translations therefore maintain a fine line of seeming continuity across different contexts. This fine line is what distinguishes translations from other kinds of transformations, for example full absorptions or outright rejections. Translations consequently unfold in a productive tension of continuity and change.

[1] Although all of these elements are familiar to the established literature on the diffusion of norms within IR (e.g. Meyer et al. 1997; Finnemore and Sikkink 1998; Risse et al. 1999), they have not been kept analytically apart.

To change the social and political dynamics within a specific context, arriving norms need to resonate there. More precisely, they need to resonate with what Charles Taylor (1997) calls background knowledge, i.e. the knowledge that is tacitly taken for granted and implicitly relied upon. Making norms resonate with this kind of knowledge is, in turn, the task of translators. As Walter Benjamin (1977) has famously argued, the 'Task of the Translator' is not to faithfully adhere to the meaning of the original, but to transform it in ways that allow original meanings to resonate in novel ways within receiving languages. It is the translators who alter the meaning of norms so that they not only resonate but, by resonating, also change the contexts in which they are being translated. The ardent work of translators is therefore the central scope condition for norm translations to take place.

As they do take place, the translated norms develop a life of their own. Translations are therefore not mere derivates of established global 'originals'. Instead, as Benjamin has argued, every translation creates a new original, thereby undermining assumed hierarchies between alleged originals and their translations. In the case of norm translations, this means that global norms do not have priority over local ones or vice versa. Instead, the global and the local are intricately intertwined in recursive processes of translation in which neat dividing lines between 'the global' and 'the local' start to blur. This undermines the spatial imagination of much IR scholarship on the diffusion of norms and ideas that equates the global with the universal and the local with the particular. In contrast, I argue that the international is nothing but its own particular context. It is the world of international policy experts, diplomats, and aid workers—and it is between this context and rural Bangladesh that translations of 'the rule of law' unfold in a recursive back and forth movement.

Following this recursive back and forth movement poses a significant methodological challenge. What exactly do we follow when we follow global norms? Their normative aspirations might be articulated in a multiplicity of different vocabularies; for example—as the following analysis will show—liberal demands for gender equality might be expressed in the language of Islam and Islamic law. If one only focused on the discursive appearance of liberal vocabularies, these translations would be easily lost from sight. Norm translations can therefore not simply track explicit references to the norm in question. Neither can they simply follow institutional templates as these templates might well be adopted but subsequently filled with a life of their own and quite distinct from what institutional designers originally had in mind. What can be tracked, however, are the artefacts through which norms travel from one place to another. Following things rather than the norms themselves is thus imperative for the analysis of the myriad ways in which global norms are translated as they travel back and forth between different spaces. In the following analysis, I have therefore followed the artefacts through which international donor agencies aim to take 'the rule of law' to non-state justice institutions in rural Bangladesh (see also Section 1.3).

Empirically, I follow the artefacts of one large-scale project that aims at using the village courts as vehicles for the promotion of the liberal rule of law. These artefacts include the flip-charts used by fieldworkers like Tapathi (see above) as well as posters, billboards, official paperwork, and magnificently decorated wooden village courtrooms that have been built in approximately 350 villages in five regions of Bangladesh. There is a large-scale social experiment built into the project design, as in four out of these five regions the village courts ought to be activated through grassroots-level employees of local NGOs. In the fifth region, however, it has been directly implemented by UNDP's Dhaka-based project team. The experiment bears clear results. In the four regions, the ardent work of local NGOs alters established dynamics of conflict resolution. In contrast, in the one region where it is implemented directly through international agencies, nothing happens; the project's artefacts simply turn into empty ruins, devoid of meaning or impact in the landscape of local conflict resolution in rural Bangladesh.

In the four regions where the project is implemented by local NGOs, the fieldworkers operating at the grassroots level give these artefacts new meaning. They do so by making the artefacts as well as the norms they ought to carry resonate with the background knowledge of people in rural Bangladesh. This background knowledge encompasses a detailed understanding of the ways in which state and non-state institutions are entangled in what I conceptualize as the logic of non-enforcement. Following this logic, people frequently file cases with the state courts, not to get binding and enforceable verdicts but to change the dynamics of non-state courts in their favour. This works even though enforcement capacities of the formal judiciary are highly limited and, in most cases, the state does not cast a credible 'shadow of hierarchy' (Börzel 2010). Yet the symbols of the state, like uniforms and official documents, retain a high degree of authority; they are habitually recognized and tightly woven into the background knowledge of people in rural Bangladesh. In addition to the logic of non-enforcement, this background knowledge also includes sophisticated understandings of social order and its underlying hierarchies, a desire to maintain the integrity of village communities, and the professed imperative to live a pious life (though what that means exactly is itself subject to controversy). It is against this complex background knowledge that global notions of 'the rule of law' need to be translated.

The fieldworkers and court assistants translate 'the rule of law' as it is understood by international donors in three ways. Firstly, they *translate the normative vocabulary of the secular rule of law into the language of Islam and Islamic law*. Especially for the empowerment of women, the local fieldworkers draw on explicitly Islamic rather than secular human rights discourses. They also translate ideal-typical notions of retributive justice into the language of community harmony and reconciliation and thereby allow global notions of the liberal rule of law to resonate with the normative background assumptions of people in rural Bangladesh. Secondly, rather than approximating the village courts to the formal judiciary (as envisioned by the EU and UNDP), the fieldworkers integrate the village courts into the universe of informal justice institutions like the *shalish* in rural Bangladesh. Thirdly, the fieldworkers also translate one of the key practices of the rule of law into a locally intelligible and politically potent form: namely, *the production of bureaucratic paperwork*. Instead of using the files and forms provided by the project as a means for the neutral recording of village court proceedings, the local NGOs use precisely these documents as a form of symbolic capital that allows poor and marginalized people to access local elected politicians like the Union Parishad chairmen. As this access would have been otherwise blocked, the local NGOs *do* change the social and political context in which they are operating by empowering marginalized groups and in particular women, but only because they *do not* promote the rule of law as it is understood by international donor agencies.

By translating 'the rule of law', the fieldworker and court assistants develop what Shareen Hertel (2006) has called 'unexpected power'. This unexpected power highlights the persistent agency of the recipients of global norms. Their agency is not limited to the mere approximation of local contexts to existing global scripts but includes the capacity to change global norms in ways that render them meaningful in the social and political worlds they are navigating. This power of the seemingly powerless is often subtle or even hidden (Scott 1985); and bringing it into focus requires detailed attention to the specific complexities of the contexts in which norm translators are embedded. In the case of the following analysis, one of these contexts is rural Bangladesh.

Bangladesh

Bangladesh separated from Pakistan in 1971 after a short but brutal war that cost 1–3 million lives. The numbers are themselves subject to ongoing political contestation and only a second wave of historical writing has recently started to disentangle some of the complexities of the conflict (Mookherjee 2015; Siddiqi 2013; D'Costa 2011; Saikia 2011; Bose 2010). Embedded in Cold War rivalries, this was a local struggle with global ramifications as not only India and Pakistan but also the US, the Soviet Union, and China had competing interests and rather different strategic understandings of what was happening in the Bay of Bengal in 1970/1 (Raghavan 2013). The conflict itself had been long in the making. After the first partition on the Indian sub-continent had divided India and Pakistan, the latter was left without most of the colonial state's central institutions as the majority of the bureaucratic corps of the

Indian civil service as well as the bulk of the army and police forces stayed in India. At the same time, Pakistan emerged as an independent state consisting of two unconnected territories. Tensions between the eastern and the western wing of the country soon accelerated as resources were systematically transferred from east to west while access to the newly built institutions of the state remained largely blocked for Bengalis. In addition, questions over the status of Bengali as a national language have remained equally contentious so that for the first two decades, Eastern Pakistan remained 'economically exploited, politically suppressed, and culturally dominated' (Karim 2011, 6).

Upon gaining independence, Bangladesh literally faced all the odds. It was left without a functioning state apparatus and only highly diminished bureaucratic corps, much of its infrastructure had been destroyed, significant parts of its intellectual elite had been murdered just before the war ended, millions of people were internally displaced, and more than 10 million refugees who had escaped to India awaited the possibility of return. The overwhelmingly agricultural economy went into steep decline as its only export—jute fibre—suffered as the world discovered plastic in the 1970s. Given widespread poverty and weak state infrastructure, Henry Kissinger infamously labelled Bangladesh as a 'bottomless basket case' (White 1999, 307). A few years later, the World Bank economists Faaland and Parkinson (1976) upgraded the country to 'a test case of development', arguing that if development initiatives could succeed in Bangladesh, they could also succeed anywhere else. It is this status as a 'quintessential developing country' and a 'testing ground for new development ideas' that Bangladesh has retained until today on the international stage (Lewis 2011, 17, 5).

On this testing ground, the citizens of Bangladesh have achieved some extraordinary results. They have reduced the number of people living in absolute poverty from 70.2 per cent in 1990 to 43.3 per cent in 2012. During the same time, the number of people suffering from insufficient daily energy intake has also declined significantly (UNDP 2013, 110); and over the past two decades, Bangladesh has started to outperform India and Pakistan in a number of key social indicators, including life expectancy, health, infant mortality, education, and gender equality (Drèze and Sen 2013). This ongoing social transformation is not reducible to external intervention but rooted in a long trajectory of civic engagement and political activism within the country. This trajectory runs from the colonial period to the language movements of the 1950s and 1960s and the famine relief of the mid-1970s when 'private voluntary organisations all over the country began providing free cooked food and relief, and government sponsored gruel kitchens followed a little later' (van Schendel 2009, 181).

Bangladesh is thus a weak state in a strong society (White 1999). This strong society consists not only of robust informal networks able to capture key institutions of the state but also of NGOs that assume some of the state's key competences. The Bangladesh Rural Advancement Committee, for example, was founded in 1972 and later simply rebranded as BRAC. Today, it is the world's largest NGO and engages in projects across all sorts of sectors, including micro-crediting, education, health, and food security (Lewis 2011, 114). BRAC also owns a number of social enterprises, maintains its own university, and has started to set up its own projects in different African, Asian, and Latin American countries; it also currently runs more legal aid clinics than there are police stations in the country (Pereira 2013). Similarly, the Grameen Bank has also been transformed from a local organization to a multifaceted enterprise with global reach. Whereas BRAC and the Grameen Bank constitute large-scale development conglomerates, there also exist a myriad of smaller and medium-sized organizations in Bangladesh.

These organizations are not simply the expression of an exceptionally vibrant civil society. Instead, they have increasingly developed parallel structures to the state, creating what Lamia Karim (2011) has analysed as 'the NGO Shadow State' in Bangladesh. This shadow state undermines a strict conceptual distinction between the state, civil society, and the private sector (Ahasan and Gardner 2016, 4; Lewis 2004). On stylized accounts, civil society is the space where relationships between the state and its citizenry are mediated so that the former is held accountable to the latter.[2] Yet in highly aid-dependent countries, the externally funded proliferation of NGOs reverses these lines of accountability. Instead of simply allowing the citizenry to hold the state accountable, NGOs are themselves held accountable by their international donors (White 1999, 320–5). Bangladesh has historically been such a highly aid-dependent country. Throughout the 1950s and 1960s, the East Pakistani economy depended heavily on aid flows and the immediate post-war decade had an average annual per capita aid of $35 per citizen (van Schendel 2009, 220). Although the per capita aid has decreased since the 1990s, aid dependency has persisted as almost half of all public investment continues to be financed by aid (Khan 2013, 8–10).

External funds have therefore had a deep impact in Bangladesh; they have altered the nature of both the state and civil society. Whereas the state has rapidly reduced its responsibilities by outsourcing the provision of basic services to NGOs, the activities of these organizations have also changed dramatically. Since the mid-1980s, shifts in the politics of international aid have increasingly diverted attention away from grassroots-level mobilization towards market participation as a route to empowerment (Kabeer 2003). This shift has also coincided with a rapid expansion of the number of NGOs, which increased

[2] It is this stylized model to which the World Bank as pace setter of international development has subscribed since the late 1980s—and many other bi and multilateral donor organizations have followed suit. For an exposition as well as early critique of the Bank's conceptualizations of civil society, see Williams and Young (1994).

significantly as international donors diverted funds from the government to the non-governmental sector. Although strongly influenced by transnational development discourses, this sector has never been just the passive recipient of foreign ideas. Instead, drawing on a long history of civic engagement, Bangladesh continues to have an unusually high number of local initiatives; and, as David Lewis has argued, '[a]lthough foreign organisations have played important roles in the establishment of many of these local organisations, today the NGO sector in Bangladesh displays a strongly indigenous character and can be seen as a local formation of globally determined influences' (Lewis 2011, 109).

Understanding NGOs in Bangladesh as a local formation of globally determined influences has significant methodological implications for the investigation of the role of non-state actors in processes of norm translation. It means, firstly, that public statements by local NGOs cannot be simply taken at face value. As NGOs in Bangladesh are structurally depended on transnational flows of funds, they are also forced to at least partially cater to the dominant discourses within international development discourses. Secondly, however, this also means that not all activities of local NGOs can be even-handedly dismissed as ideological interpellations. As the NGOs are specific local responses to global forces, there is an agency of the governed; and a key task for research on processes of norm translation is to highlight this agency. This, in turn, requires moving beyond seemingly familiar actor categories. Instead of simply focusing on NGOs as translators of global norms, a nuanced analysis of the transformations that these norms undergo as they travel has to start with the reconstruction of translation chains (Latour 1987, 132–44). Along these translation chains, different people within the same organization produce diverging translations of global norms, for example when the top-level executives of Bangladeshi NGOs translate such norms differently than their grassroots employees. Although the preceding analysis has shown why such a disaggregation of actor categories is vital in the context of Bangladesh, where neat levels of analysis start to blur as the international, the national, and the local are inseparably intertwined, this point is of general relevance for the analysis of norms in translation. It imposes the broader question of how norms can be followed as they move back and forth between different people in different places.

1.3. DOING TRANSLATION RESEARCH

In the intricate interplay of institutional reference points, normative aspirations, and specific sets of practices that ground both institutions and normative aspirations in the regularly reoccurring patterns of everyday life, focusing exclusively on only one element is likely to mislead. For example, although following institutional designs as they travel from one place to another is relatively easy, it reveals remarkably little about how these designs actually come to life as they are embedded within new contexts. In the same way, normative aspirations can be smoothly tracked across different contexts if they are always expressed in the same words. Yet these very words might also change, for example when secular norms are translated into religious discourses or vice versa. As an alternative to following only institutional designs and discursive iterations, I have proposed to trail the material artefacts through which norms are transported back and forth between different actors located in different contexts.

Literally following things rather than words thus allowed me to track translations of 'the rule of law' across different sites (Cook 2004; Marcus 1995). The things that I have followed were primarily the artefacts used within the AVCB project. These artefacts include posters, flip-charts, billboards, and other education materials through which the village courts, and with them transnational notions of 'the rule of law', ought to be brought to rural Bangladesh. In addition to the educational materials, two further artefacts stood out. The first are the courtrooms that the project installs in the villages where it is operating. Usually including wooden judges' benches, a witness stand, and a table for the court assistant as well as seats for the audience, the village courtrooms have been designed to symbolically enhance the authority of the courts. The second artefact is not made from wood directly, but from paper. It is the trail of bureaucratic paperwork that the project produces. This includes both government and non-government prescribed forms delivered by international donors for the administration of village court justice. It includes further documents required for purposes of project monitoring and evaluation. These documents as well as the courtroom, billboards, and posters were all artefacts exclusively designed to make 'the rule of law' move between the headquarters of international donors in Brussels and New York, their country offices in Dhaka, an assemblage of regional and district outposts, and more than approximately 350 villages in rural Bangladesh.

These villages are spread across five different regions in Bangladesh; and although I pursued an ethnographic approach to analyse the translation of travelling norms (see below), a second methodological approach entered my research, albeit involuntarily. This is the experimental project design already indicated above. Building on a colonial legacy of experimentation in the social world, primarily though not exclusively in Sub-Saharan Africa (Bonneuil 2000), contemporary donor interventions pursue increasingly experimental project designs for the generation of what international bureaucrats deem to be policy-relevant knowledge (Rottenburg 2014). And in the case at hand, the project through which I investigate the translations of the rule of law in rural Bangladesh started out in Sylhet and was subsequently expanded to include four further regions (Madaripur, Rangpur, Chittagong, and Khulna). Yet, the set-up of the project in Sylhet and the four other divisions differs in one crucial respect—the presence of local NGOs. Without my choosing, this experiment unavoidably permeates my own analysis; and explicitly attests the decisive importance of local NGOs. Yet it cannot account for why these NGOs are so important. Explaining why the project fails in the region where it is directly implemented by UNDP's Dhaka-based experts but succeeds (albeit in unexpected ways) where it is run by the employees of local NGOs recruited from the immediate vicinities of the villages where the courts are activated requires an ethnographic approach.

Political ethnography encompasses both a specific approach to the collection of data as well as a distinct strategy for its interpretation; and both are insuperably intertwined (Schatz 2009). For the collection of data, I have conducted a cumulative total of eight months of fieldwork carried out over four research trips between 2011 and 2016. During this time, I attended about two dozen *shalish* and village court sessions as well as several training sessions, workshops, and courtyard meetings similar to the one described at the beginning of this chapter. In addition to observations on non-state justice proceedings, I have conducted over 120 interviews and a dozen group discussions with people in rural Bangladesh as well as with staff members of international organizations, legal experts, and representatives of various civil society organizations in Dhaka (I provide a list of all interviews and group discussions at the end of the book). To protect my respondents, I have anonymized all interviews, unless otherwise stated in the text.[3] While conducting interviews with people in rural Bangladesh, I worked with colleagues and translators from the respective localities.

My colleagues and I visited different villages and had conversations with people directly involved in the project, for example as court assistants or fieldworkers, as well as ordinary villagers. The latter were easy to get hold of: usually, my colleague and I would sit down at a local tea stall, have a cup or two, and exploit the other guests' open curiosity at the presence of this strange white person in their village. Tea stalls in rural Bangladesh, like anywhere in South Asia, are a privileged site for political ethnography as here the boundary between the state and civil society frequently blurs: in these roadside tea stalls low-level state officials, politicians, and local elites meet, discuss, and *do* local politics (Gupta 1995, 384; Hull 2012b, 67). Starting at the tea stalls, I also deliberately tried to broaden the social base of my respondents by

[3] The interviews are numbered and prefixed to give further information about the positions of my respondents: I indicate the sex of the interviewee by prefixing f for female and m for male; as group discussions always involved both female and male participants, I here only indicate gd. Secondly, for all respondents working within the AVCB project, I prefix EU, UNDP, and NGO. Interviewees outside the project are prefixed with CSO for members of civil society organizations (broadly construed), RB for people living in rural Bangladesh, and ST for representatives of the state. An interview with a female fieldworker of one of the four NGOs would therefore be indicated as, for example: NGO-f-009.

facilitating interviews with Hindus and Christians as well as by trying to have more interviews with women. The latter continued to prove challenging throughout my field research, especially in Chittagong and Sylhet Division. Together with my colleagues and translators, we developed different strategies to counter the male bias of our initial tea stall approach, for example to ask female project staff from the four local NGOs to facilitate interviews with women who had appealed to the village courts as well as to female members of community-based organizations of any sort.

Asking questions about quotidian conflicts within a village community, the different strategies deployed to solve them, and the underlying normative logics that informed these strategies, I waited for the village courts to appear. Instead of opening a conversation with direct questions about village court justice, I waited until my interlocutors pointed to the village courts themselves, for example by recounting a village court session they had been involved in, or by showing me documents related to a village court case. My interlocutors' ways of making sense of the village courts were thus the empirical entry point for the reconstruction of different translations of 'the rule of law' as international donors understand it. This reconstruction needs to start on the ground where the norm in question is being translated. It also needs to remain open enough to take notice of specific local translations without reducing them to mere print-offs of established global norms. The notion of translation conceptually undermines the plausibility of incontestable originals. Instead of being faithful copies of global originals, local translations produce new originals. Investigating these translations is an analytical challenge; it requires categories which do not reify global norms by reducing local translations to more or less pathological deviations from these seeming originals. For translations of 'the rule of law', I develop such categories in Chapter 2. They build on my tripartite account of norm content and draw on arguments advanced in the academic field of jurisprudence, political philosophy, and legal anthropology to capture the ways in which the institutions, normative aspirations, and practices of 'the rule of law' are translated as it moves back and forth between metropolitan centres, the capital of Bangladesh, and the country's villages. It is these translations that constitute the empirical backbone of the following chapters.

1.4. OUTLINE OF THE BOOK

The book is divided into two parts with three chapters each. Part I starts with developing a theoretical account of norm translation and outlines the analytical framework with which different translations of 'the rule of law' can be captured in Chapter 2. Having laid the theoretical groundwork, Chapter 3 introduces the village courts as a quasi-formal institution. It locates them in the complex legal landscape of rural Bangladesh and analyses how they relate to both state and non-state institutions. In addition to situating the village courts in relation to their state and non-state counterparts, this chapter also contextualizes contemporary donor interventions in village court systems in rural Bangladesh historically. Both at the beginning of the twentieth and at the beginning of the twenty-first century European efforts at introducing or later 'activating' the village courts followed very similar lines of reasoning, displaying remarkable though largely unacknowledged continuities between colonial and contemporary projects with the village courts. After having discussed the legal integration of the village courts into the state-backed legal system in Chapter 3, Chapter 4 turns to the analysis of the ways in which state and non-state law actually interact in practice. These interactions amount to what I call 'the logic of non-enforcement', which constitutes the background knowledge in rural Bangladesh. It is against this background knowledge that transnational notions of 'the rule of law' need to be unavoidably translated. The second part of this book turns to the analysis of these translations.

Part II starts by introducing the key actors within the project aiming at the activation of village courts in Bangladesh. Highlighting the underspecification of contemporary transnational liberal scripts, Chapter 5 shows how the EU, UNDP, and the four local NGOs all make sense of the village courts in different ways, translating them as functional equivalents to the state-backed judiciary, local institutions of democratic governance, and sites for the promotion of community-based justice, respectively. Whereas these translations stay within the broad confines of transnational liberalism, the subsequent translations in rural Bangladesh do not. Chapter 6 analyses the outcomes of the transnational experiment in justice that currently unfolds in rural Bangladesh. It shows how, without the intervening agency of the fieldworker and court assistants of local NGOs, the artefacts of the project remain nothing but ruins in the landscape of conflict resolution in rural Bangladesh, devoid of meaning and purpose. In contrast, in those regions where the project is implemented by local NGOs, the village courts emerge, but not as extensions of the state-backed courts (as envisioned by the EU), but as one further non-state institution within the universe of rural conflict resolution. Ironically, through the introduction of the village courts as yet another de facto non-state institution the fieldworker and court assistants enhance participatory spaces for poor and marginalized people, and women in particular, precisely because they do not promote the rule of law as understood by international donors.

Chapter 7 explains why this is the case. It shows how the local NGOs' grassroots-level staff translate 'the rule of law' in ways that resonate with the background knowledge of people in rural Bangladesh. They use the files and forms provided by the EU and UNDP not for the orderly keeping of village court records, but as symbolic capital that allows poor people to approach local elites they could not otherwise access; and they translate the liberal secularism of the rule of law into notions of (a) community harmony and (b) Islam and Islamic law. In conclusion, Chapter 8 shows how these translations of the rule of law are lost as the project outcomes are fed back into transnational policy paradigms. Through the analysis of the project's monitoring and evaluation apparatus, I show how the boundaries of these paradigms are carefully policed, how anything that threatens contemporary canonical notions of 'the rule of law' as they currently circulate through the international system is systematically eradicated, and how the translational work of people like Tapathi is lost in retranslation.

Part I

2

Norms in Translations

In his *Philosophical Investigations*, Ludwig Wittgenstein asked a seemingly very simple question: what does it mean to follow a rule? Yet, the answer he gave to that question was intricately complex. He argued that the ability to follow a rule necessarily presupposes the possibility of understanding it in the first place—and of course the attempt to understand something always also bears the risk of misunderstanding it. Now, one could argue that the difference between understanding and misunderstanding is explanation: if only a rule is properly explained in full detail, the possibility of misunderstanding it would be minimized. Yet, for Wittgenstein such a full explanation, which could eliminate the possibility of misunderstanding, is impossible. Thus, he argues that there can never be a final explanation, which would need no further explanations:

> But then how does an explanation help me to understand, if after all it is not the final one? In that case the explanation is never completed; so I still don't understand what he means, and never shall!—As though an explanation would be hanging in mid-air, unless it was supported by another one.
>
> (Wittgenstein 1984, §87, my translation)

Although rejecting the possibility of a final explanation that would render a rule perfectly intelligible and thus unambiguous, Wittgenstein did of course not conclude that we cannot follow rules at all. Instead, he argued that we can understand rules, but not through conscious reflection alone; we ultimately understand rules only against a background of what is taken for granted. This background is unarticulated—and maybe even unarticulatable (Taylor 1997, 167). Thus, Wittgenstein argued that sooner or later, we would have exhausted the explanations for the ways in which we understand, and thus also navigate, the worlds we inhabit. As he put it: 'If I have exhausted my justifications I have reached bed-rock, and my spade is turned. Then, I am inclined to say: "This is simply what I do" . . . [Thus], when I obey a rule, I do not choose. I obey the rule *blindly*' (Wittgenstein 1986, 217–19; emphasis in the original). This Wittgensteinian insight that our ability to obeying rules rests not only on conscious reflections alone but also on social practices constitutes the overall philosophical frame of this chapter. It is of direct relevance to research on processes of norm translations within IR, in which norms are generally understood to be standards or *rules* of appropriate behaviour (Finnemore and Sikkink 1998, 891). This chapter investigates what happens when these standards or rules of appropriate behaviour travel back and forth between different social and political contexts.

It is the central argument of this book that, given the ardent work of translators, the meaning of norms changes as they move from one context to another. If—and only if—their meaning is changed in processes of translation will norms also alter social and political dynamics of the receiving context. This dual change has been largely neglected within IR scholarship on both the diffusion of norms and their localization, as I show in the following section. The subsequent section then outlines my theoretical account for norm translation and shows how it is the central task of translators to recreate the meaning of norms in ways that resonate in the receiving context. More precisely, arriving norms and ideas need to resonate with the background knowledge, i.e. the kind of tacit knowledge that, without saying, gives specific meaning to our actions and utterances but also underpins institutions, practices, and normative orders. When translators recreate the meaning of norms in ways that resonate with this kind of background knowledge they, in fact, create new norms, thereby undermining neat analytical distinctions between original norms and their subsequent translations. Instead of being derivate of some kind of 'original' global norms, local translations are therefore originals in their own right. Yet this poses an analytical challenge as it requires categories that capture both global norms and local translations without reducing one to a mere cliché of the other. The final section of this chapter develops such categories for 'the rule of law'. Before developing these analytical categories that capture translations of 'the rule of law' as it travels from the global to the local and back again, I start by discussing these crooked ways of norms.

2.1. THE CHEMISTRY OF DIFFUSION AND THE CROOKED WAYS OF NORMS

The movement of norms from one socio-political context to another is usually described as a process of diffusion within the social sciences. This notion of diffusion is borrowed from the natural sciences; and there it refers to a process by which particles move from a space with a higher density of particles to a space with a lower one. This implies that particles travel into empty space; an implication that also pervaded the early beginnings of diffusion research within IR.[1] Pioneered by the Stanford School of sociological institutionalism, it comes most clearly to the fore in a seminal article by Meyer, Thomas, Boli, and Ramirez on 'World Society and the Nation-State' (Meyer et al. 1997). In contrast to functional explanations, Meyer et al. argue that many features of the contemporary nation-state are derived from global cultural scripts. These global cultural scripts contain institutional prescriptions, which are simply 'downloaded' into specific national contexts where they lead to institutional isomorphisms that cannot be accounted for by exclusive reference to endogenous functional necessities. Throughout the article, Meyer et al. use a hypothetical example to illustrate their point. They ask what would happen if 'an unknown society [was] "discovered" on a previously unknown island' (Meyer et al. 1997, 146). Soon after discovery, they argue, a government would form, a familiar ensemble of ministries and other state agencies would be opened, the island would by recognized by other states and admitted to the UN, the island's population would be counted and classified according to the standards of the world census models, and modern educational, medical, scientific, and family law institutions would develop. The authors conclude that 'without knowing anything about the history, culture, practices, or traditions that obtained in this previously unknown society, we could forecast many changes that, upon "discovery", would descend on the island' (Meyer et al. 1997, 146). The island itself, however, on which global cultures' scripts descend, remains empty in the spatial imagination of the Stanford School.

Instead of accounting for local responses to global cultural scripts in any detail, scholars of the Stanford School simply posit the generic notion of 'decoupling' (DiMaggio and Powell 1983). The institutional reference points that are downloaded from global cultural script are simply decoupled from existing social practices; the global does not intrude the local. This is the case for many properties of modern statehood cited above, including the rule of law as 'decoupling occurs precisely at the point where the law intrudes' (Boyle and Meyer 2002, 82). This approach helps to explain the striking similarities of, for example, national constitutions in spite of the deep diversity of socio-political realities in countries around the globe (Boli 1987). Yet it does not account for the variation in the ways in which these constitutions affect socio-political processes differently in different countries. It does not account for the variety of ways in which state-backed law and social practices are intertwined in dialectal processes in which the former affects the latter (to varying degrees) without ever being fully independent of it (Eckert et al. 2012; Benda-Beckmann and Benda-Beckmann 2007). In sum, the works of Meyer et al. do account for the striking similarity of institutional forms around the globe, but they cannot explain the different effects that global scripts have in different contexts.

[1] I would like to thank Rahul Rao for this analogy, I owe this point to him.

In order to explain the varying effects that global norms have on local contexts, constructivist scholars in IR have populated the empty islands that still pervaded the spatial imagination of the Stanford School. They have introduced agents into the structural account of the Stanford School and shown how it is only their ardent work that allows global norms to affect local practices. Margaret Keck and Kathryn Sikkink, for example, have shown how domestic actors in repressive states can align with transnational advocacy groups so that 'boomeranging effects' pressure authoritarian governments from above and below (Keck and Sikkink 1998, 12–13). By showing how 'ideas do not float freely' (Risse-Kappen 1994), constructivists have thus highlighted the decisive importance of actors both above and below the state. This importance has been theorized in Cascade, Boomerang, and Spiral models, through which constructivists have reconstructed the complex itineraries of global norms (Keck and Sikkink 1998; Risse et al. 1999). They have shown how norms are moved back and forth between the local and the global by a multiplicity of state and non-state actors. Constructivists have thereby developed dynamic models of the ways in which norms travel; but these models have persistently relied on static assumptions about the content of norms (Krook and True 2012, 106). In other words, although constructivists have reconstructed the crooked ways of norms, the ways in which norms change as they move back and forth between different places has remained unexplored.

2.2. THE NOTION OF TRANSLATION

These changes are at the heart of the following chapters where I show how global norms about 'the rule of law' change as they travel from the desks of EU bureaucrats in Brussels to UN offices in Dhaka and on to local NGOs in rural Bangladesh—and how there the socio-political dynamics of conflict resolution change correspondingly. This dual change is what I analyse as a process of translation. Translations are the transformation in the content of norms that occurs as these norms are transported from one place to another; translations are therefore transportation plus transformation (cf. Callon 1986; Latour 2005; Best and Walters 2013; Barry 2013). Yet the transformations are not limited to the content of norms. As norms are translated, the social and political contexts in which they are translated change as well. Thus, processes of translation are different from 'norm localizations' in which local elites actively transform and reconstruct norms to make them resonate with local practices. This localization perspective as developed by Amitav Acharya (2004, 2009) thus inverses constructivist accounts of norm diffusion. It is no longer the norm that remains fixed, but the local context assumes prime of place. The dual transformations of (a) the content of norms and (b) the contexts in which they are translated have been largely ignored by scholarship on the diffusion of norms and their localization.

To understand the transformations, the content of norms first needs to be disaggregated. As intersubjectively shared standards of appropriate behaviour, norms consist of three interrelated yet analytically separable elements. Firstly, they consist of institutional reference points. This is the focus of the Stanford School (Buhari-Gulmez 2010, 256). Yet institutional shells remain meaningless if they are not connected to specific sets of practices (Risse et al. 1999, 2013). Finally, norms also contain an unavoidably normative component that points beyond existing practices by establishing what is—and is not—considered to be appropriate (Finnemore and Sikkink 1998, 891). Norms therefore consist of a dynamic interplay between these three constitutive elements, i.e. institutional reference points, specific sets of practices, and normative aspirations. In processes of translation, these elements change—but they change to different degrees so that a fine line of seeming continuity is maintained as norms are translated between different actors located in different contexts. This fine line is important. It distinguishes translations from other kinds of transformation, for example full appropriations or outright rejections. Translations therefore unfold in a productive tension of continuity and change. While their core content does change, these changes nonetheless remain recognizable to different actors that are located in different contexts. Yet what drives the changes in the content of norms that occur as they travel back and forth between one context and another?

Background Knowledge

When norms travel, they never encounter empty islands. Instead, they encounter pre-existing social and political worlds in which a diversity of actors navigates complex landscapes of pre-existing institutions, practices, and normative convictions (Chakrabarty 2008, xii). These institutions, practices, and normative convictions, in turn, are connected and interwoven in what Charles Taylor has termed 'background knowledge'. Background knowledge refers to all that is taken for granted and simply relied upon; it is the unarticulated assumptions against which understanding becomes possible and actions meaningful (Taylor 1997, 167).[2] Inspired by Wittgenstein's account of what

[2] Taylor's notion of background knowledge does bear some resemblance to Jürgen Habermas's notion of the lifeworld. According to Habermas, the lifeworld is a 'culturally and linguistically organized stock of interpretive patterns [which] circumscribe action situations in the manner of a pre-understood context that, however, is not addressed' (Habermas 1987, 124, 132). I prefer Taylor's notion for two reasons: firstly, its intuitive plausibility of a background against which understanding becomes possible and action meaningful. Secondly, and more importantly,

it means to follow a rule, Taylor strongly criticizes the methodological individualism of the social sciences and the epistemological tradition that underpins it for reducing human understanding to the conscious representations of the world by a single agent. In contrast, Taylor argues that we cannot consciously reflect on all that we know. The conscious representations of the world by a single individual are not 'the primary locus of understanding, they are only islands in the sea of our unformulated grasp on the world' (Taylor 1997, 170). Of course, this does not mean that human beings do not act, or do not act deliberately or intentionally. Instead, Taylor argues that the deliberate choices we make only become meaningful against the background of a socially shared knowledge, which is unarticulated and, at least in its entirety, unarticulatable. Thus, we are able to critically reflect on some of the things we take for granted, but we can never question all that we take for granted at the same time. For Taylor, this knowledge is not reflexively available in thought but embodied, which means that 'our bodily know-how, the way we act and move, can encode components of our understanding of self and the world' (Taylor 1997, 170).

Although deeply internalized and generally taken for granted, background knowledge is not the same as 'culture'. Reductionist sociologies of culture define the latter as a clearly delineable whole, which is thought to be congruent with particular population groups (Benhabib 2002, 4). Yet, such a view risks essentializing cultures and reifying them as separate entities (Turner 1993, 412). Thus, when I argue that different background knowledges shape the translation of travelling norms, I am *not* concerned with differences in culture. As Andrew Hurrell has argued in his analysis of 'Norms and Ethics in International Relations', differences in culture are less significant than 'differences in national and regional histories, in social and economic circumstances and conditions, and in political contexts and trajectories' (Hurrell 2003, 150). In other words, different contexts are constituted by different background knowledges, which are not only inscribed in people's bodies but also sedimented in institutions and woven into our threads of moral reasoning, which emerge out of long trajectories of philosophical thinking (Ricœur 2006, 6; Bourdieu 1990, 56–7). Being imbricated in all aspects of social and political life, the background knowledge that people tacitly hold, and that underpins everything we do, is structured not by cultural divisions but by complex processes of social differentiation and, consequently, by unequal relations of power.

Habermas's notion of the lifeworld is embedded in a complex social theory of the interaction of lifeworlds and what he calls 'the system'. This social theory, however, has been developed for what Habermas understands as advanced capitalist societies. This is a significant limitation as Bangladesh clearly does not fall into this camp.

These structuring effects of unequal distributions of power on background knowledge have been theorized by Pierre Bourdieu. They are embodied in what he calls 'habitus', which is a 'system of durable, transposable dispositions, which integrates past experiences and functions at every moment as a matrix of perception, appreciation, and action' (quoted in Pouliot 2008, 273). Embedded in power relations, habitus is acquired through learning processes starting in the very first years of life, they reflect the social conditions in which they are produced, and they become so deeply engrained in the body that they last a lifetime. Thus, habitus is not a set of consciously held ideas but, quite literally, inscribed into people's bodies; it is 'social necessity turned into nature, converted into motor schemes and body automatisms' (Bourdieu 1990, 69). Through habitus social relations become so deeply internalized that they affect the aesthetic perception of art but also preferences for food, sports, dresses, and hairstyles (Bourdieu 1984, 6–7). This is a specific kind of socially mediated background knowledge which is so deeply internalized that it works automatically. It allows us to navigate the social worlds we inhabit and only comes to the forefront in moments of crisis or as a response to novel and unprecedented situations (Hopf 2010, 541–3).

Although deeply ingrained in the body and generally not reflexively available in thought, habitus is not deterministic. Instead, it is located at the intersection of structure and agency. The background knowledge that is embodied in habitus is socially structured. Yet, at the same time, this socially structured background knowledge does not exhaust all possible situations an actor might confront in her lifetime. Instead, habitus is also transposable as it influences perceptions and produces reactions to novel phenomena or unprecedented situations (Bourdieu 1991, 12–13). These reactions, however, are in turn conditioned by the historically grown background knowledge that is embodied in habitus. Thus, what Bourdieu adds to Taylor's philosophical investigation of background knowledge is a social theoretical account of its extraordinary durability without falling back into some kind of cultural essentialism. Whereas the strength of Taylor's interpretative approach is his attention to meaning, his weakness is the obliviousness to relationships of power. The awareness for the importance of power relations in the ways in which background knowledge is differentially structured within and across contexts is the strength of the work of Pierre Bourdieu; its main weakness is his disregard for meaning.

The Task of the Translators

Translations are processes of meaning making (Lendvai and Stubbs 2007, 177); and in these processes, the work of translators is decisive. As I will explicate below, it is only the proactive work of translators that (a) changes the meaning of arriving norms in ways that resonate with people's habitually held background knowledge while thereby also (b) changing the social and political dynamics within a given context. The ardent work of translators is therefore the central scope condition for translations to take place. While this scope condition can be derived from the mobilization literature within IR (Risse et al. 1999, 2013), this literature, as argued above, underestimates the at times extraordinary extents to which the meaning of norms changes in processes of translation. These changes are the complex tasks of the translators.

As Walter Benjamin argued in 1923, the 'Task of the Translator' is not to simply transfer meaning from one language into another by means of literal translation. Instead, the task of the translator is to find in his or her own language the closest approximation to the original's intended meaning. This approximation, however, cannot hope to simply copy the original as correctly, precisely, and faithfully as possible. Literal translations often fail; they do not become meaningful in the receiving language. Instead, the approximation of the original's intended meaning has to recreate this meaning within the resources as well as the long intellectual histories of the receiving language itself. Thus, Benjamin has argued that: 'The translation...does not live within the dense forest of its own native language; instead, from the outside and without entering it, the translation calls the original into this forest, precisely at that point where the echo of its own language allows for the reverberation of the foreign language's original' (Benjamin 1977, 66, my translation). This task of the translator, according to Benjamin, amounts to nothing less than the recreation of meaning in the receiving language. Yet, this recreation does not simply copy the original; instead, it reproduces the original in a way that is understandable to the new language. This translation, then, becomes an original in its own right; it is not fully resembling the foreign language's original anymore, but neither is it fully native to the receiving one. Instead, it is a fusion of meaning. As Sudipta Kaviraj has argued, even in literary translations, the interaction between two languages amounts 'more [to] a fusion of meanings, rather than a simply one-way writing of the meanings of a text into an entirely different passive language. Language is never passive to that extent' (Kaviraj 2005, 519).

Language is never passive to that extent precisely because it is always embedded in a wider social context. Given this intimate relationship between language and social contexts, Benjamin's account of the task of the translator is not only relevant for the translation of languages, but also for the translations of norms and ideas more broadly. His key insight is to highlight the productive component inherent in any translation. Every translation produces a new object (Freeman 2009, 435); and whereas the translation of texts produces new semantic objects, the translation of norms produces new social, political, and legal objects. This production of new social, political, and legal objects is, first and foremost, a political task. Translators operate in social contexts structured by at times severely unequal relations of power; and their translation work upsets these relationships. The translation of norms therefore not only recreates the meaning of seeming 'originals' in innovative ways; it also alters the social and political dynamics of the contexts in which they are being translated. Translations therefore develop powers of their own. These include not only the Habermasian ideals of 'the unforced force of the better argument' but also the use of symbolic power of the Bourdieusian kind. By recreating the meaning of norms in ways that resonate with the in habitus embodied background knowledge of the people surrounding them, translators therefore exercise power, at times to quite significant degrees.

In order to develop these powers, translations depend on the work of translators as well as on further conditions that need to be met:

(1) Translators need to have an intimate knowledge of the social and political dynamics of a specific context; they need to at least know what can, and cannot, work as symbolic power against the backdrop of particular background knowledges.

(2) Translators also need access to (at least minimal) material resources through which this symbolic power can be expressed (see Holzscheiter 2005).

(3) Translators need enough room for manoeuvre that allows them to translate material resources into symbolic power. This room or manoeuvre can be circumscribed by:
   a. Restrictions imposed by the context from where norms and ideas are sent, for example through narrowly defined implementation criteria by international donor agencies (see also Fung 2004; Hajer 2009).
   b. The social and political dynamics in the contexts where translators operate, for example if their movement and activities are circumscribed by governmental authorities (Risse and Ropp 2013, 16–17), when their work is strongly contested within civil societies (Jetschke and Liese 2013; White 1999), or when other powerful non-state actors limit their room for manoeuvre.

These three aspects further specify the conditions under which the work of translators can materialize in ways that change (a) the content of norms and therefore also (b) the social and political dynamics of a particular context. As argued above, the ardent work of translators undermines the idea of fixed and incontestable originals. Transposed to the context of norm translations, this has significant consequences as it undermines the idea of global norms as originals of which local translations would be mere derivates. This, in turn, challenges the spatial imagination of IR.

Translation Circles and the Spatial Imagination of IR

As an academic field of knowledge, IR is based on a specific spatial imagination that distinguishes between international, national, and local levels. This spatial imagination is hierarchically structured as 'the international' is equated with the universal whereas 'the local' is equated with the particular. Consequently, most scholarship on norm diffusion has followed top-down rather than bottom-up approaches and thereby contrasted the universal appeal of global norms with the particularistic qualities of local ones (Acharya 2004, 242).[3] This particular spatial imagination is not only descriptive, but also evaluative: in the equation of the global with the universal, the global is at least implicitly credited with both moral and technical expertise. In this combination of moral and technical expertise, the authority of 'the international' is constructed vis-à-vis 'the local', whose cultural practices are perceived to be the primary obstacle to the realization of universal rights, and whose forms of social and political organization are constructed as the endogenous culprits of economic stagnation and poverty (Rao 2010, 55; Merry 2006, 100). Yet, this kind of universalism that is constructed in 'the international' is a rather narrow one: it tends to reduce the world to 'the West' and rests on the certainty that 'the Rest' shall follow its path (Chan 2010).

Yet rather than being the universal, 'the international' is also nothing but a particular context. It is made up of diplomats, foreign aid workers, the bureaucrats of international organizations, and transnational activists who can only understand each other because of a shared horizon of implicit assumptions that do not need to be explicated but are simply taken for granted by all participants within a conversation (Risse 2000, 16). As the international is also just another context, Anna Holzscheiter has argued that it is important to at least entertain the possibility that 'the international perspectives propagated by NGOs are by no means "universal" but rather limited to specific cultural understandings' (Holzscheiter 2005, 746). Instead of simply descending from the global to the local, norms are therefore translated in a back and forth movement between different actors located in different contexts; and none of these contexts can claim analytical primacy: as much as there is not context-independent global universalism, there are hardly any genuinely 'local' places that would be unexposed to, and thereby untainted by, transnational influences (Merry 2006, 216).

[3] An important exception is the collaborative work of Kathryn Sikkink with Margret Keck and Martha Finnemore, which combines a bottom-up account of norm emergence with a top-down account of norm socialization. However, as I have shown above, they argue (a) that norm entrepreneurs play a more important role in processes of norm emergence than in processes of socialization, and (b) this implies a degree of stability of the content norms at the international level. Implicitly, therefore, the works of Sikkink et al. also reproduce the spatial imagination of IR, in which the global is equated with the universal and the local with the particular.

As norms move back and forth between different contexts, they are translated in what I call a translation circle. The notion of a translation circle flattens the spatial imagination of IR and thereby also challenges the assumption that global norms are incontestable originals. This view prominently informs much scholarship on the diffusion of norms and ideas that equates the effectiveness of global norms with the degree to which their realization on local contexts deviates from global norms as incontrovertible yardsticks. In contrast, from the perspective of a translation circle, there are, in the words of Anna Tsing, 'no originals, but only a heterogeneous continuum of translations, a continual process of rewriting in which meaning—as well as claims of originality and purity—are made' (Tsing 1997, 253). This is important as it has far-reaching analytical implications. Analysing translations as continuous processes in which claims to originality are—first and foremost—claims to authority rather than to translational fidelity requires analytical frameworks that can capture various translations in their own right and do not rank them hierarchically. More precisely, the analysis of global norms within translation circles requires analytical frameworks that circumvent two twin dangers, especially for the translation of norms in the Global South: the uncritical acceptance of global norms as incontestable universal originals, and the equally uncritical reification of post-colonial difference.

This problem is particularly acute in cases where global norms are congruent with analytical categories within the social science, for example in the case of 'democracy' or 'the rule of law'. Dethroning these global norms from their claim to incontestable originality requires a simultaneous distancing from the conceptual languages of the social sciences, which have emerged out of the political history of Western Europe and North America and took it as their primary task to represent that history. Thus, Sudipta Kaviraj has argued that:

> An implicit European reference works from the heart of the conceptual apparatus of modern social sciences, turning it 'naturally' to Euro-normality, much as the magnetic properties of a compass needle always make it point north. European history is the natural north of social science. (Kaviraj 2009, 180)

This gravitation of the social sciences towards the political experiences of Western Europe and North America is far from coincidental. Instead, it was produced in processes of colonial expansion, which globalized not only the modern political institutions that developed in the North Atlantic, but also the analytical vocabularies deployed to describe and analyse them.

This globalization of political institutions in the wake of colonial expansion has left neither the colonizers nor the colonized untouched (Randeria 2000). Yet the historical entanglements between colonies and metropoles have been insufficiently reflected within the social sciences so that '[i]n the universal language of modern social theory the history of the West is always written as world history' (Randeria 2002, 288). By writing the history of the West as the history of the world, the plurality of the social and political practices across the globe is translated into the familiar conceptual languages of the social sciences. As Ashis Nandy has argued, these translations constitute an imperialism of categories, in which '[i]ntellect becomes IQ, the oral cultures become the cultures of the primitive or the preliterate, the oppressed become the proletariat, social change becomes development' (Nandy 2002, 61). What Nandy criticizes here is the unidirectional translation of diverse social and political practices into the conceptual languages familiar to the West.

This implicitly elevates the political history of Western Europe and North America to the analytical yardstick against which all other social and political practices across the globe are measured (Draude and Neuweiler 2010, 5). Within this measurement, those social and political practices that do not straightforwardly correspond to the historical experiences of the North Atlantic can only be understood as pathological deviations from established Western models. These deviations are then explained through analytical dustbins like 'culture' or 'tradition' that contrast an allegedly static non-Western essence with the dynamic mobility of (Western) modernity. Alternatively, these deviations have also been approached through teleological lenses like, most recently, modernization theory, which have confined non-Western social and political practices to the waiting room of world history and an unsatisfying 'not yet'. Here, non-Western societies are 'not yet' civilized, developed, or fully democratic in a liberal sense (Berger 2012). Both strategies affirm the inferiority of non-Western societies vis-à-vis their Western counterparts. In the first case, this inferiority is inherent and essential, in the second, it is temporary as non-Western societies have 'just not yet' fully caught up with the analytical and normative yardsticks defined by the social and political practices in the North Atlantic.

Post-colonial scholars have thus developed powerful critiques of Western universalisms. Yet these critiques run the danger of resulting in equally uncritical appreciations of post-colonial difference. Ironically, this appreciation of post-colonial difference tacitly perpetuates two of the main problems of Western universalism that post-colonial scholars have so vigorously attacked themselves. On the one hand, the appreciation of post-colonial difference reifies the ontological distinction between 'the West' and 'the Rest' (Hall 1992) that has been identified by Edward Said (1978) as the key characteristic of Orientalist discourses. On the other hand, the defence of post-colonial difference against Western universalisms also undermines the possibility of post-colonial agency, which is channelled through the translation of hegemonic global cultural scripts. Thus, Rochana Bajpai has argued that global liberalism is an internally highly diverse and thus flexible conceptual edifice, which allows for the transformation of its meanings in post-colonial contexts (Bajpai 2011, 289). Therefore, the investigation of translations of global norms in a variety of local contexts can only proceed through analytical categories which circumvent the twin dangers of affirming Western superiority and the reification of post-colonial difference. The following section develops such a framework for 'the rule of law'.

2.3. ANALYSING TRANSLATIONS OF 'THE RULE OF LAW'

'The rule of law' is a surprisingly polarizing concept. On the one hand, it has been presented as a panacea to many of the world's problems, including ongoing crises of governance and economic growth in many countries of the Global South. While much of the early enthusiasm of 'the Rule of Law Revival' in the late 1980s has started to fade, advocates like Thomas Carothers keep on emphasizing its 'useful non-ideological appeal in an international climate of heightened sensitivity about ideological impositions' (Carothers 2009, 60). Until today, the rule of law is seen as a technical, and therefore unideological and non-political, solution to contemporary challenges of governance. On the other hand, critics of the rule of law have rejected these appeals to its 'purely technical' character and argued that any notion of the rule of law unavoidably contains 'deep ideological and political commitments which require a whole host of presumptions about justice and how best to achieve it' (Salomon 2011, 201). It is, as Dezelay and Garth have argued, a 'new legal orthodoxy' and the current 'rallying cry for global missionaries' (Dezalay and Garth 2002b, 307, 2002a, 2). Diametrically opposed as they are, both arguments reify 'the rule of law' as a distinctly Western concept. In the first case, the diffusion of this concept is considered to be progressive and hence normatively desirable; in the second case, it is resisted on the ground that it would constitute a neo-colonial imposition. Neither of the two approaches is very helpful in understanding translations of the rule of law as they unfold as it travels back and forth between the world of international experts, national elites, and people in rural Bangladesh.

Understanding these translations requires an analytical perspective that appreciates the plurality of rules of law; and the ways in which these change between different contexts. Such perspectives have been advanced by scholars of legal pluralism like Werner Menski (2006), who has developed what he calls a 'global perspective on law' that operates through three interrelated coordinates: (1) the legal institutions of the state, (2) the social relationships that fill these institutions with life as well as constitute their own non-state law, and (3) the moral, ethical, and religious principles that inform a specific legal system. All three coordinates are inseparably linked so that none can be analytically prioritized at the expense of the others. However, these three coordinates have generally been studied in isolation from each other in almost hermetically sealed sub-disciplines. Thus, whereas the investigation of systems of state-backed laws has been predominantly the domain of jurisprudence, anthropologists have embarked on socio-legal studies of the 'living law' (discussed below). The moral, ethical, and religious principles that are unavoidable parts of any legal system have been the subject domain of legal and political philosophers or religious scholars (Menski 2006, 173–91). The strength of Menski's global conceptualization of law is that it challenges this academic division of labour and thus does not need to prioritize state-backed law over non-state legal orders as it is often found in the jurisprudential literature. At the same time, his plurality-sensitive conceptualization of law does not reduce all kinds of law, state-backed as well as non-state, to social processes, as many legal anthropologists have done (Benda-Beckmann and Benda-Beckmann 2007, 56). Approaching law from a global perspective through the three coordinates outlined above also prevents the divorce of law from normative contestations that unavoidably exist in any legal system (Dworkin 1986).

The three coordinates that Menski proposes offer a more complex picture of a legal system in *any* society, Western or non-Western. They also circumvent the specific colonial hierarchies that have been established through the prioritization of, for example, state-backed law over non-state legal systems or of secular over religious law as Menski insists that all three coordinates of law are of equal analytical importance. Consequently, his model satisfies the epistemological demands of a translation perspective by avoiding the uncritical affirmation of Western superiority without falling back into the reification of post-colonial difference. With some modifications, this model can be adopted to my tripartite account of norms outlined above. Both state and non-state courts as well as the ways in which they are formally integrated fall within the broad category of legal institutions. Morality, ethics, and religion are all part of broader normative orders; and socio-legal processes are constituted by practices that endow institutions and normative orders with specific meanings. The remainder of this chapter introduces the analytical vocabulary through which the plurality of institutional designs, normative orders, and correlative practices can be navigated as 'the rule of law' is translated while moving back and forth between bureaucrats in Brussels, UN personnel in Dhaka, the fieldworkers of local NGOs, and the people inhabiting the complex legal landscape of contemporary rural Bangladesh.

Institutions

In terms of institutions, the rule of law is tightly linked to the modern state; and until recently, the vast majority of rule of law-related projects by international donor agencies were directed at the official judiciaries of recipient states. Yet having increasingly grown disillusioned with the prospects of furthering the rule of law exclusively through state judiciaries, international donors have recently turned their attention towards non-state justice mechanisms and the prospects of promoting the liberal trinity of democracy, human rights, and the rule of law through these institutions (UNDP et al. 2013; Tamanaha et al. 2012). As a major study published by UNDP, UNWomen, and UNICEF attests, contemporary rule of law programming has to start with the 'recognition that Informal Justice Systems are an empirical reality, albeit a complicated one' (UNDP et al. 2013, 7). On the one hand, non-state justice institutions are considered to be more accessible than their state-backed counterparts. They are geographically close, fast, and more in sync with local normative convictions. For international donor agencies, non-state justice institutions harbour the dual promise of enhanced efficiency and greater legitimacy for the delivery of justice. On the other hand, however, non-state justice institutions around the world are frequently criticized for their non-compliance with international human rights standards, their patriarchal biases, and their overall perpetuation of unequal power hierarchies. International donor organizations are now confronted with the task of evacuating the perceived benefits of non-state justice institutions from their seeming shortcomings (Berger 2017).

A key strategy pursued by international donor agencies is the integration of non-state justice institutions into the state-backed judiciary. This integration unfolds along two lines. The first concerns procedural or substantial requirements that might be imposed on non-state justice institutions for at least partial recognition of their verdicts by the state. Such requirements include prescriptions of fair trial, the documentation of hearing, or the refrain from physical punishments. These requirements then bring non-state justice institutions closer to the formal logics of the state-backed judiciaries in whose territories they are functioning. The second dimension concerns institutional linkages between state and non-state institutions, for example in the form of judicial oversight or rights of appeal. In the first case, decisions by non-state institutions are subjected to regular oversight by state officials. In the second case, the decisions of non-state institutions are formally recognized by the state and appealable in its courts (Kötter 2012). More complex than the analysis of how non-state courts are institutionally integrated with state-backed judiciaries, however, is the analysis of the various normative orders that underpin both state and non-state law.

Normative Orders: Liberalism, Harmony, Islam

Despite widespread and frequently repeated appeals to the rule of law's non-ideological character (Carothers 1998, 2009), few international experts would share the following position articulated by legal philosopher Joseph Raz.

Raz pushed the claim about the rule of law's normative neutrality to its logical conclusion when he argued that the rule of law:

> is not to be confused with democracy, justice, equality (before the law or otherwise), human rights of any kind or respect for persons or for the dignity of man. A non-democratic legal system, based on the denial of human rights, on extensive poverty, on racial segregation, sexual inequalities, and religious persecution may, in principle, conform to the requirements of the rule of law better than any of the legal systems of the more enlightened Western democracies. This does not mean that it will be better than those Western democracies. It will be an immeasurably worse legal system, but it will excel in one respect: in its conformity to the rule of law. (Raz 2009, 211)[4]

A rule of law that perpetuates extensive poverty, racial segregation, sexual inequalities, and religious persecution is clearly not on the minds of international legal and development experts currently advocating the spread of the rule of law. The strength of Raz's account and his insistence on a definition of the rule of law exclusively through procedural criteria without reference to any normative content is that it reveals the implausibility of theorizing the rule of law revival as 'non-ideological' or 'technical'.

No legal order can gain social traction without at least some degree of legitimacy; the facticity of law and claims to its normative validity are inseparably intertwined (Habermas 1998, 95). Also, the existence of widespread poverty, racial segregation, or sexual discrimination would be in need of some kind of normative justification (albeit highly implausible or ideological ones) to render the kind of rule of law that Raz has described above justifiable in the eyes of those who live within its jurisdiction. Thus, even thin conceptualizations of the rule of law include the criterion that 'laws must be reasonably acceptable to a majority of the populace or people affected... by the laws' (Peerenboom 2004, 4). The rule of law has to *make sense* to its subjects—whatever sense that might be; and '[n]o set of legal institutions or prescriptions exist apart from the narratives that locate it and give it meaning' (Cover 1983, 4–5). Consequently, for the investigation of translation of the rule of law the pressing question is not whether there can be a non-ideological conceptualization of the rule of law. Instead, the central question is: in which normative orders are different notions of the rule of law embedded, and how do these orders relate to processes of translation?

[4] One possible objection to Raz's account regards his exclusion of 'equality' from the conceptual terrain of the rule of law. Thus, it might be argued that the introduction of formal equality before the law would, on the one hand, prohibit the kinds of scenarios that Raz draws while, on the other, still hold on to a technical rather than a normatively loaded conceptualization of the rule of law. Yet, it is to simply hold on to a notion of equality without any further normative reflection on the 'Equality of What?'—for a sophisticated account of the complexities of the concept of equality, see Cohen (1990).

Before addressing this question, it is, however, important to first specify the notion of a normative order. Normative orders are complex structures of values and normative aspirations that legitimize the exercise of political authority as well as the distribution of basic goods.[5] As Rainer Forst and Klaus Günter have argued, normative orders are orders of justification that have a dual existence in the sense that they refer, on the one hand, to already existing social and political orders while, on the other, also pointing beyond these orders by raising claims to validity that transcend the status quo. Thus, they not only mediate between past, present, and future but also legitimize existing political conditions without foreclosing the possibility of critique and change (Forst and Günter 2011, 15–16). Such justifications of political and/or legal authority can never stand alone but are always embedded in what Forst has called narratives of justification (*Rechtfertigungsnarrative*). These narratives embed abstract principles, values, and normative aspirations within specific contexts and thus endow them with historical plausibility as well as emotional appeal (Forst 2013, 6–17).

The emotional appeal of 'the rule of law' as it currently circulates among global development specialists and policy experts is its intimate connection to liberalism. This connection is forged as, conceptually, the rule of law is closely tied to adjacent notions of democracy and human rights as well as free market capitalism (Ehm 2010). Yet this normative liberal order is far from monolithic as the precise meaning of the rule of law changes, depending on the ways in which certain concepts are prioritized over others (Freeden 1998, 77). The World Bank's notion of the rule of law, for example, is closely tied to notions of the market and economic growth; it prioritizes property rights over socio-economic ones and understands democracy primarily in terms of accountable governance. In contrast, international human rights organizations prioritize inalienable rights over economic development and thereby understand the rule of law first and foremost as a way of translating universal moral aspirations into legal guarantees (Schuppert 2009, 212–18). Further shifts in the meaning of the liberal rule of law are easily imaginable: a strong emphasis on participatory democracy combined with a comprehensive notion of human rights that includes socio-economic entitlements pushes the rule of law in the direction of social democracy. In contrast, a strong emphasis on the

[5] There is an ongoing debate in international political theory about the precise relationship of authority and legitimacy: whereas Ian Hurd (1999) has argued that the two are synonymous as authority is recognized legitimacy, Zürn et al. (2012a) have argued that authority and legitimacy are intertwined but distinguishable concepts. Both operate through recognition, but on different levels: whereas authority refers to the basic recognition for the need of an institution (broadly conceived), legitimacy is the recognition that this authority is exercised in desired and desirable ways. This distinction is very helpful for my investigation of translations of the rule of law in rural Bangladesh: here, the authority of the state is recognized on a very basic level, but the ways in which this authority is exercised are considered to be highly illegitimate.

rule of law at the expense of democratic participation and a limited set of unalienable political rights alone pushes liberalism towards libertarianism (Freeden 2008, 201).

Within the broad confines of contemporary global liberalism, various different understandings of the rule of law become possible; and some of these different translations of the rule of law within contemporary global liberal scripts will be further discussed in Chapter 5. Beyond the confines of global liberalism, however, rules of law can also be embedded in different normative orders—and in the remainder of this book, two such orders stand out. The first is built around notions of community harmony, the second around Islam and Islamic law.

The Harmony Ideology

State and non-state justice mechanisms are often associated with different underlying logics of conflict resolution: whereas the former aim at retributive justice and the punishment of the offender, the latter aim at reconciliation and the recreation of harmonious ties within a community. Although this distinction seems overdrawn, as non-state justice mechanisms impose at times severe punishment on offenders, it is still indicative of two logics of conflict resolution, which exist on a sliding scale rather than as mutually exclusive alternatives. Thus, Anke Draude and Sonja Neuweiler have argued that in many parts of Sub-Saharan Africa non-state justice institutions prioritize the reconciliation of conflicting parties and the subsequent recreation of social peace and harmony over the kind of retributive justice available in the state-backed courts (Draude and Neuweiler 2010, 17). The legal anthropologist Laura Nader has described this kind of prioritization of social harmony over justice as the *Harmony Ideology* (1990). Historically contextualizing her ethnographic fieldwork in a Zapotec mountain village in Mexico, Nader argues that this prioritization of harmony over justice has a long historical trajectory and was first introduced through the Spanish colonizers in the form of missionary courts. These missionary courts facilitated processes of mediation and reconciliation as a deliberate strategy to pacify the population and thus undermine possible resistance against the Spanish colonizers (Nader 1990, 3–10).

Not limiting herself to the investigation of Zapotec mountain villages, Nader has identified—and fiercely criticized—a similar move from state-backed justice to alternative dispute resolution (ADR) in the United States in the late 1960s. As Nader rightly observes, the shift 'away from a concern with justice to a concern with harmony and efficiency, from a concern with right and wrong to a concern with therapeutic treatment, from courts to ADR' (Nader 2002, 139) occurred precisely at the point when the feminist and civil rights movements started to advance their political struggles *through* the state-backed law. Thus, in the United States, as in Mexico, the move from state-backed justice to an increasing focus on ADR and its underlying normative arguments about harmony and reconciliation functioned as a pacifying strategy that served nothing but the perpetuation of social privilege and power. As Nader persuasively demonstrates, this relegation of government to private realms has been highly influential beyond the United States. Mediated by US-trained legal experts, ADR has travelled to the international level and become a new 'standard of civilisation' (Nader 2002, 150–1). This expansion from the United States into international legal discourses has also facilitated an environment in which non-state justice mechanisms—like the village courts in Bangladesh—can be understood by Western donor agencies as meaningful ways to promote the rule of law *as such*.

Although the recent enthusiasm about ADR as a way of bypassing state-backed justice delivery through an emphasis on reconciliatory processes has been fuelled to a significant degree by socio-legal developments in the US, it is important to disentangle what turn out to be very different motivations for a prioritization of ADR-facilitated harmony over state-backed justice. In the case of the US and Western Europe, ADR is particularly prominent in cases of business disputes as well as matters of family law. In both cases, the predominant motivation for ADR is that it promises to be both faster and cheaper. Thus, ADR is primarily fuelled by a desire for the efficient resolution of conflicts. This also applies to conflicts within the realm of family law as, for example, in divorce cases the aim of ADR in the West is generally not to save the marriage, but to prevent costly and prolonged court cases. In contrast, ADR and its underlying notions of harmony and reconciliation can also be fuelled by a very different set of motivations: as Laura Nader has argued herself, the prioritization of non-state over state-backed conflict-resolution mechanisms can also be a counter-hegemonic tool; and many communities in Asia, Africa, and Latin America have used non-state conflict-resolution mechanisms precisely to keep first the colonial and later the post-colonial state out. Here, the kind of harmony facilitated by ADR is not desired because of its high efficiency and low costs; instead, it is a matter of identity, belonging, and resistance.

The two motivations for seeking reconciliation and harmony through ADR actually constitute different normative orders. The difference between these normative orders becomes most visible in the relationship of ADR to the state-backed laws: in the first case, the wish for efficiency and the speedy and cheap resolution of justice is not an attack on the normative order(s) embodied in the state-backed law. Instead, it is at best an implicit dissatisfaction with the way in which this normative order is realized in the performance of the state-backed judiciary. Therefore, the outcomes of ADR are also not expected to diverge significantly from the kinds of verdict that the state courts might have passed in similar cases. In the second case, however, ADR becomes a direct attack on the normative orders of state-backed justice and its underlying principles. Here, ADR is an explicit withdrawal from the state-backed justice delivery *because* the kinds of judgements that this judiciary would pass are not considered to be legitimate. They would not be considered legitimate because the space in which harmony is sought is a different one: it is not the entire citizenry of the state to which the state-backed laws apply—rather, it is a particular community that is incongruent with the citizenry of the state. In that sense, the notion of social harmony that Nader identified in the Zapotec mountain village, and which also underpins the dynamics of local conflict resolution in Bangladesh (see Chapter 4), is different from the harmony ideology that Nader has also criticized in the US.

Although ADR-facilitated harmony can be both an extension of the normative order embedded in the state-backed laws and a form of resistance against it, this itself does not illuminate the relationship between 'harmony' and the liberal rule of law. Whereas resistance to liberal state-backed laws might violate the liberal rule of law, resistance to illiberal state-backed laws might actually enhance it. Consequently, the prioritization of harmony over justice can be both compatible and incompatible with the liberal rule of law that is currently being diffused by Western donor agencies. Harmony is compatible with the liberal rule of law if it reproduces the basic justice principles that liberals associate with the state-backed rule of law, i.e. the firm protection of individual rights and at least procedural equality. At the same time, the notion of harmony becomes incompatible with liberalism if it does not adhere to these principles. Although not clear cut, there is thus a normative boundary that distinguishes between different notions of community harmony as compatible or incompatible with the liberal rule of law. A similar and equally not clear-cut normative boundary is often constructed between Islam and liberalism. In the next section, I critically investigate this boundary and side with both Muslim and liberal intellectuals who advance a more nuanced understanding of the relationship between Islam, Islamic law, and the rule of law.

Islam and Islamic Law as Normative Order

As a normative order, Islam is at least under constant suspicion of being incompatible, or only very partially compatible, with liberalism.[6] Although the

6 The by now classical statement of this is, of course, Huntington (1993). The list of Huntington's critics is long, but for a particularly pertinent one within the field of IR see Chan (1997), who documents how Huntington's thesis of 'The Clash of Civilizations' is simply 'Too Neat and Under-Thought a World Order'.

debate that followed the publication of 'The Clash of Civilisations' in a *Foreign Affairs* article in 1993 is too long (and often far too polemical) to be revisited here in detail, I would like to highlight one aspect that feeds into the thesis that liberalism and Islam constitute incommensurable normative orders: the notion of participation, and how it relates to law. Whereas the liberal rule of law is conceptualized as highly flexible, as it allows citizens to translate political participation into the articulation of state-backed laws, Islam is considered to be fixed and immutable, as the Qur'an is, at least by some, equated with the final and immutable articulation of positive law (Menski 2006, 284). This equation is articulated by Muslims and non-Muslims alike; the dividing lines between Islam and liberalism are therefore constructed from both sides. To pick an arbitrary though not entirely unrepresentative example of such an argument as advanced by Bernard Lewis:

> To a Western observer, schooled in the theory and practice of Western freedom, it is precisely the lack of freedom—freedom of the mind from constraint and indoctrination, to question and inquire and speak; freedom of the economy from corrupt and pervasive mismanagement; freedom of women from male oppression; freedom of citizens from tyranny—that underlies so many of the troubles of the Muslim world. (Lewis 2003, 115)

All the issues Lewis touches upon are couched in the language of freedom but evolve primarily around the possibilities of participation: participation in the form of speaking one's mind, engaging in unconstrained economic activities as well as the political life of one's community, and the right to participate in all of the above activities regardless of one's identity, gender, or otherwise. Thus, Lewis assumes that there is an essence of Islam, and that this essence is fixed across time and space. Both views are wrong, as I show below.

Although Islam is probably the scriptural religion par excellence, Gudrun Krämer and Sabine Schmidtke have argued that 'like any text, sacred or other, the Qur'an requires active minds to explore its meaning(s) and implement its directives under changing circumstances' (Krämer and Schmidtke 2006, 4). Yet, who precisely the 'active minds' are, and who is allowed to speak for Islam, is far from clear and first and foremost a question of authority. Thus, Krämer and Schmidtke have argued further that '[t]he nature, scope and locus of religious authority, then, is far from clear with regard to the pre-modern period. It is even less so in the modern period. More and more groups and individuals are claiming the right to speak on Islam and in the name of Islam' (Krämer and Schmidtke 2006, 12). Claiming the right to speak for and in the name of Islam are thus claims to authority, and also claims to recognition within a particular normative order. This normative order centres on the Qur'an but is also informed by a wide array of complementary materials like the collected reports of the sayings, deeds, and practices of Mohammed (*hadith*), long and distinguished traditions of Islamic jurisprudence (*fiqh*), and the opinion of religious experts (*ulama*).[7] The variety of legal and normative resources within Islamic scriptures already introduces a high degree of flexibility into what is often misrepresented as a fixed and immutable body of law. Thus, Wael Hallaq has concluded that Islamic legal authority 'has always encompassed the *power* to set in motion the inherent processes of continuity and change' (Hallaq 2005). Hallaq's argument is pitched at the level of Islamic legal doctrine alone. At the level of Muslim legal practices the diversity, and thus the internal flexibility of Islam as a living normative order, is further accelerated, as Matthew Nelson (2007) has shown. Thus, none of the claims that Bernard Lewis makes about Islam are written in stone (or in the Qur'an, for that matter) as fixed and immutable facts. Both Muslims and non-Muslims alike are engaged in lively debates over the relationship between Islam and democracy (Ahmad 2000), women's rights (Mernissi 1996), human rights (Baderin 2005), political and moral economies (Tripp 2006), free speech, and apostasy (Schaefer 2015). All of these debates, in one way or another, evolve around the same question: who has the right to speak for Islam?

The answers given to this question depend not only on the textual sources selected but also on the interpretations that are applied to these texts. Both the selection of sources and the strategy of interpretation chosen depend, in turn, also on contextual factors and the ways in which Islam interacts with local customs, national identities, migration flows, transnational linkages, etc. Thus, Islam represents a complex and internally diverse normative order that houses a variety of narratives of justification, which, in turn, legitimize and delegitimize a multiplicity of claims to religious and political authority—as, again, both Muslim and non-Muslim scholars have shown (Ahmad 2000; Laborde 2008). In this sense, Islam and liberalism are not diametrically opposed or mutually exclusive. Instead, both Islam and liberalism are normative orders with rich and often internally conflicting narratives of justification that legitimize political authority and thus endow law, whether state-backed or not, with particular meanings. For my investigation of translations of the rule of law in Bangladesh, this highlights the imperative to disentangle the core values of a justification narrative as much as possible from the specific vocabularies in which these values are clothed. More specifically, the following investigation has to ask *for whom* participatory spaces are created through the activation of village courts, *how* these spaces are created, and through *which justification narratives* this happens—regardless of whether the specific vocabulary of the justification narrative is distinctly liberal or Islamic. Furthermore, I am not primarily concerned with the question of whether these spaces actually amount to the full realization of liberal rights or Islamic principles. Instead,

[7] This is only a cursory glance at what is a highly complex and internally diverse intellectual tradition. For further discussion of the sources of Islamic law, see Hallaq (2009).

I only concentrate on the degree to which more participation becomes possible through the deployment of specific narratives of justification.

Practices of Documentation

Besides institutional arrangements and normative orders that justify these arrangements, 'the rule of law' is conceptually linked to specific sets of practices. One central practice of enacting the rule of law is the production of bureaucratic paperwork. Without the production of paperwork, the modern rule of law would be virtually unimaginable as all state-backed legal proceedings are unavoidably mediated by written records. These records embody promises to neutrality, impersonality, and objectivity that already Max Weber had placed at the conceptual heart of 'the rule of law'. As Weber argued in 1921: 'Equality before the law and the demand for legal guarantees against arbitrariness demand a formal and rational "objectivity" of administration, as opposed to the personal discretion flowing from the "grace" of the old patrimonial domination' (Weber 1978, 979–80). In order to administer this formal equality before the law, bureaucratic paperwork is essential to facilitate what Weber understood as the formal and rational objectivity of the administration. For Weber, it was precisely this objectivity which endowed the rule of law with legitimacy (Habermas 1998, 98). This demanded objectivity, however, requires that the paperwork through which any administration is bound to function could be nothing more than the neutral medium of social and legal facts.[8] This understanding of paperwork as a simple carrier of information has deeply pervaded legal systems around the world. It has also left its imprint on the social sciences and humanities so that Ben Kafka could argue that scholars 'discovered all sorts of interesting and important things looking *through* paperwork, but seldom paused to look *at* it' (Kafka 2009, 341). Yet what happens if we pause and look at paperwork, and not only through it?

Instead of treating paperwork as a neutral carrier for the representation of legal facts, Matthew Hull has argued that bureaucratic objects, and in particular files and other forms of paperwork, always need to be enacted in practice (Hull 2012a, 2012b). As they are enacted in practice, the meaning of the files as material objects becomes intimately connected to the people that use them (Reckwitz 2002). This means that files that circulate in state-backed judicial

[8] There is a long line of critique against Weber's account of the bureaucracy, and the role of paperwork within it. For the by now classical statement, see Crozier (1964), who argued that although documents do not facilitate rationalization in the Weberian sense, they facilitate a high degree of organizational control. This line of critique is less relevant for my argument, as I do not focus on bureaucratic documentation as such but much more on legal documents.

processes are not simply the passive carriers of information. Neither are they the equally passive canvases upon which social power structures could simply inscribe their existing hierarchies. Instead, they mediate between different people as well as the social worlds these people inhabit. As mediators, the documents of legal proceedings transform, distort, and modify the meanings of what they are supposed to carry (Latour 2005, 39). Therefore, Matthew Hull has argued in this study of the *Government of Paper* in urban Pakistan that within the administration of Islamabad 'documents often function less as instruments of documentation than as tools for building alliances or oppositions among government functionaries, property owners, businessmen, and builders' (Hull 2012b, 22). The documents Hull analyses enable different actors to forge alliances and form oppositions which they could not have otherwise forged or formed. Although not all of the documents he analyses are legal, some are; and the analogy certainly holds: legal paperwork develops a life, and thus also a power, of its own.

This social life of documents has been thoroughly analysed within anthropology and the anthropology of bureaucracies in South Asia in particular (Riles 2006; Gupta 2012, 2013; Hull 2012b; Mathur 2015; Cody 2009). Julia Eckert, for example, has shown in her studies of legal pluralism in Mumbai how the symbolic power of state-backed legal institutions, and thus also of the documents that are issued there, is often deployed as a social capital by exactly those people who do not have access to any other kinds of social capital that could influence the outcomes of non-state justice mechanisms (Eckert 2009, 199). This symbolic power emerges as official paperwork speaks both *with* and *to* the authority of the state. It does not necessarily need to rely on the material back-up of strong enforcement powers of the state. Instead, this sense of authority is habitual; it is inculcated and locked into the background knowledge through which actors navigate the social worlds they inhabit. This habitual and inculcated power is precisely what Bourdieu (1990) has conceptualized through the notion of habitus: it is the pre-reflective response to a marker of authority. In this case, authority is symbolically mediated. When it is symbolically mediated and not backed up by strong enforcement powers, authority does not necessarily lead to rule compliance. Instead, it merely prompts people to change their course of action. Consequently, in areas of limited statehood (Risse 2013), where the enforcement powers of the state are by definition low, the symbolic mediation of the state's authority through bureaucratic paperwork changes people's actions, but not necessarily in accordance with the state-backed laws.

Nonetheless, bureaucratic paperwork and documents are highly important: birth, marriage, and divorce certificates, documents of land ownership, school certificates, national ID cards, and petitions or complaints to government officials are all essential artefacts to negotiate encounters with the state, even in areas where statehood itself is limited. As they mediate encounters with the state, these documents also carry traces of its authority. Francis Cody (2009), for example, has shown in her study of marginalized women in southern India that the submission of written petitions to district-level government offices can itself be an instance of enacting and performing political power. Thus, rather than being the neutral conveyer of the content of a petition, the piece of paper onto which it is actually written is itself a highly important artefact without which formal entitlements to citizenship cannot be *practised*. For my investigation of translations of the rule of law in Bangladesh, this means that there are strong reasons to be 'cautious about relying on files themselves as evidence of the practices that involve them. Much of what is important about the use of files is not documented within them' (Hull 2012b, 218). Thus, the documents that circulate in processes of conflict resolution must not be taken at face value. Instead, the central question is how these documents are enacted in practice—and what kinds of effects the specific ways of enacting them in practice have.

The Living Law as Background Knowledge

The ways in which people make sense of bureaucratic documents is intimately linked to the background knowledge in which they are embedded. It is this background knowledge that gives official paperwork meaning beyond the information that is inscribed in the files themselves; and this is not only the case in South Asia, as Akhil Gupta has forcefully argued (Gupta 2013). Instead, the symbolic power of paperwork that unfolds beyond the legal prescripts of the state are also part of what Eugen Ehrlich has called 'the living law' (Ehrlich 1986). Criticizing positivist jurisprudence in 1913, Ehrlich defined the living law as 'the law which dominates life itself even though it has not been posited in legal propositions' (Ehrlich 2002, 493). Ehrlich's definition of living law encompasses two distinct phenomena. On the one hand, the living law refers to the kind of non-state law discussed above under the heading of legal institutions. On the other hand, however, Ehrlich's definition also includes the specific social meaning that the state-backed laws acquire within a particular context. Thus, he argues that the living law is not enshrined in the legal texts 'that the courts recognize as binding when they decide a legal controversy, but [it is] only that part which the parties actually observe in life' (Ehrlich 2002, 497). This point of the living law points to the complex ways in which state and non-state law become entangled *in practice* within a particular context.

In Bangladesh, state and non-state law interact in practice through a logic of non-enforcement. Matthew Nelson has developed the idea of the logic of non-enforcement in his investigations of the politics of state-backed Shari'a law in Pakistan. Focusing on the laws of inheritance in Punjab, Pakistan, Nelson has shown how local elites expected their elected politicians to undermine the enforcement of the state-backed laws of inheritance. This, according to Nelson, led to a surprising logic of post-colonial accountability: accountability not through, but *against* the state-backed laws as locally elected politicians were held accountable for their ability to prevent the implementation of state-backed laws (Nelson 2011). According to this logic of non-enforcement, the goal of political participation was not to change the content of state-backed laws. Instead, the goal of political participation was the systematic non-enforcement of state laws and a prioritization of localized conflict resolution through non-state justice mechanisms. This logic of non-enforcement therefore connects state and non-state legal institutions in an unexpected way. Although the state-backed laws are systematically not enforced, filing a case with these courts nonetheless changes the dynamics of non-state institutions. The logic of non-enforcement is decisively mediated by official paperwork as producing a file in a non-state court, like in a *shalish* in Bangladesh, actually changes the course of the *shalish* session in favour of the person in possession of the file.[9] This logic of non-enforcement is also saturated with normative expectation about the recreation of community harmony and thereby connects institutions, practices, and normative orders in a complex web of the living law. The living law is the background knowledge against which arriving norms about 'the rule of law' unavoidably need to be translated.

2.4. CONCLUSION

Reflecting on her experiences of arriving in North America, the Polish émigré and later editor of the New York Times Eva Hoffmann wrote, 'Because I don't know the background, I don't always grasp the foreground' (Hoffman 2008). This chapter has brought the background to the foreground by arguing that norms and ideas encounter pre-existing institutions, practices, and normative orders when they travel from one context to another. These institutions, practices, and normative orders are woven together in complex sets of background knowledge; and in order to have an impact on the social and political dynamics within a given context, arriving norms need to resonate with this background knowledge. Making norms resonate is the task of translators; and their ardent work is the central scope condition for translations to take place. Yet at the same time, their creative work undermines the plausibility of global original norms of which local translations would be mere derivates. Instead, every translation creates its own original. This, in turn, requires the

[9] For a similar account about the importance of documents in Indonesia, see Benda-Beckmann and Benda-Beckmann (1994).

development of analytical categories that capture the multiplicity of possible translation in their own right with pre-emptively degrading certain translations to pathological deviations from established global yardsticks. Having established such a framework for 'the rule of law' in this chapter, the remainder of this book turns to the empirical analysis of translations of 'the rule of law' in rural Bangladesh. It starts by introducing the village courts as the institution around which these translations materialize in Chapter 3.

3

The Village Courts in Bangladesh

The project that is at the heart of this book aims at 'activating' the village courts in Bangladesh. It proceeds through a large-scale social experiment that tries to promote the rule of law through non-state justice institutions. The project is considered to be a visible departure from orthodox rule of law programming that has exclusively targeted state-backed institutions. Yet although only very recently rediscovered by international donors as a seemingly 'local' solution to persistent problems of governance in Bangladesh, the village courts are neither very new nor very local. Their first traces can be found not in Bangladesh but in Britain where colonial reports, which already recommended the experimental introduction of the village courts at the dawn of the twentieth century, are stored in the India Office Records of the British Library in London. The village courts that contemporary donors aim to activate thus emerge out of a long historical trajectory in which foreign influences and local practices have continuously affected each other. This chapter reconstructs part of this trajectory and situates the village courts within recursive processes of translation, in which 'the global' and 'the local' have become inseparably entangled. It shows how the village courts were initially invented by the British colonial administration in the second half of the nineteenth century, how this invention was fraught with uncertainties, and how it followed a specific logic in which the accumulation of empirical data about processes of conflict resolution in rural communities was used to alter allegedly universal standards of law in light of local circumstances. A similar logic applies today; and recent donor-driven projects to 'activate' village courts in rural Bangladesh are strikingly similar to their colonial predecessors. After having shown these similarities, the chapter embeds the village courts in the legal landscape of contemporary Bangladesh and analyses the ways in which they are formally integrated into the state-backed justice system. Whereas this chapter focuses on the formal institutional relationship between state and non-state law, Chapter 4 will look at this interaction in practice and focus on the living law in rural Bangladesh.

3.1. HISTORICAL TRAJECTORY

The motivations that underpinned the British promotion of 'the rule of law' in colonial India were varied. They included the protection of commercial interests as well as the protection of British citizens against judgments by exclusively indigenous courts. Yet, in addition to the protection of British interests (narrowly conceived), there was a further, distinctly moral justification for the colonial promotion of the rule of law: the elimination of local customs considered to be 'repugnant' as well as the introduction of 'rational principles of justice' as part of an overall 'civilizing mission' (Benton 2002, 127–8; see also den Otter 2007). Although nineteenth-century British colonial administrators agreed almost unanimously on the superiority of the British rule of law over the legal practices they identified in colonial India, the precise shape that British rule of law promotion in India should take remained contentious. In the late eighteenth century, both the Governor General of Bengal Warren Hastings and the appointee to the Crown Court in Calcutta William Jones rejected the direct transfer of British laws to colonial India as these laws would be, in Jones's words, unsuitable for 'the natives of Bengal' (quoted in Cohn 1996, 86). These natives of Bengal and the ways in which their lives ought to be governed continued to occupy the minds of colonial administrators as well as philosophers like Jeremy Bentham, who extensively referred to the province of Bengal, part of which later would become Bangladesh, in his 'Essay on the Influence of Time and Place in Matters of Legislation' (1843).

In this essay, Bentham argued that although the principles of good legislation were universally valid, their specific realizations would need to be adapted to the specific contexts in which the laws ought to apply. For Bentham, good laws should be informed by the universal 'principles of human nature' and the 'science of utility', both of which he considered to non-controversial. Bentham thus set England as the standard that best approximated these principles and then chose Bengal as a province that formed 'as strong a contrast with England as possible' (Bentham 1843, introduction) in order to see how the universal principles of good legislation could be applied there. Bentham concluded that it was the task of the legislator to translate the universal principles of law to the particular context in which they were to be applied. This translation would need nothing more than a sufficient amount of empirical data to facilitate the translation of universal principles for a context like Bengal. As Bentham argued:

> To assist him in the execution of it, the legislator should be provided with two sets of tables. Those of the first set would exhibit a number of particulars relative to the body of laws which has been pitched upon for a standard, as contemplated in different points of view; for example, a table of offences; tables of justifications, aggravations, extenuations, and exemptions; a table of punishments; a table of the titles of the civil code; a table of the titles of the constitutional code, and so on.

> Those of the other set will be: a general table of the circumstances influencing sensibility; tables or short accounts of the moral, religious, sympathetic and antipathetic biases of the people for whose use the alterations are to be made; a set of maps, as particular as possible; a table of the productions of the country, natural and artificial; tables of the weights, measures and coins in use; tables of its population, and the like. These tables, if a man would work with accuracy, he should have, not metaphorically only, but literally and materially, before his eyes.
>
> (Bentham 1843, chapter 1)

Central to Bentham's argument about the translation of law is the accumulation of empirical data. These data should include not only socio-economic indicators but also the wider discursive environments in which the alterations of universal principles of legislation ought to apply. Analysing Bentham's argument, Partha Chatterjee has argued that this kind of translation is by no means exceptional but rather representative of nineteenth- and twentieth-century Western political thought. As Chatterjee has argued, this style of thought takes the West as the highest standard of civilization and then uses empirical data to show how non-Western societies deviate from this standard. This empirical deviation, in turn, justifies the modification of allegedly universal normative principles to match empirically deviant non-Western contexts in which they ought to be applied (Chatterjee 2011, 6–7). This style of thought cements the West's standing as the closest approximation to the realization of universal principles and, at the same time, constitutes the non-West as empirically abnormal and normatively deficient.

Bentham's logic of translating allegedly universal principles of law for local circumstances surfaces in late nineteenth- and early twentieth-century law reform in colonial Bengal. In 1870, the colonial government established the *panchayat* system for the administration of the rural parts of the province. The Bengal Village Chaukidari Act divided the countryside into 'unions' that were to be administered by a *panchayat* committee comprised of three to five members that were appointed by the colonial magistrates. The tasks of the *panchayat* were primarily the collection of taxes and the appointment and supervision of village police for the maintenance of law and order. In 1870 '[t]he act was introduced experimentally in a few places only' (Kabeer 1965, 7–8). This experiment, however, did not prove to be effective as the *panchayats* that were set up by the colonial administration were not accepted by the rural population. Thus, the colonial administrator Rivers Thomson remarked in 1886: 'I am sorry to find that after several years of experiment the idea of leaving the law to work itself…has not been realised' (quoted in Banerjee 1978, 240).

In response to the failures of the Bengal Village Chaukidari Act, the colonial government commissioned a number of reports. The Fraser Commission Report of 1902–3, the Hobhouse Commission of 1907–9, and the Levinge Committee in 1913 all proposed the creation of village-level courts for the trial of minor cases among the village population (Khan and Rahman 2009, 29). The Hobhouse Commission (1908) examined the desirability of the decentralization of colonial authority in India more generally. The Commission embarked from the argument that this question could not be answered 'by the mere enunciation of general principles, or without taking into account previous and existing conditions' (p. 25). Central to their investigation was the question 'whether the people are sufficiently advanced in education and independence for any measure of village autonomy' (p. 239). Here again there is an attested difference between Europe and India and this difference needs further empirical investigation; in light of these investigations, supposedly universal principles of law and government can then subsequently be translated. In its report, the Commission cautiously concluded that '[i]t is most desirable to constitute and develop village *panchayats* for the administration of certain local affairs [including the administration of justice] within the villages. This system must, however, be gradually and cautiously worked' (p. 306).

A few years later, the Levinge Report (1914), which focuses exclusively on the province of Bengal, strongly supports these recommendations by using exactly the kinds of tables that Bentham had proposed: it enumerated the rising number of civil cases that had almost quadrupled between 1873 and 1912 (p. 26). The report also listed the growth of the population, the number of criminal cases conducted, the number of witnesses examined in them, the spread of primary schooling, growth in middle and high school attendance, the expansion of jute cultivation, and overall growing wealth in the district of Mymensingh as evidence for much needed administrative reforms (p. 25). This evidence is combined with detailed lists about the different districts of Bengal, their respective population numbers, their areas in square miles, as well as the number of sub-divisions, police stations, municipalities, and village unions within them (p. 39). Based on detailed maps (pp. 47, 55, 57, 61, and 65) the report recommended redrawing administrative boundaries and to reform in particular 'the management of local affairs in rural areas' (p. 73).

At the heart of this reform was the recommendation for expanding the competences of the village *panchayats* as '[i]t is chiefly in the exercise of judicial functions... that local authorities acquire importance, but it is also essential that the exercise of these functions should be closely and carefully supervised by sympathetic officers on the spot' (p. 106). This combination of enhanced competences for local authorities and increased supervision of their activities runs through the entire report. It had also been a central theme of the Hobhouse Commission, and the Levinge Report referred extensively to the Commission's argument, in particular with regard to the formal establishment of village courts (p. 114):

> The [Hobhouse] Commission contemplated a system of village courts of equity, which would be freed from the observance of complicated rules of evidence and the technicalities of the ordinary legal procedure, and would bring to bear on

> cases before them their own intimate acquaintance with village sentiment and their local knowledge of the facts... They were partly designed to give petty litigants the opportunity... of settling their disputes by a simple and inexpensive procedure near their homes, but their main purpose was educative, to develop the sense of communal responsibility within the Union, and to teach people to manage the affairs of their own village. At the same time it was hoped that the creation of these village courts would enhance the influence of the *panchayats* and strengthen and encourage them in the performance of their other duties, thus gradually paving the way to the exercise by them of higher powers.

The Levinge Report endorsed most of the ideas presented already in the Hobhouse Commission and recommended the introduction of village courts that ought to trial minor civil and criminal cases by forming a bench around the head of the union *panchayat* as well as two further representatives. As shown in the quote above, the stated motivation for the introduction of village courts was the wish for a fast and cheap provision of justice that would operate without too many procedural constraints, take local concerns into consideration, and thereby also strengthen the authority of the local government institutions.

As with the 1870 Chaukidari Act, the introduction of village courts was conceptualized as a social experiment. Thus, the Levinge Report states that '[t]here is a strong body of opinion in favour of the creation of such [village courts]. We think that the experiment should be given a trial in Bengal... The experiment should be introduced gradually and cautiously, as soon as the necessary legislation has been undertaken' (p. 119). The necessary legislation was eventually passed in 1919 in the form of the Bengal Village Self Government Act. Chapter VII of the Act established so-called 'Union Benches' in which specified civil and criminal cases could be trialled while the respective provisions of the Penal Code, the Code of Criminal Procedure, and the Code of Civil Procedure were suspended. These Union Benches are the predecessors of the contemporary village courts that the EU, UNDP, and four local NGOs currently try to 'activate' in Bangladesh (Murshed 2012, 13).

The official reasoning behind the contemporary project is quite similar to the arguments advanced in the British reports of the early twentieth century; they now include the promotion of 'justice delivery down at the grassroots level', the 'resolution of conflicts in an expeditious, transparent, and affordable manner', and to 'strengthen local government institutions to be responsive to local needs'.[1] Similarly, whereas the Hobhouse Commission argued in 1908 that the village courts were 'most desirable to relieve the regular courts [and] to prevent the people from having to undertake long journeys for the

[1] These quotes are taken from various project publications, including Barkat (2012).

settlement of paltry disputes' (Hobhouse 1908, 242), the AVCB project stated exactly one century later that '[i]t is expected that the activation of village courts will reduce the pressure created by the backlog in the upper-level courts, and permit easy access to justice at the lower levels' (UNDP 2008, 70). And as in the late nineteenth century, the contemporary activation of village courts by the EU and UNDP was anticipated by a long trail of reports, fact-finding missions, and baseline surveys. On the basis of these data, contemporary transnational ideas about the rule of law are translated (see also Chapter 5). As the preceding analysis shows, these translations between European norms and local circumstances have therefore unfolded in long historical trajectories. Within these trajectories, knowledge about what is seemingly 'local' have been produced by the colonial administration, translated into policies, and experimentally introduced. As colonial interventions were introduced in rural Bengal, they were translated further on the ground, ultimately blurring all too neat distinctions between 'the global' and 'the local'. As I have argued in Chapter 2, the global only emerges in friction with the local (Tsing 2005), and the local—in turn—is always already a highly transnationalized space. In the end, the village courts are neither fully indigenous to rural Bengal nor are they an exclusively foreign invention; instead, they are the outcome of complex interactions. These interactions have not only shaped the development of secular but also of religious state-backed laws in South Asia.

Codifying Religious Laws

During the rule of the East India Company from the 1750s to 1858, legal policies had followed a broader strategy of imposing a British layer of authority onto already existing structures of governance in the Mughal Empire. Working from within the legal structures of Mughal governance, the Hastings Reforms of 1772 introduced civil and criminal courts at the district level. Whereas the civil courts were to apply Hindu law to Hindus and Muslim law to Muslims, the criminal courts were to universally apply Islamic law. Trying to preserve the original sources of law, the company officials argued that these courts did not impose British legislation. Instead, they argued that the distinguishing feature of the now British-administered indigenous laws was a higher degree of procedural precision (Benton 2002, 143–9). Initially relying on local religious experts for the administration of religious law, the British court officials from the beginning distrusted their local counterparts and were irritated by what they perceived to be the grossly inconsistent and thus arbitrary application of religious law to different cases (Giunchi 2010, 1126). Thus, from the late seventeenth century onwards, significant resources were mobilized to rehabilitate the textual bases of religious law by translating Sanskrit, Persian, and Arabic sources of both Hindu and Islamic law into

English. By relying primarily on textual sources, the British administrators and scholars that codified Hindu and Muslim law therefore quite literally reduced the complexities of the pre-colonial legal system(s) to 'arrested, frozen forms of representation [that] often had more to do with a limited kind of textual accuracy than a genuine appreciation of the norms by which people actually lived' (Anderson 1993, 180). Although the contextualized legal practices of *pre-colonial* India were always informed by legal scriptures, they were not reducible to texts alone. Instead, the interpretation and application of religious principles always unfolded through local religious authorities that were firmly embedded within particular contexts into which they translated the principles that permeated from religious texts.

The codification of religious laws, and the aspiration to national uniformity this codification represented, thus led virtually to the 'Reinvention of Shari'a under the British Raj' (Giunchi 2010). This reinvention of Shari'a as well as of Hindu law was increasingly limited to personal matters and family law. Thus, by the 1870s most civil and criminal laws in colonial India were based on secular legal codes, written by the British. At the same time, the family laws continued to be based on religious laws, also written by the British. Yet, although 'colonial administrators may never have changed Islamic legal arrangements quite so profoundly as when they were trying to preserve them' (Anderson 1993, 169), this did not mean that the Anglo-Mohammadan laws that were codified by the British remained alien to South Asian Muslims. Instead, the transformation of religious legal practices into text-based religious laws was also paralleled by indigenous movements as Islamic scholars in Deoband, Aligarh, and Lucknow responded to colonial domination through movements of Islamic revival that followed, despite a significant degree of internal diversity, a similar path of 'scriptualism' (Metcalf 2002, 6–15). These scriptualist movements, in turn, altered the processes of law making in colonial India. As Anderson has argued, the influence of the scriptualist movements epitomized in the 1937 Muslim Personal Law (Shariat) Application Act, which stated that '[n]otwithstanding any custom or usage to the contrary, in all questions (save questions relating to agricultural land) regarding... Personal Law... the rule of decision in cases where the parties are Muslims shall be the Muslim Personal Law (Shariat)'.[2] Abrogating what some Islamic scholars perceived as 'non-Islamic customs', the Act further homogenized Muslim

[2] The full text of the first paragraph specifies the concerns of Personal Law more clearly. It reads: 'Notwithstanding any custom or usage to the contrary, in all questions (save questions relating to agricultural land) regarding intestate succession, special property of females, including personal property inherited or obtained under contract or gift or any other provision of Personal Law, marriage, dissolution of marriage, including talaq, ila, zihar, lian, khula and mubaraat, maintenance, dower, guardianship, gifts, trusts and trust properties, and waqfs (other than charities and charitable institutions and charitable and religious endowments) the rule of decision in cases where the parties are Muslims shall be the Muslim Personal Law

legal practices by equating Muslim identity with the state-backed application of a specific interpretation of Shari'a law. Anderson concludes that '[i]t was an Act of indigenous instigation, but its form and purpose reflected a view of the Shari'a that had been reshaped in the British administration of Anglo-Muhammadan law' (Anderson 1993, 184).

The long history of British rule of law construction in colonial India is thus a history of translation: with substantial help from Orientalist scholars and legal experts, British colonial administrators translated what they believed to be local circumstances into colonial law. Local recipients, however, were far from passive. Instead, local actors appropriated, resisted, and translated colonial laws in accordance with their own understandings, preconceptions, and political agendas (Benton 2002, 151). Thus, in contrast to what Marc Galanter has argued in his classic study of *Law and Society in Modern India* (1989), the colonial state never fully succeeded in displacing local legal agency. At the same time, however, ostensibly, 'local' manifestations of law like Hindu or the South Asian version of Muslim Personal Law cannot be conceptualized in isolation from transnational influences, generally quite powerful ones as in the case of the colonial state. Thus, contemporary European efforts to promote the rule of law in Bangladesh are not an instance of a global norm diffusing into a particular local context. Instead, they are just one more pebble in the complex mosaic of European-Bengali rule of law translations that have been created throughout the past two and a half centuries. Before turning to a more detailed discussion of the contemporary legal landscape in the last part of this chapter, the next section first turns to the recent political history of Bangladesh to situate current translations of 'the rule of law' in their broader socio-political context.

3.2. BANGLADESH'S RECENT POLITICAL HISTORY

Bangladesh is a young country with a long history. It separated from Pakistan only in 1971 after the so-called 'second partition' on the Indian sub-continent. The first partition separated India and Pakistan in 1947. This partition

(Shariat).' Available at: http://bdlaws.minlaw.gov.bd/print_sections_all.php?id=173, accessed on 26 March 2017.

What was left open was the equally important question: who is a Muslim? This question had been answered by the Madras High Court in 1922 as the court decided that anybody who 'accepted the prophethood of Mohammed and the supreme authority of the Qur'an would be treated as a Muslim in the eyes of the law' (Anderson 1993, 184). The questions of who is (and is not) a Muslim, who gets to decide this, and how are complex, fascinating, and in need of further research. Unfortunately, they go beyond the scope of this book. I have, however, discussed the related question of who has the right to speak for Islam in Chapter 2. I will also take up this question again in the final section of this chapter.

followed the logic of the 'two-nation theory' that prioritized religion over linguistic or regional identities and argued that Muslims and Hindus are distinct nations with distinct claims to separate independent post-colonial states.[3] Carved out of the Muslim majority areas in the northern part of colonial India, Pakistan comprised two discrete territorial entities—East and West Pakistan—separated by 1,500km of Indian territory. In 1947, Pakistan did not inherit many of the colonial state's central institutions as the capital New Delhi, the majority of the bureaucratic apparatuses of the Indian civil service, and the army as well as police forces stayed in India. In many ways, this was a uniquely challenging situation. As Willem van Schendel has argued: 'no other postcolonial state combined the loss of its administrative hub, the need to govern two unconnected territories, and the ambition to found a national identity upon a religious one' (van Schendel 2009, 107). In particular, the last aspects proved to be extremely difficult and, in the end, insurmountable: within the already unequal division between India and Pakistan, Pakistan's eastern wing fared even worse than its western counterpart. In 1947, East Pakistan had only *one* member of the former elite bureaucratic cadre of the colonial state, the capital of the new state was located in its western wing, administrative staff were centralized there and also resources were transferred from east to west.

Questions about Urdu as the national language soon became the focal point in the conflict between East and West Pakistan (van Schendel 2009, 111) as it involved both questions of power and identity: on the one hand, the push for Urdu as the national language seriously undermined the possibility of the Bengali-speaking East Pakistanis to enter the new state's bureaucratic ruling elite. On the other hand, the imposition of Urdu and the related defamation of Bengali as 'un-Islamic' powerfully symbolized the marginalization of the eastern part in the political life of Pakistan. Thus, since the late 1940s, various language movements emerged in East Pakistan—and were repeatedly crushed by the military and police forces. What these movements generally demanded, however, was not independence but greater autonomy within a federal structure and the recognition of *Bangla* as an additional national language (Hossain and Khan 2006, 329). It was only during the late 1960s that the demand for *Bangla* was seriously combined with a demand for a *desh*, i.e. with the demand for an independent country. This shift occurred in the context of national parliamentary elections. In East Pakistan the leftist parties refused to contest this election as they were dissatisfied with the (West) Pakistani emergency relief after a cyclone had cost between 375,000 and 500,000 lives earlier that

[3] There is a prolific amount of scholarship on the 1947 partition—and intense historical debate about its causes and consequences. A sophisticated introduction to these debates can be found in Bose and Jalal (2004, 135–66).

year. Without competition from the left, the Awami League (AL) secured a landslide victory and won all but two of the parliamentary seats reserved for the eastern wing of the country. As 55 per cent of the total population of Pakistan lived in the eastern part, this meant an absolute majority for the AL. This, however, was unacceptable to the West Pakistani elites—and the parliament was never constituted.

As the elections took place in December 1970, Pakistan was ruled by the former commander-in-chief of the armed forces Yahya Khan. Facing pressure from Zulfikar Bhutto and his Pakistani People's Party (which had won the majority in the western wing of the country), Yahya postponed the first session of parliament in March 1971, provoking mass demonstrations in East Pakistan and, ultimately, a short but brutal war of independence/separation. The history of this war is not only complex but also heavily contested in popular discourse while remaining under-researched academically. As van Schendel has argued, this history involves not only the confrontation between Bangladeshi freedom fighters (*Mukti Bahini*) and the Pakistani military, but also 'the victimization of various groups (women, Hindus, ethnic minorities); local vendettas and the settling of personal scores; tensions between [Bangladeshi] nationalists of different hues . . . and thousands of stories of personal courage and sacrifice' (van Schendel 2009, 161). These stories of personal courage and sacrifice unfolded within a highly polarized international context: as war broke out in the middle of the Cold War, superpower involvement was unavoidable. While India and the Soviet Union supported Bangladesh, China, and the US sided with Pakistan. At that point, Pakistan was of pivotal importance to Sino-US relations: during a visit to Pakistan in July 1971, US National Security Adviser Henry Kissinger embarked on a first secret diplomatic mission to China where he laid the groundwork for Nixon's visit the following year. Pakistan and Yahya Khan thus did play an essential role in the re-establishment of channels of communication between Washington and Beijing—and as the atrocities in Bangladesh started to appear in the international media, Nixon scribbled an order to his staff on 2 May 1971 clearly stating: 'To all hands. Don't squeeze Yahya at this time. RN' (quoted in van Schendel 2009, 169).[4]

Only more recent historical scholarship has introduced some much needed nuances that push the analysis of the war beyond nationalist narratives of various kinds.[5] The conflict itself lasted only nine months but still claimed

[4] The international history of the war in Bangladesh is currently receiving increased scholarly attention, with two monographs published at the end of 2013: Gary J. Bass's *The Blood Telegram: Nixon, Kissinger, and a Forgotten Genocide* (2013) and Srinath Raghavan's *1971: A Global History of the Creation of Bangladesh* (2013).

[5] See, for example, Mookherjee 2015; D'Costa 2011; Siddiqi 2013; Bose 2010.

1–3 million lives.[6] Furthermore, at least 10 million people fled the country between March and December 1971 into India's West Bengal. As the high number of refugees was combined with Pakistani air strikes on Indian military bases in the north west of the country, India intervened militarily in the conflict on 3 December 1971. Two weeks later, the West Pakistani army surrendered—and East Pakistan became Bangladesh. Before surrendering, however, West Pakistani soldiers and pro-Pakistan militias abducted intellectuals, professors, doctors, artists, journalists, and other professionals and executed them in Dhaka. Left with only a very diminished intellectual elite and bureaucratic corps, but with high numbers of internally displaced people, millions of refugees in India, a largely destroyed infrastructure, and an overwhelmingly agricultural economy whose only significant export—jute fibre—went into steep decline as the world discovered polypropylene (i.e. plastic) in the early 1970s, the newly born Bangladesh literally faced *all* the odds as it became independent. The immediate post-war years consequently saw rapid economic decline, an accelerating political crisis, a famine in 1974 that claimed a further 1.5 million lives, and a first military coup in 1975. Between 1975 and 1990, the country was ruled by two consecutive military dictatorships. Since the return to electoral democracy in 1991, the country has been ruled by the alternation of two dominant parties: AL headed by Sheikh Hassina and the Bangladesh National Party (BNP) under the leadership of Khaleda Zia. Whereas the former is the daughter of the independence leader, first president, and so-called 'Father of the Nation' Mujibur Rahman, the latter is the widow of Bangladesh's first military dictator. These two parties continue to dominate Bangladeshi politics today.

While deeply divided along party lines, the overall economic policies of both prime ministers have, however, been remarkably similar: both continued the piecemeal economic liberalization that had started in the mid-1980s. This liberalization, however, has been neither 'planned gradualism nor shock therapy' (Islam 2005, 380). Since the early 1990s, Bangladesh has sustained an average growth rate of 5 per cent per year while income inequality has sharply increased from a Gini coefficient of 38.8 in 1992 to one of 46.7 in 2005 (UNDP 2013, 115; Lewis 2011, 158). The key drivers behind this economic growth are the rise in ready-made garment and shrimp exports, the increasing remittances of Bangladeshis working abroad, and the revenues from Bangladesh's role as the second-largest provider of soldiers and police to UN peace-keeping missions. Yet although contributing only about one quarter to the country's GDP, the basic centrality of agriculture to the economy remains as approximately two in three Bangladeshis work in rice or jute production, livestock farming, forestry, or fisheries (Lewis 2011, 137–66; van

[6] The official Bangladeshi figure is 3 million. The official Pakistani figure is 26,000. Figure quotes in van Schendel (2009, 173).

Schendel 2009, 239–41). With the majority of the population still living in rural areas, land is a scarce resource; and it is disappearing fast as multinational companies, often with the support of local government and non-governmental elites, appropriate increasing amounts of agricultural land in the name of 'development' (Ahasan and Gardner 2016).

The consequences of this 'dispossession by development' are all the more severe as Bangladesh is today the most densely populated country in the world (if city states like Singapore are excluded). With 154 million inhabitants, it is the third-largest Muslim-majority country (90 per cent of the population are Muslim, about 8 per cent Hindu, and 2 per cent Buddhist and Christian); and contestations over Bangladesh's national identity persist: independence from Pakistan could only be achieved by undermining the religious reductionism of the two-nation theory and moving other markers of identity—in particular culture and language—back to the forefront. Emphasizing Bengali language, however, immediately started to blur the boundaries between Bangladesh and the population of the Indian state of West Bengal. Carving out a space for a distinct Bangladeshi identity is therefore an ongoing political process—and in this process, the legacies of the 1970/1 war still loom large: in 2011, the current AL government established an international war crimes tribunal (which is 'international' only in name) to put the collaborators with the Pakistani Army during the liberation war on trial. One of these collaborators was Abdul Quadar Mollah, who was accused of involvement in the killing of intellectuals during the last days of the war as well as other war crimes. As the international tribunal sentenced him to life imprisonment, mass protests broke out in Dhaka with hundreds of thousands demanding capital punishment. Only a few weeks later, a counter-movement emerged accusing the protesters of blasphemous comments and demanding a stronger role of Islam in national politics. Abdul Quader Molla was hanged on 12 December 2013 on the grounds of Dhaka Central Jail—and predictably strong protests followed.[7]

The ensuing legitimacy crisis of the state was not resolved through the subsequent national election in early 2014, which was boycotted by the main opposition party and anticipated by an upsurge in political violence. As the AL stayed in power for a second consecutive term, the space for dissent has continued to shrink after the national election. State repression against the opposition, mass arrests, forced disappearances, and extra-judicial killings have significantly increased (International Crisis Group 2016; Human Rights

[7] Several international human rights organizations have strongly criticized the international war criminals tribunal for violations of principles of due process. Before the execution of Abdul Quader Molla, the UK, US, UN, and EU all issued statements calling for the stay of the verdict. For a detailed account of the events that preceded the execution of Quader Molla as well as the war tribunal in general, see the blog of Dhaka-based journalist David Bergman at http://bangladeshwarcrimes.blogspot.co.uk.

Watch 2016). At the same time, targeted attacks against religious minorities, atheists, and political activists have been on the rise, as have assaults on foreign aid workers, culminating in the attack on a café in Dhaka's diplomatic quarter in July 2016, which left almost thirty people dead. In response to this escalating violence, the ruling AL has repeatedly affirmed its vision of a secular Bangladesh; but it has thereby also resorted to an increasingly authoritarian vision of the country's national identity and left little room for legitimate opposition (Berger 2016). Such specific narratives of national identity, the precise relationship between religion and secularism that they define, and the political histories in which they are embedded have historically been key tools for the legitimation of political regimes. These tools have also left their imprint on the country's legal system.

3.3. THE LEGAL LANDSCAPE IN CONTEMPORARY BANGLADESH

The State-Backed Laws

Bangladesh's contemporary legal system is strongly influenced by the legacies of the colonial rule of law as well as the legal history of Pakistan. Most significantly, Bangladesh inherited from the colonial state a legal system in which civil and criminal codes were based on secular laws while all personal matters were legislated through religious family law.[8] Thus, in contemporary Bangladesh, Muslim family law applies to Muslims, Hindu family law to Hindus and Buddhists, and Christian family law to Christians. The different religious family laws are administered through the state-backed court system. The family courts that apply Muslim, Hindu, and Christian family law belong to the subordinate courts, together with a set of district and magistrate courts for civil and criminal cases, respectively (Rahamāna 2010, 15–17).[9] Besides the three different sets of rules constituting the family laws, there are, however, some civil and criminal laws that cover specific aspects of family life but apply to members of all religious communities uniformly. These include the Child Marriage Restraint Act (1929) and the Guardian and Wards Act (1890). The former renders the facilitation of a marriage between boys under the age of 21 and girls under the age of 18 a criminal offence that

[8] For a recent account of the persistent continuities between colonial and post-colonial conceptualizations of the relationship between law and religion, see Sezgin and Künkler (2014).

[9] The precise nature of the judicial hierarchy among various district and magistrate courts is irrelevant in the context of this study. For a precise overview, see Rahamāna (2010, 15–20).

is punishable with up to one year of imprisonment.[10] Such a marriage, however, would still be legally valid. The Guardian and Wards Act establishes that the implementation of religious family laws regarding the custody of children is always conditional on what is considered to be in the best interest of the child. Both acts date back to colonial times and thus highlight a long-standing dynamic of South Asian legal systems; as changes in religious family laws generally provoke a lot of resistance (Nelson 2013), colonial administrators as well as contemporary legislators have generally found it easier to pass supplementary civil and criminal legislation to undermine those practices that they disapprove of.

The resistance that changes to religious family laws provoke has also affected the reception of international norms in Bangladesh. Although Bangladesh has signed some of the most significant human rights treaties, including the Convention on the Elimination of All Forms of Discrimination against Women (CEDAW, in 1984), the Convention on the Rights of the Child (CRC, in 1990), and the International Covenant on Economic, Social, and Cultural Rights (ICESCR, in 1998), all of these treaties have only been signed with reservations and a suspension of those clauses that were considered incompatible with the current religious family laws in Bangladesh.[11] At the same time, however, CEDAW, for example, has been used to improve the legal protection of women by changing the criminal law codes. Again, this highlights the internal tensions that have emerged from the legacy of the colonial rule of law as it had created a unitary legal system in which different laws are based on different legal sources: secular legislation thus coexists with codified religious principles within the same body of state-backed laws. This tension also surfaces in the constitution of Bangladesh as commitments to secularism and Islam coincide.

Bangladesh adopted its first constitution in November 1972. The principles enshrined in the constitution were the same ones that had informed the struggle for independence: secularism, socialism, nationalism, and democracy (Riaz 2003, 308). The meaning of all four has been continuously contested over the past four decades (Menski 2015). Between 1975 and 1991 Bangladesh was ruled by two military dictators. The first, General Ziaur Rahman, changed the designation of citizens from 'Bengali' to 'Bangladeshi' in order to highlight differences with the Bengali-speaking population of the Indian province of West Bengal in 1977. In the same year, the principle of secularism was abandoned and substituted with an emphasis on 'absolute trust and faith in

[10] The age threshold was amended in 1984. In its original version of 1929, the minimum age for marriage was 14 for girls and 18 for boys.

[11] The reservations concern: Articles 2, 13 (a) and 16.1 (c) of CEDAW: equal rights in marriages and upon its dissolution; Article 14(1) on children's freedom of religion in CRC; and Articles 2 and 3 of ICESCR regarding equal rights to inheritance.

the Almighty Allah' in the preamble as well as a new sub-clause (1A) in the constitution that prescribed that all government actions should be guided by this absolute trust. The second, General Husain Muhammad Ershad, altered the constitution in 1988 by introducing the Eighth Amendment that declared Islam to be the state religion.[12] Ershad's amendment encountered strong resistance from both secular and religious forces within the country as the strongest Islamic political party, the Jamaat-e-Islami, denounced Ershad's move as 'hypocritical' and not genuinely Islamic (Riaz 2003, 308–12). A 2010 Supreme Court verdict reinstated secularism as a cornerstone of the constitution and banned Islamic parties.[13] Through the following Fifteenth Amendment of the Constitution in 2011, Article (1A) was deleted and replaced by Article 8 (1) stating that '[t]he principles of nationalism, socialism, democracy, and secularism . . . shall constitute the fundamental principles of state policy'. At the same time, however, article (2A) was left intact. It declares that '[t]he state religion of the Republic is Islam, but the State shall ensure equal status and equal right in the practice of the Hindu, Buddhist, Christian and other religions'.[14] Thus, under the current constitution Bangladesh is a secular state with Islam as a state religion and constitutionally guaranteed equal rights and statuses of *all* religions.[15]

Within the short constitutional history of Bangladesh, the role and position of Islam has thus been a subject of constant debate and amendment. Although these debates can be read as the attempts of different governments to legitimize their respective rules (Riaz 2003), they also point to the somehow deeper question: *which role should the state play in the realization of Islamic principles, what exactly are these 'genuinely Islamic' principles, who gets to decide all this, and how?* These debates did not emerge only after 1971. Instead, as shown above, they informed the 1937 Muslim Personal Law (Shariat) Application Act. They also informed a piece of Pakistani legislation that is still in force in Bangladesh today and particularly relevant for my investigation of translations

[12] Ershad's Amendment also further 'indigenized' national identity by changing the spelling of 'Bengali' to 'Bangla' and 'Dacca' to 'Dhaka'.

[13] This decision currently seems highly controversial as in the run-up to the national elections in January 2014 the Election Commission has withdrawn the registration of the Jamaat-e-Islami. A High Court verdict from November 2013 confirmed the deregistration of the Jamaat-e-Islami. The judges argued that although Islam is the state religion under article (2A), 'the Jamaat had misinterpreted Islam from its inception' (quoted in the *Dhaka Tribune*, 4 November 2013).

[14] *The Constitution of Bangladesh*, accessed from the website of the Bangladeshi Ministry of Law at http://bdlaws.minlaw.gov.bd/sections_detail.php?id=367&sections_id=24549 on 7 November 2013. This is the slightly altered version of 2011. The earlier version from 1988 read: '[t]he state religion of the Republic is Islam, but other religions may be practiced in peace and harmony in the republic'. Quote taken from http://www.law.emory.edu/ifl/legal/bangladesh.htm, last accessed on 7 November 2013.

[15] For a detailed discussion of the Fifteenth Amendment, see Menski (2015).

of the rule of law: the 1961 Muslim Family Law Ordinance (MFLO).[16] The MFLO was the first attempt of the Pakistani state to codify Muslim personal law. Although the 1937 Shariat Act lay the foundation for the MFLO, Mumtaz Ahmad concludes that 'having been promulgated by the British colonial administration, [the 1937 Act] could not claim any Islamic legitimacy' (Ahmad 1993, 39). Like the 1937 Act, the MFLO covers questions of inheritance, marriage, polygamy, divorce, and maintenance. Based on the recommendations of a seven-member commission of Islamic legal experts, the MFLO established that marriages under Muslim family law should be registered with the state, a requirement that did not exist before. Regarding polygamy, the MFLO established the formal rule that it was only permissible with the explicit consent of the first wife. This consent had to be validated by an arbitration council (discussed in more detail in Section 4.3). The Arbitration council was also the only way to initiate a divorce under Muslim family law as the MFLO required that a husband seeking a divorce had to submit a letter to the local council as well as a copy to his wife. Any divorce would—according to the statute—only become effective after a 90-day mediation phase in which the chairman of the local council, the still married couple, and their representatives would try to solve those problems that had led to the application for divorce in the first place. Controversially, this insistence on the 90-day mediation phase undermined the possibility of immediate verbal divorce, which husbands before could obtain by uttering the word *talaq* (i.e. 'divorce') three consecutive times.

The MFLO was welcomed in particular by women's rights groups as its provisions for the first time involved the state more directly on a legislative level in the administration of Muslim personal law and thus opened the possibility of seeking legal remedies in cases of non-consensual polygamy or default of maintenance payments; it also undermined the constant insecurity that had emanated from the possibility of immediate divorce through *triple talaq* (Ahmad 1993, 39–41). Yet at the same time the MFLO encountered fierce resistance. Islamic religious scholars including Abul Ala Maududi and the Jamaat-e-Islami rejected the MFLO as un-Islamic (An-Na'īm 2002, 230). They argued that the MFLO violated the 'fundamental nature of Islam' and that the codification constituted an illegitimate infringement of the state upon the authority of Islamic scholars (Ahmad 1993, 42). Over the past five decades, these contestations over the MFLO have repeatedly surfaced in both Pakistan and Bangladesh. In February 2013, the Hefazat-e-Islam Movement organized a number of mass demonstrations in Bangladesh in order to advance their 13 Point Program, of which Point 5 concerns '[t]he

[16] There have been some minor amendments to the 1961 MFLO in Bangladesh. These amendments, however, do not concern the content of the MFLO but its administration by the respective government bodies; see An-Na'īm (2002).

Abolishment of the anti-Islamic inheritance law'—a clear reference to the 1961 MFLO's explicit recognition of the inheritance rights of orphaned grandchildren.[17] Thus, the 1961 MFLO has frequently been the topic of fierce debate at the level of legal doctrine. At the level of legal practice, however, the changes in legislation had less tangible effects than the intensity of the debate over the MFLO at a doctrinal level would suggest. In fact, in Pakistan the MFLO has only had marginal effects on the lives of women, if at all (Nelson 2011; Ahmad 1993). As I will show in the following chapters, this is also the case in Bangladesh where the overall enforcement of both secular and religious state-backed laws is highly irregular, in particular in the rural areas of the country. Instead of exclusively running through state-backed laws, the living law in rural Bangladesh unfolds primarily through non-state institutions.

Non-State Justice Systems: the *Shalish*

The most prominent non-state justice mechanism in Bangladesh is called *shalish*. A *shalish* is 'the practice of gathering village elders for the resolution of local dispute' (Jahan and Shahan 2009, 6–7), whereby the notion of 'elders' is less a generational category but refers to respectable and influential people, often including elected local politicians, schoolteachers, doctors, and religious authorities. The *shalish* is a pre-colonial institution; and although it is often described as 'an age-old tradition' it is far from static. As an institution, the *shalish* constantly changes, takes different forms in different places, and thereby also reflects broader social transformations within rural Bangladesh (Lewis and Hossain 2008b, 56). In contemporary Bangladesh, *shalish* appear in all shapes and sizes. I have attended *shalish* with five, 50, and 150 or more participants that negotiate anything from family disputes to conflicts over cattle trespassing but also serious criminal offences, including rape and murder cases. As *shalish* courts are not regulated by the state, both their composition and the ways in which they reach decisions are not uniform but vary, often even within the same village community. In terms of substance, *shalish* decisions are frequently equated with facilitating restorative rather than retributive justice (e.g. Hossain 2015; Jahan and Shahan 2009). Whereas retributive justice demands the punishment of the offender, restorative justice aims at reconciliation and tries to heal the wounds as well as to bring back social harmony. Yet, as I have argued in Chapter 2, this distinction between retributive and restorative justice is often overdrawn, as non-state justice institutions like the *shalish* can be highly retributive and impose different kinds of punishment, including corporal ones (Siddiqi 2011d; Siddiqi 2011a, 2011c). At the same

[17] For the 13 Point Program, see http://www.kaagoj.com/details?id=139, last accessed 10 May 2013; for a detailed discussion of inheritance in the MFLO, see Nelson (2012).

time, the restoration of harmonious relationships always runs the danger of perpetuating local power relations as the resolution of conflicts might simply amount to 'the arbitrary imposition of solutions upon reluctant disputants by powerful personnel of local communities' (Khair 2008, 97). Embedded in local power relations, the internal dynamics of a *shalish* are thus influenced by a number of factors, of which two stand out. Firstly, distribution of land and land ownership play a significant role in the constitution of village authorities (Lewis and Hossain 2008b). Secondly, land as the material basis for power in rural Bangladesh is interwoven with multiple and overlapping hierarchically structured markers of identity that encompass religion, caste, age, and gender.

The complexities of village politics are further accelerated as the *shalish* is also embedded in an intricate web of transnational influences. On the one hand, transnational Islamic movements since the early 1990s have increasingly targeted the *shalish* as a way to institutionalize their respective interpretations of Islamic principles in rural Bangladesh (Riaz 2005, 171).[18] On the other hand, international liberal donor organizations have displayed an increasing interest in the *shalish* as a way of promoting human rights and the rule of law. In doing so, they have followed the lead of local NGOs, thereby once again undermining categorical distinctions between transnational and local influences on Bangladesh's non-state justice institutions. The NGO that pioneered inclusionary *shalish*-based conflict resolution is the Madaripur Legal Aid Association (MLAA). Starting its work in 1978, MLAA has become a key influence on international donors' engagement with non-state justice institutions, not only in Bangladesh (see Golub 2003). It has not only been a decisive inspiration for the project to activate the village courts in Bangladesh (discussed in more detail in the following chapters) but has also actually shaped the ways in which international donor organizations currently conceptualize non-state justice institutions (UNDP et al. 2013). According to its own historical narrative, MLAA 'looked to Bangladesh's traditional form of dispute resolution—"Shalish" or "mediation" in English—and modified it to be participatory and promote human rights, gender equality, and justice' (Madaripur Legal Aid Association 2011).

MLAA's initial projects with *shalish*-based conflict resolution in rural Bangladesh have been taken up and developed further by different organizations in Bangladesh like BRAC, Ain-O-Shalish Kendro, and Nagorik Uddyog (Siddiqi 2003; Alim and Ali 2007; Golub 2012). In response to such projects,

[18] These movements include donations from Saudi Arabia as well as remittances from the Bangladeshi diaspora in the Gulf States, the UK, and the US. Besides Riaz's very general account of 'Traditional Institutions as Tools for Political Islam in Bangladesh' (2005), little is yet known about the translation of transnational Islamic norms in rural Bangladesh. Although this kind of investigation is beyond the scope of the present study, it certainly constitutes an important area of future research.

international donors like the World Bank and various UN agencies have started to shift their focus to reformed *shalish* as a cheap and efficient way of facilitating access to justice for the poor and marginalized segments of society (Akmeemana et al. 2008). This growing enthusiasm about the potentials of Bangladesh's non-state justice institutions as an instrument for the promotion of human rights and justice has been carried by two assumptions: on the one hand, the *shalish* is understood to be authentic. It is portrayed as 'an age-old tradition of local justice in Bangladesh that goes back to the practices developed in Ancient South Asian village communities' (UNDP 2008) or as 'an indigenous method of dispute resolution which has prevailed in rural areas of Bangladesh for centuries' (Mikhail 2007). On the other hand, international donor agencies have pointed to the speed and efficiency with which cases are resolved within *shalish*. Both notions of authenticity and efficiency resonate well with contemporary international discourses about development, as they link local ownership and participation to the realization of pre-defined objectives—the delivery of justice as a public good by non-state institutions (Bliss and Neumann 2008, 4).

Shalish and Islam

What resonates less well with international donor agencies is the role of Islam in *shalish*. Although neither Islamic principles nor Islamic religious authorities are necessary ingredients of a *shalish*, references to Islam are a prominent strategy of village authorities to further legitimize a *shalish* decision (Siddiqi 2011b). In particular, the use of Islamic principles to police and maintain gendered hierarchies in rural Bangladesh has been the subject of much debate, both within the country and abroad. As the enthusiasm about the potential of *shalish* for the realization of human rights and access to justice for the poor started to grow since the mid-1990s, a second issue entered public debate: the detrimental effects of *fatwa* on women's rights.[19] Since 1990, about thirty to fifty *fatwa* cases per year have been reported in the national and at times also the international media.[20]

[19] I here rely on Dina Siddiqi's definition of *fatwa*: 'In Sunni Islam a *fatwa* is a non-binding opinion or interpretation, issued by a recognized authority or legal scholar, on a point of Islamic law or practice. *Fatwa* are usually produced in response to queries by individuals on specific points of contention or confusion. The weight or social acceptability of a *fatwa* depends on the reputation and authority of the mufti or jurist approached, and his/her standing within a given community of scholars. Conventionally, *fatwa* are issued in writing. In Islamic states as well as in countries in which there exists an official government-sanctioned *Shari'a* board (e.g. Malaysia) *fatwa* from these boards can provide the basis for court decisions and government actions' (Siddiqi 2011b, 200–1).

[20] In Bangladesh, *fatwa* entered the public debate only after the return to electoral democracy in the 1990s (Shehabuddin 2008). This, however, does not mean that before the 1990s what then started to be reported as '*fatwa*' did not exist.

These cases often revolve around allegations of pre-marital sex or extra-marital affairs and result in severe violence inflicted upon the accused women in the name of religion. In these cases, corporal punishment (at times so severe as to cause the death of the accused) was inflicted by a *shalish*, but justified through a *fatwa*. In these cases, however, the target of national and international critique is not the *shalish* itself, but only the *fatwa*. In fact, most of these critiques collapse the complex interplay of *fatwa* in *shalish* into the rather simplistic conclusion that Islam causes violence against women.

This conclusion is not only drawn by international media outlets, but also by some members of the Bangladeshi judiciary. In 2000, the High Court issued a *suo motu*, i.e. a ruling on its own initiative, to declare *fatwa* illegal. The court declared that: 'Giving a fatwa by unauthorised person or persons must be made a punishable offence by the Parliament immediately, even if it is not executed' (Daily Star 2001). This decision to declare *fatwa* illegal was welcomed by human rights organizations in Bangladesh and abroad; Amnesty International, for example, concluded that '[t]he division bench of the High Court which made the ruling, and the Bangladeshi women's rights activists who presented the court with evidence against the practice of fatwa, are to be congratulated' (Amnesty International 2001). The court's emphasis on *fatwa* but not on *shalish* or extra-judicial punishments in general provoked strong resistance in Bangladesh. Following the verdict of the High Court Division, several Islamic organizations organized a series of strikes (*hartals*) all over the country and Fazlul Haq Amini, Secretary General of the Islamic political party Islami Oikko Jote, declared the two judges who had passed the verdict heretics. Subsequently, two religious scholars filed an appeal against the verdict with the Appellate Division of the Supreme Court (Riaz 2003, 315–16). It took the Supreme Court ten years to pass a judgment on the appeal. Eventually, in 2011, the Appellate Division decided that non-enforceable *fatwa* were legal—but that they could (a) only be passed by a 'learned person', although it remained vague about the exact qualifications needed to be classified as a 'learned' person, and (b) that *fatwa* should only apply to 'religious matters', which again have not been defined precisely.[21]

The decision by the Appellate Division, however, upheld a second High Court decision following writ petitions by human rights organizations in 2010

[21] Talking to the senior barristers who represented the opposing sides in the 2011 *fatwa* case at the Appellate Division of the Supreme Court, both expressed partial satisfaction with the verdict when I interviewed them in January and February 2012. Both stressed the Court's attempt to find a compromise between two very hardened fronts, and both acknowledged that this compromise was somehow uneasy, especially because the decision remained deliberately vague on the key points of (a) the necessary qualifications to pass judgment and (b) a precise definition of 'religious matters' (CSO-f-035; CSO-m-067).

that declared *all* extra-judicial punishments illegal.[22] This case was filed by a number of prominent Bangladeshi human rights organizations with the explicit aim of disentangling punishments imposed by non-state conflict-resolution mechanisms from questions about Islamic *fatwa* (NGO/CSO-f-035). In its decision, the High Court attempted to establish a typical collision regime in 2010 (p. 14) by arguing that:

> The trial of any offence and imposition of penalties may only be done by established courts and tribunals. To the extent that traditional dispute resolution or alternate dispute resolution takes place, it is also required to be carried out in accordance with law and this cannot involve the imposition of penalties for conduct not recognized as offence under Bangladesh law... In addition, traditional dispute resolution processes through the shalish for resolution of inter alia family disputes take place, but imposition of penalties, such as caning, whipping etc. or fine in such shalish by a private person is bereft of any legal authority and is illegal.[23]

Although the High Court recognized that non-state conflict-resolution processes take place, it was very clear in its decision to point out that non-state justice institutions do not have the authority to impose any kind of corporal punishment or to punish crimes which are not recognized as such in the law books of Bangladesh. Furthermore, the High Court's decision also affirmed the state's monopoly on the legitimate interpretation and execution of Islamic law. Referring to the 1937 Muslim Personal Law (Shariat) Application Act as well as its amended versions in the 1961 MFLO and the 1974 Muslim Marriages and Divorces Registration Act, the court argued that '[t]here is no such provision in the Act here that a private person such as Mufti, Moulana or Imam is given power to administer/execute marriages or divorces on behalf of the concerned' (p. 16). Here, the judgment of the High Court clearly states that Islamic law is enforceable in Bangladesh only to the degree that it is recognized and codified by the state; any alternative interpretation of Islamic law is devoid of state-backed legal authority within the territory of Bangladesh. This and the 2001/11 *fatwa* cases that were negotiated at the High Court and Appellate Divisions of the Supreme Court point to a set of questions that I have discussed in Chapter 2, i.e. the relationship between state and non-state justice institutions from a judicial point of view. Although firmly rejecting the execution of extra-judicial punishments, there is some room for state-regulated non-state justice

[22] The five petitioners were all NGOs: Bangladesh Legal Aid and Services Trust; Ain-O-Shalish Kendro; Bangladesh Mahila Parishad, BRAC, and Nijera Kori.

[23] Judgment of the Supreme Court, High Court Division, in response to Writ Petition 5863 of 2009 with Writ Petition 754 of 2010 and Writ Petition 4275 of 2010. Judgment passed on 8 July 2010. Full text available at: http://www.blast.org.bd/content/judgement/ejp-judgment-8July2010.pdf, accessed 17 November 2013.

institutions within Bangladesh. The next section turns to two of these institutions, which are central to this book: the village courts and arbitration councils.

Quasi-Formal Institutions: Village Courts and Arbitration Councils

In-between the state-backed courts and the non-state system of the *shalish* are two 'quasi-formal' institutions—the arbitration councils and the village courts. Both operate at the level of the Union Parishad (UP). The UP is the second smallest administrative unit of Bangladesh and consists of nine smaller sub-units called wards and each ward is presided over by an elected representative called 'the ward member'. Together with three elected female representatives, the nine ward members form the Union Council. At the head of this council is a directly elected local politician—the UP chairman. These chairmen are the focal point of local politics (Lewis and Hossain 2008a) and they also play a decisive role in both the village courts and arbitration councils.

The Arbitration Councils

The arbitration councils were introduced in 1961 through the MFLO, but they only deal with four kinds of cases falling within the jurisdiction of the Ordinance, namely divorce, maintenance, polygamy, and dower. They are headed by the UP chairman who together with one representative of each conflicting party forms a three-member jury. As argued in Chapter 2, the formal integration of non-state institutions into the state's judiciary needs to be analysed along two lines, i.e. (a) the procedural and substantive requirements imposed on non-state justice institutions and (b) their judicial oversight through state agencies. Substantially, the arbitration councils are bound by the existing state-backed Muslim family laws. Section 6 of the MFLO establishes that Muslim men may enter another marriage with the explicit consent of their first wife. This consent needs to be verified by the arbitration council. Entering another marriage without this consent is punishable with up to one year's imprisonment and/or a fine of up to 10,000 thaka (100 euro), yet the marriage is nonetheless valid in law.[24] For the dissolution of marriages, the 1961 MFLO stipulates that only those divorces that are verified by the arbitration council are legally valid. The application for divorce has to be filed with the arbitration council by either the husband or wife. Following the application with the arbitration council, there is a ninety-day mediation phase facilitated by the council. Applications for

[24] To give an estimate of the purchasing power of Bangladeshi thaka (BDT): in the region of Sylhet, market prices for cattle outside of festive seasons are about 9,000 BDT for unfattened and about 20,000 BDT for fattened cattle. The estimates are quoted in Sarma and Ahmed (2011, 144).

divorce have to be submitted in writing, and a copy of the application has to be sent to the other party involved. Divorces that do not proceed through the arbitration council constitute criminal offences, punishable with up to one year's imprisonment and/or a fine of up to 100,000 thaka (1000 euro).

Besides matters of polygamy and divorce, the arbitration councils also deal with disputes about maintenance and dower. Section 8 (1) of the MFLO establishes women's rights to maintenance by their husband. If a husband fails to maintain his wife, or fails to maintain his wives equally, the UP chairman can constitute the arbitration council and issue a certificate that determines the amount of maintenance to be paid. Finally, Section 10 of the MFLO specifies that the wife can seek recourse from the arbitration council if her husband fails to pay her dower upon demand. Dower is a payment by the husband to his future wife; it is both a sign of respect and a financial security for the wife. The arbitration councils are thus bound by the substantial provisions of the state-backed Muslim family laws. At the same time, the relevant state-backed Civil Codes of Procedures are suspended. There is no right to appeal against decisions reached by an arbitration council, but sub-section (4) of section 6 and sub-section (2) of section 9 allow for the application for revision with the Assistant Judge for cases concerning polygamy. The Assistant Judge might also stay specific arbitration council proceedings if one party has objected to the UP chairman and questioned his impartiality. Besides this provision, there is no formal judicial oversight over the activities of the arbitration council (Islam 2012).

The Village Courts

Importantly, prior to their 'activation' through international donor agencies, the village courts in Bangladesh have existed largely on paper, but not in the practices of rural conflict resolution. On paper, i.e. in terms of intuitional design, the village courts are very similar to the arbitration councils—with one significant difference. The jurisdiction of the village courts is limited to minor civil and criminal cases; and, whereas the arbitration councils are bound by the substantial provisions of the state's Muslim family laws, the respective substantial provisions of the civil and criminal laws are suspended in the village courts. As section 3 of the 2006 Village Court Act specifies, the village courts override the Code of Criminal Procedure and Civil Procedure in cases that fall within its jurisdiction (Murshed 2012, 17–18) so that 'all cases relating to offences in part of the schedule and to matters specified in part II therefore shall... be triable by Village Courts, and no civil or criminal court shall have jurisdiction to try any such case or suit'. The offences that are specified in parts I and II refer to the criminal and civil cases triable in the village courts; they include the dishonest misappropriation of property, theft, criminal intimidation, intentional insult, killing or maiming of animals, animal trespassing, recovery of money due on contracts or other documents, and the recovery of immovable property. Although some of the offences listed in schedules I and II of the Village Court Act are punishable with imprisonment or heavy fines according to the civil and criminal laws of Bangladesh, the village courts can neither imprison offenders nor impose fines on them. Instead, the village court has only the legal authority to impose compensation payments of up to 75,000 thaka.[25]

The village courts therefore effectively substitute the impositions of state-backed civil and criminal laws for pecuniary compensation to be negotiated within the village courts. There are two caveats to this. Firstly, if the village court considers the imprisonment of an offender necessary, it can send the case to the state-backed judiciary (Murshed 2012, 18). Secondly, the state-backed judiciary preserves the right to evacuate cases from the jurisdiction of the village courts and feed them back into the state's legal system. Section 16 of the 2006 Village Court Act establishes that:

> where the District Magistrate is of opinion that the circumstances of a case relating to a matter falling under Part I of the Schedule and pending before a Village Court are such that the public interest and the ends of justice demand its trial in a Criminal Court he may, notwithstanding anything contained in this Act, withdraw the same from the Village Court and send it to the Criminal Court for trial and disposal.

The superiority of the state-backed laws is therefore affirmed. Beyond these two caveats, only procedural requirements apply to the village courts. They concern primarily its composition. Like the arbitration councils, the village courts are presided over by the UP chairman. Additionally, in the village courts each of the conflicting parties nominates two representatives, of which at least one ought to be a member of the Union Council unless the UP chairman permits the nomination of two non-Council members as representatives (section 5 of the 2006 Village Court Act). The 2013 Village Court Amendment Bill further specifies that at least one member of the village court panel has to be a woman. In order to initiate a village court, the aggrieved person files an application with the UP chairman. The fines for the application are 2 thaka (0.02 euro) for civil and 4 thaka (0.04 euro) for criminal cases. If the chairman accepts the application, he fixes a date for the trial and summons both parties as well as potential witnesses to the first court hearing. During this hearing, however, the accused might apply 'Rule 33' by admitting and satisfying the claim(s) of the

[25] After intensive lobbying through the project, the Village Court Act was revised in 2013. The main changes included: extending the financial ceiling of the village courts from 25,000 to 75,000 thaka and the mandatory inclusion of at least one female representative in the village court jury. As most of my field research was conducted when the 2006 Village Court Act was still in place, throughout the book I reference this Act rather than the 2013 one. For the project's press release about the 2013 Village Court Act, see: http://villagecourts.org/news.php, accessed 6 December 2013.

applicant in front of the UP chairman. In this case, the 'Compromise Sheet' is signed and the village court is not formally constituted. If the village court is constituted, the five-member jury passes the judgment after hearing both parties and potential witnesses.

The specific nature of the majority by which a decision is reached is decisive for the possibility of appealing against a decision reached in a village court. Only if the decision was passed by a 3:2 majority is there a right of appeal to the Magistrate of First Class for criminal and the Court of Assistant Judge for civil cases. If the decision is passed with a 4:1 verdict or unanimously, there is no right to appeal with the state-backed courts. The state-backed courts, however, can refer cases to the village courts if they consider them to be within the jurisdiction of the latter. Although in cases of failure of justice, the magistrate or assistant judge may set aside decisions of the village courts or refer cases back to the village courts for reconsideration (Murshed 2012, 18); the village courts are not formally supervised by the Ministry of Law but by the Ministry of Local Governance and Rural Development (MLGRD). This creates a peculiar tension within the village courts as a quasi-formal institution: although there are judicial provisions that ensure the supremacy of the state-backed judiciary over the village courts, for example through the possibility of lifting cases from the village courts to the magistrate courts or through the revision of village court decisions through magistrate and assistant judges, the village courts remain a fundamentally rural institution that are largely separated from the state's justice system.[26]

3.4. CONCLUSION

As a quasi-formal institution, the village courts are located in-between the state and non-state justice systems in rural Bangladesh. As I have shown in

[26] In many ways, this separation again dates back to colonial times: the village courts were introduced as part of a larger decentralization scheme that increased the powers of local authorities. Mahmood Mamdami has identified a similar pattern of colonial governance in Uganda. Reflecting on his personal experience of working with the Ministry of Local Governance in Uganda, Mamdami writes: '[t]he Ministry of Local Government was like a state within the state. I realized that this was the ministry for peasants. It was the heart of the colonial state' (Mamdani 2001, 656). It was the heart of the colonial state as British colonialism in Sub-Saharan Africa operated largely through a form of indirect rule that created a bifurcated state and distinguished between *citizen* and *subject*. Whereas citizens were subject to the 'civilized' laws of the state, subjects were under the administration of 'tribal' laws that governed non-market relationships, family, and community affairs (Mamdani 1996, 17). In many ways, the village courts that were introduced in Bengal in 1919 and are currently activated in Bangladesh through the combined efforts of the EU, UNDP, and four local NGOs are positioned directly at this dividing line.

this chapter, they emerge out of a long historical trajectory in which some striking continuities persist between the introduction of the village courts through the British colonizers at the dawn of the twentieth century and the most recent attempts of 'activating' these courts through international donor agencies. In both cases, the departure from the state-backed rule of law has been conceptualized as a large-scale social experiment; and in both cases, this experiment has been preceded by the production of expert knowledge about processes of rural justice. After having outlined the institutional legal landscape within which this experiment unfolds in this chapter, Chapter 4 turns to the living law that fills this landscape with a life of its own. It is this living law that constitutes the background knowledge that underpins all processes of conflict resolution in rural Bangladesh; and it is this background knowledge with which transnational notions of the rule of law have to resonate in order to affect the established dynamics of conflict resolution within rural communities.

4

Between the State and the *Shalish*

The Logic of Non-Enforcement

This chapter complements the previous analysis of the formal institutional structure of the legal landscape in rural Bangladesh through the investigation of the ways in which state and non-state laws interact in practice. As argued in Chapter 2, these interactions constitute the living law and therefore the specific kind of background knowledge against which all processes of conflict resolution are made sense of. In rural Bangladesh, this background knowledge is characterized by what I call the logic of non-enforcement. According to this logic, people frequently appeal to the state courts, but not in order to get binding and enforceable decrees, but in order to alter the dynamics of non-state justice institutions. This chapter shows the logic of non-enforcement at work by, firstly, offering a thick description of a *shalish* session on an attempted murder case in rural Bangladesh. Secondly, I contextualize this description with further evidence from representatives of the judiciary, police, and local elected politicians in rural Bangladesh. After having shown how the logic of non-enforcement is mediated through the symbols of the state, and in particular through bureaucratic paperwork, in the final section of this chapter I turn to the normative vocabularies that underpin the systematic non-enforcement of state-backed law. In this chapter, I therefore reconstruct the background knowledge against which all subsequent translations of 'the rule of law' analysed in the second part of this book unfold. Before turning to this analysis, the following section exemplifies the logic of non-enforcement through the thick description of an emblematic *shalish* session in rural Bangladesh.

4.1. THICK DESCRIPTION: A *SHALISH* IN HATHAZARI

It is the beginning of November 2012 and I have just arrived in Bangladesh for my second round of fieldwork. After a couple of days in Dhaka, I travelled to

Hathazari in Chittagong Division to revisit the area where I had started my research on translations of the rule of law in Bangladesh in October 2011. This time, I stay in the house of my colleague and thus live directly in the UP, where I had already conducted two dozen interviews before. We visit the UP chairman in his office. He is clearly surprised to see me again; he did not really believe me when I told him in 2011 that I would return the following year. We talk for some time, then he asks me if I am still interested in *shalish*. As I confirm that I am, he tells me that there is currently a very complicated *shalish* case in his UP; it involves attempted murder and very strained relations between two villages. The final *shalish* session is on Saturday night in the building of the primary school—and I am invited.

On Saturday night, my host and I drive to the primary school. The sun had set an hour earlier. About fifty people have gathered outside the flat concrete building which houses the classroom. The classroom itself is also packed as approximately 150 people—all of them male—have squeezed into the single room, looking towards the front where the chairman of the UP, some ward members, and the conflicting parties are seated around a large desk. The walls are decorated with educational material, displaying the Bengali alphabet, a map of Hathazari District, and paintings by the school children. The room is filled with the noise of countless conversations. As the chairman starts to address the audience and welcomes everybody, the noise slowly fades away and we can finally hear him clearly:

> and this is actually a case for the police; someone was badly injured and almost died. But if you go to the police, you will have to pay lots of money—and the police will not restore peace in our community. The police are partial; they only work for their own benefit. But we don't work for the benefit of anybody, except the victim and our community. We have invited all involved parties and the chairmen of their wards; we will discuss the matter thoroughly. We will try to forget all the quarrels and fights and find friendship again ... This is already the third shalish, but first we will hear the statements of all parties again.

Hearing all statements takes about an hour. It unfolds as a discussion, at times very emotional, between the conflicting parties, their representatives, the chairman, and the general audience. As I could not follow the entire discussion, what follows here is a reconstruction of the case that builds on the accounts given in the *shalish* as well as supplementary discussions I had with the chairman, the victim's family, and my translator before and after the *shalish*. The case involves three parties (A, B, and C): the conflict escalated three months ago, in mid-August, as Khairul and his family (A) went to visit some of their distant relatives, Shamsul's family (B), to celebrate *Eid-al-Fitr*. Khairul and Shamsul live in different villages that belong to the same UP. Soon after Khairul's family arrived at Shamsul's house, a fight erupted and some members of Shamsul's family started throwing stones and beating Khairul and his relatives. Eventually, Khairul and his family managed to escape from the village—but returned in the evening. Just before sunset, Khairul, some of his male relatives, and some other men from his village, about twenty men in total, returned to Shamsul's house and dragged him and his son into the yard, where they started insulting him and beating him with canes and the blunt sides of harvesting knives. At the same time, Yafi (C) was taking a bath in the nearby pond as he heard the fight. Although a neighbour of Shamsul, he also knew some of Khairul's family members and tried to intervene in the conflict and persuade both parties to stop the fighting. Some men from group A now also started to attack Yafi, driving a large harvesting knife into his skull. As Yafi's brother Asif arrived, Khairul (A) and his people escaped. Asif started chasing them, mobilizing some men from their village. They stopped group A at a bridge and started to beat them. By then, the conflict had fully escalated as people from Khairul's (A) village as well as from the village of Yafi (C) and Shamsul (B) faced each other at the bridge. Someone called the chairman of the UP, who arrived and tried to calm everybody down. After an attempt at resolving the conflict through a *shalish*-on-the-spot had failed, the chairman called the police, who eventually arrived and managed to dissolve the crowd. In the meantime, Yafi (C) was transported to Hathazari Medical College for treatment.

As the respective parties gave their statements, most disagreement concerned the question of who had initially instigated the fight between parties A and B, with both parties blaming each other. After the statements, the chairman asked the audience to leave the classroom. Inside the room, only the conflicting parties, the ward members of their respective villages, a couple of religious leaders and other honourable members of the community, the chairman, my colleague, and I stayed. Intense negotiations started as a crowd of 150 to 200 men waited outside while two dozen men continued their discussion inside the classroom. The negotiations lasted almost four hours, eventually reaching the following settlement: party B had to pay 30,000 thaka (approximately 300 euro) to party A for starting the fight. Party A, in turn, was split into two offenders, Khairul and Salim. Khairul had to pay 190,000 thaka (1,900 euro) to Yafi's family; Salim had to pay 125,000 thaka (1,250 euro). The 40,000 thaka (400 euro), three goats, and one cow that Khairul (A) had already given to Yafi's family (C) were not deductible; instead, they would be considered as a present and sign of good will. Yafi's family would refrain from pursuing the case with the state's law-enforcement agencies, if Khairul and his accomplices formally apologized and asked for forgiveness.

The negotiations lasted four hours and revolved around two main questions: who bears the responsibility for the escalation of conflict? And who should pay how much compensation for what to whom? For the first question, Khairul and his representatives (A) claimed that the origin of the conflict was Shamsul's (B) insult against them. The later injury of Yafi (C) was nothing but an unfortunate accident. In contrast, the representatives of Shamsul (B) and

Yafi (C) highlighted the offence of Khairul and his family (A) against their village community as a whole and thereby argued that Khairul was the primary culprit of disrupting the harmony within the UP. In the end, most men sitting around the table in the classroom agreed that although Shamsul was wrong in insulting his relatives, Khairul and his accomplices should not have reacted the way they did. Consequently, they (A) bore the primary responsibility for the incident—and should thus also pay the highest amount of money. Whereas party B should pay 30,000 thaka to party A for insulting them, party A should pay a total of 315,000 thaka to party C. Party C, represented primarily by Yafi's brother, hesitantly accepted the compromise. He repeatedly pointed out that the amount they would receive did not even cover the current costs of medical treatment, which already on that day had exceeded 400,000 thaka. However, establishing the fines of 190,000 thaka for Khairul, 125,000 thaka for Salim, and 30,000 thaka for Shamsul was anything but arbitrary: a lot of discussion between the ward members of the respective villages as well as the chairman and other community representatives very carefully investigated how much each of the parties could be expected to pay without financially harming them so much that they and their families would be in danger of losing the possibility to sustain their own livelihoods.

After the compromise was reached, the chairman of the UP allowed the audience, which had patiently waited outside, to enter the classroom again. He announced that a compromise had been reached, and said:

> it is the ability to forgive, which makes us truly great. And forgiveness is one of the most important virtues for Muslims: because those who forgive their enemies will also be forgiven by God! And Yafi and his family forgive those people who have harmed them so much. We are very thankful for them to forgive their enemies and to not think only about themselves, but to think about our Union Parishad. They could have killed the people who almost killed their family member; but they were wise and agreed to a mediation, so that we can live in peace and harmony.

Then, Khairul approached Yafi's brother, bent down, touched his feet, and asked for forgiveness. Yafi's brother took a deep breath, looked down, and hesitated—but eventually signalled Khairul to move up again. They embrace each other, albeit hesitantly—and thereby closed the case. It was well past midnight when the *shalish* was over.

The next day, my colleague and I went to see Yafi and his brother at their home in the village, where the fighting had started. We met Yafi and his brother who was primarily talking. He told us that Yafi and he both worked in Saudi Arabia and returned to Bangladesh only for the *Eid* celebrations, a few days before Yafi got injured. Their house was new and spacious, resembling the latest architectural fashions of the new remittances-funded buildings that had emerged in the dozens in and around the UP. Inside their house, we had a long conversation, in which Yafi's brother recalled the events of the last couple of months: on the day when Yafi was injured, some local leaders tried to solve the conflict on the bridge before the police came—but they failed. The same night, the police then also came to his house and asked him for his testimony. But his neighbours urged him to not give any testimony, so he only said that his brother was in hospital. The next day, the higher-ranking sub-inspector of Hathazari Police Station came to his village to investigate the case. He gave a full testimony as the health of his brother had deteriorated. He was treated at Hathazari Medical College, but his condition got worse and he had to be transferred to the larger and better-equipped Medical College in Chittagong, where the wound was opened and cleaned again. They showed me pictures of Yafi the day after the injury: he had a large open wound on his skull, in which I could see pieces of cracked bone and uncovered brain matter. Yafi was sitting just opposite me, a large scar running for nine centimetres right across his shaved head. He had empty eyes, did not say a word, and only stared at the wall behind me.

His brother goes on: after the sub-inspector of the police had left, the ward members, some representatives of Khairul's family, and the UP chairman came. Khairul's family offered him some money and some animals to sacrifice for his brother. They also asked him to withdraw the case with the police—but he refused. Instead, he maintained that he would only withdraw the case once he was sure that his brother would be alive and well. On that day, the chairman and a congregation of fourteen respectable people from the UP travelled to Chittagong to see his brother in the Medical College. The chairman also called the regional leader of his party and asked him to contact Chittagong Medical College to make sure that Yafi would receive the best possible treatment. But even with this treatment, it took almost two months for Yafi to recover, that's why he only agreed to a *shalish* now. I asked him what he would do now with the court case. The police were investigating a case of attempted murder, as he had told me earlier. He nodded and said that there was a court hearing in one week's time. He would go to the court and lie, saying that he did not remember who injured his brother; and his brother would do the same. His brother Yafi slowly nodded.

'So do you think you got justice from the *shalish* yesterday?' I asked, again Yafi's brother, as it was almost impossible to have a conversation with Yafi directly. He hesitated, and then said: 'what happened, happened. God wanted it this way. And we have to accept this'. Silence—then I tried again: 'that's very true! Of course, we cannot change the will of God. But we can make decisions, we can decide to live piously or in sin; we can decide to live a just or unjust life... And do you think it was a just decision? In the *shalish* yesterday?' He seemed to be struggling and took some time before he answered; then, he said:

> if I wanted revenge, I should have taken it myself, the day they almost killed my brother. But I live in a community, in a social system—and I will honour the

> decision of the Chairman. See, Khairul apologized; he put his hand on my feet and would keep them there until I have forgiven him. I have forgiven him now, he has apologized and he contributes all the money he can. His family is not very wealthy; they cannot even pay all the hospital bills. But we can pay them, so I accept his apology and his contribution. And now we can live in peace again; we have restored the peace to our Union Parishad'

He then turned the tables and asked me: 'do you think I have sold my brother? Honestly, please, I want an honest answer from you—have I sold my brother?' Now it was me who hesitated. I thought for a moment—and decided to tell him what I thought: 'No, I don't think you have sold your brother. But I also think that you did not get justice, in the *shalish* or from the police. But you got something else; you got peace for your Union Parishad, probably that's also very important. But it's not the same as justice.' He thought, nodded slowly, offered me a last cup of tea, and thanked me for my answer. After three hours, our conversation was over.

This conversation and the *shalish* I have described above highlight two important aspects of the dynamics of non-state justice mechanisms in the context of rural Bangladesh. Firstly, in the case of the *shalish* the state-backed laws were not enforced but explicitly circumvented. This circumvention, however, did not mean that the state-backed laws or their enforcement agencies would have been insignificant for the dynamics of conflict resolution. Instead, the formal case, which was filed by the sub-inspector of Hathazari police, constituted a pressure point, which forced the chairman to (a) intervene with the hospital and ensure appropriate treatment, and (b) organize a further *shalish* as previous mediations had left party C unsatisfied. Paradoxically, although the involvement of state agencies did alter the dynamics of conflict resolution, virtually nobody in the case study presented above actually assumed that these agencies would have any tangible enforcement capacity.[1] I have addressed this paradox at greater length in Chapter 2 and argued that it is an integral part of the logic of non-enforcement, in which state-backed institutions are used to alter the dynamics of non-state justice mechanisms; even though the state does not constitute a shadow of hierarchy as it lacks substantial enforcement capacities. This is possible because the symbols, and in this case the representatives, of the state are habitually recognized as markers of authority in rural Bangladesh. This recognition is inculcated and operates almost automatically; it does not produce adherence to the state-backed laws but makes people change their courses of action nonetheless. Secondly, the *shalish* session described above shows how the logic of non-enforcement is

[1] Even Yafi's brother, who did keep the police involved as long as he was not sure if Yafi would survive, did not seriously consider the possibility of actually pursuing this case through the state-backed courts. In our conversation quoted above, the only serious alternative to the *shalish* mediation he considered was personal revenge.

inseparably linked to a vocabulary of social harmony and the integrity of the community, which constitute the key values that inform processes of decision making in non-state justice institutions. In the remainder of this chapter, I argue that both the logic of non-enforcement and the values of social harmony and the integrity of the community constitute the living law, and therefore also the background knowledge against which the resolution of conflicts is understood in rural Bangladesh.

4.2. THE LOGIC OF NON-ENFORCEMENT

When I asked people in rural Bangladesh about their preferred site for the resolution of conflict, the vast majority of them expressed a very clear preference for *shalish* courts; and virtually not a single one of my interlocutors even considered the possibility of meaningfully resolving a conflict by involving the state-backed courts. This is also confirmed in a more encompassing survey conducted by UNDP: out of the 7,667 respondents across all six divisions of Bangladesh who were asked in 2009 about how they settled their conflicts and disputes, 77.6 per cent mentioned *shalish*, while only 19.8 per cent also considered the possibility of filing a case with the formal courts (Rahamāna 2010, 85). However, this strong scepticism about the feasibility of appealing to the state-backed courts is somehow puzzling: currently, there are approximately 2.8 million cases pending in Bangladesh's judiciary; and the vast majority of them are pending with the lower courts (UNDP 2014, 2; Rahamāna 2010, 19). But who files these cases if nobody considers the state-backed courts to be meaningful sites of conflict resolution?

In the course of my fieldwork, it became clear that while most of the conflicts people experienced in the five field sites that I visited were solved in non-state fora, at times official cases were also filed simultaneously with the lower courts. The simultaneous engagement of state and non-state conflict-resolution mechanisms characterizes the logic of non-enforcement, according to which people appeal to the former in order to alter the dynamics of the latter. A very tangible illustration of how this logic of non-enforcement works was given by the UP chairman in Dhaka Division. He told me about a recent case in which he had been involved as two sons had inherited equal shares of their father's land. The older brother sold 25 per cent of the total land he and his younger brother had inherited. However, the older brother still wanted to share the remaining 75 per cent of their father's land equally between himself and his younger brother. Not surprisingly, the younger brother disagreed—and called for a *shalish*. The *shalish*, however, rejected his case and asked him to accept the decision of the older brother, as it was widely accepted that a younger brother should obey the older. Dissatisfied with the outcome of the *shalish*, the younger brother filed a case with the formal courts. As the chairman recounts:

> The older brother then asked me if I could help. And so I did: I went to the court and told them that this was a community conflict, which should be handled by the community alone. The court assured me that they won't pursue the case for some time. During this period, I organised a new shalish. This time, the shalish still confirmed that both brothers should share the remaining 75% of the land equally—but the older brother was asked to share half of the money he had earned by selling their father's land with the younger brother.
>
> I am very happy with this outcome. And I also think that the younger brother had only filed a case with the formal courts to improve the decision made in the informal forum of the shalish, this happens very often. (RB-m-005)

This example given by a local elected politician in Dhaka Division highlights two things: firstly, it shows how state and non-state courts do not inhabit different socio-legal universes but do, instead, heavily interact and are thus inseparably intertwined in rural Bangladesh. Secondly, it also shows how the systematic disengagement of the state-backed judiciary is part and parcel of the tasks of elected local politicians; and it is so across the country. Talking to a UP chairman not only in Dhaka Division but also in Chittagong, Sylhet, and Rangpur, a similar pattern emerged: one of the key tasks of the UP chairman is to intervene at the police station or even the courts to prevent the pursuit of filed complaints and to bring them back into non-state fora (RB-gd-110). This expectation towards local elected politicians to prevent the enforcement of state-backed laws and to settle disputes in the non-state justice mechanisms like the *shalish* is also well known among members of the state's judiciary.

Evidence from the State Courts

One of my closest encounters with these members was within the premises of the country's second largest court, the Divisional Court of Chittagong. The building, a blend of British colonial and Mughal architecture in red sandstone, has a long and vivid history as it was used by British, Pakistani, and Bangladeshi governments as an administrative hub and has witnessed a number of high-profile cases against government opponents and members of different independence movements since the mid-nineteenth century (Daily Star 2004). In many ways, the architectural structure of the court in Chittagong epitomizes the complex legal history that I outlined in Chapter 3. It highlights and combines multiple influences—Mughal, British, and Pakistani—and was thus the perfect location for some interviews with high-ranking representatives of the state's judiciary.

While I was talking to a public prosecutor in his office, the assistant public prosecutor, four members of the ruling AL (one of the two main political parties in Bangladesh), and a court clerk were present. Throughout the whole meeting, people came in and out of the office, briefly interrupting our conversation to have a word with the prosecutor. At some point, a UP chairman entered the office, sat down, and was offered tea. He then started talking to the prosecutor about a land dispute that had led to violent confrontations between the disputing parties. Evidently, the prosecutor was familiar with the case. After having been briefed by the chairman, he ordered the clerk to go outside and talk to the two conflicting parties, who had accompanied the UP chairman, and tell them that the party who had filed an official case with the courts should withdraw this case and agree to settle the dispute in a *shalish*, 'otherwise, they would face trouble.' Here, the logic of non-enforcement extends to the upper echelons of the judiciary. In this case, the prosecutor refrained from pursuing what was a serious criminal offence that emerged in the context of a land conflict and, in collaboration with the UP chairman, ensured that both the criminal offence and the land disputes were to be settled in non-state justice institutions. State and non-state institutions are thus intrinsically intertwined; and the representatives of both work to maintain these ties. This holds not only for the judiciary, but also for the law-enforcement agencies.

Evidence from the Law-Enforcement Agencies

Talking to one sub-inspector of police in Khulna Division, he confirmed that there is good cooperation between the police and the chairmen. I ask him if it sometimes happens that one party files a complaint—and then, a day or so later, the chairman arrives and tells him that he wants to solve the conflicts in his union directly. He laughs and comes closer: 'this happens all the time! And I always tell the chairmen: "if you can, please solve the problem in your community; I will not file a case. If you can make both parties agree to a solution. Why should I file a case?"' He goes on: 'only very serious matters should be dealt with in the courts. Otherwise, the courts will be overburdened! Justice delayed, justice denied.' He repeats the last part multiple times and concludes that 'it is much better to solve the conflicts in the communities' (ST-m-101). Later on, I also tell him about my experience in Chittagong, which I described at the beginning of this chapter, arguing that there was good cooperation between the police and the chairman in the attempted murder case, which eventually was settled in a *shalish*. I am curious as to what he thinks about my experience in Chittagong and ask him if he, as a police officer, is familiar with similar incidents in his district. He laughs again and nods in affirmation: 'the same happens here; we try to have good cooperation with the chairmen, they are very influential in their localities, they can solve many problems'. I respond that in some instances, the *shalish* itself might break the law though, for example by imposing corporal punishment on the accused offenders. He agrees: 'yes, sometimes this happens. Sometimes, people even get killed in a *shalish*. In these cases, we definitely do have to intervene! But otherwise, we are happy if the *shalish* settles the conflicts in their communities' (ST-m-101).

Evidence taken from Chittagong, Dhaka, and Khulna Divisions as well as from local elected politicians, the judiciary, and the law-enforcement agencies in Bangladesh thus attest to the widespread prevalence of the logic of non-enforcement as a regularly reoccurring pattern of conflict resolution in rural Bangladesh. In this logic, state and non-state institutions become inseparably intertwined as appealing to the state allows people to alter the dynamics of non-state justice fora in their favour, or to initiate these fora to begin with. This works not because of the enforcement powers of the state, as most of my interlocutors in rural Bangladesh have confirmed. Although being engaged in a legal conflict might be costly and burdensome, i.e. it might involve having to pay both lawyers and court fees while also requiring repeated journeys to the nearest courts, the enforcement capacities of the state are very limited and hardly ever go beyond the 'disturbance capacity' just described. Instead of being founded on the calculated fear of state-backed law enforcement, the logic of non-enforcement is decisively mediated by the symbols of the state, which are habitually recognized in rural Bangladesh. This recognition is deeply engrained in people's background knowledge and operates, at least partially, on a pre-reflective level (cf. Bourdieu 1990, 52–97). It is precisely for this reason that the symbols of the state, for example in the form of a word from a person in an official uniform or official paperwork, are endowed with the powers to change the dynamics of non-state institutions. It is this kind of change—and not the enforcement of state law—that most people in rural Bangladesh aspire to when appealing to the state's courts. The resulting systematic non-enforcement of existing state-backed laws is not limited to the civil and criminal codes, which are based on secular laws; it also extends to the state's religious family laws.

The Non-Enforcement of Religious State-Backed Laws

The most prominent example of not enforcing Islamic family laws is the case of female shares of inheritance. In particular, the inheritance of non-immovable property (i.e. land) is explicitly regulated within the Qur'an (Nelson 2013, 3). Thus, the shares of immovable property sons and daughters should inherit upon their parents' death are less open to scholarly interpretation than Islamic legal texts based, at least in part, on complementary sources. Although it is clearly stated within Islamic law that daughters should inherit half of what the sons receive, this religious principle, which has been codified and formalized in Bangladeshi state-backed family law, is rarely enforced in rural Bangladesh.

As I talk to two young women, one Muslim and one Hindu, in Chittagong Division, they outline their perspectives on female inheritance. The Hindu woman tells me that she was very happy about the absence of a legal provision for female inheritance of land for Hindus. Her Muslim friend responds that female entitlements to inherit some of their parents' land can actually become a severe problem for women: she says that she does not want any of her father's land, but her future husband might want to have some share of this land and pressure her into claiming her legal entitlement. This would, however, potentially endanger the good relationships she has with her brothers. And her brothers are the only kind of security she has: 'if I claim part of my father's land, I do not have any right anymore to go back to my father's house, as I would have acted very selfish,' she argued. So I asked her if the laws of inheritance should be changed. After hesitating for a moment, she disagreed and said:

> No, it's best to get what's written in Islamic law. So I should get some land. Or even better: if I do not need the land myself, my brothers can use it. And if I do need some money, my brothers should give me money, money the land would be worth if it was sold. In this way, there is no need to cause any trouble for anybody.
> (RB-f-030)

The swap of entitlements to (inherited) land for security and maintenance has also been confirmed as a historically grown and established practice by Rahman and van Schendel's study of inheritance practices in a village in northern Bangladesh from 1940 to 1990. They conclude that in the particular village they based their study on:

> a woman's claim to ancestral land is seen as symbolic rather than material. Land is a powerful symbol of a woman's right to maintenance by her paternal family in case her relatives by marriage cannot or will not maintain her. It is important for women to reaffirm this right to maintenance at regular intervals, and this is done by means of the institution of *nayor*, the periodic home visit by a married woman.
> (Rahman and van Schendel 1997, 53)

Similarly, in her study of two villages in Bangladesh in the early 1980s, Kirsten Westergaards found that 77 per cent of women from families with property did not intend to claim their legal shares in their paternal property in exchange for better relationships with their natal families. Finally, a more recent study of Taslima Monsoor even indicated that 95 per cent of all women interviewed considered it inappropriate to demand their rightful shares of inheritance (both quoted in Monsoor 1998, 13–14). Besides the state-backed laws regarding female shares of inheritance of ancestral land, other aspects of the state-backed Muslim family laws are frequently not enforced. Thus, in a brief study of forty Muslim women in polygamous relationships, a Human Rights Watch-commissioned report found that in no case the legal proceedings outlined in the 1961 MFLO (also discussed in Chapter 3) had been followed (Human Rights Watch 2012, 3). In a similar vein, Elora Shehabuddin has argued that the registration of marriages, the restrictions on polygamous marriages, and the security payment for women which ought to be paid upon entering a marriage (*kabin*) are frequently not enforced (Shehabuddin 2008, 84–9). In the following section, I analyse Islam as a set of justification narratives more closely to show how the deep appreciation of Islamic principles as moral guidance can co-exist with the systematic non-enforcement of the state-backed Muslim family law.

4.3. NORMATIVE ORDERS: THE LANGUAGES OF HARMONY AND ISLAM

Islam as Moral Discourse

Islam and Islamic law have a strong normative appeal to the Muslim population in rural Bangladesh. As one respondent in Chittagong told me: 'if people actually followed Islamic law, there would be no need for courts' (RB-m-018). This view, which locates the source of conflict and disorder in human disobedience with divine laws, was a prominent position among my interviewees. Another respondent told me: 'the Holy Qur'an does not change; it is our constitution, our gift from God' (RB-m-017). Thus, Islamic law is generally perceived to be fixed and unalterable by human agency. In fact, often my respondents argued that it was intervening human agency that actually caused conflicts and disturbed social harmony within their village communities. Thus, one of my interviewees in Chittagong Division complained that 'Muslims sometimes don't follow the Qur'an. They just want to make money, so they make new laws [sic.]' (RB-m-026). Here, the process of law making is not an expression of collective self-determination, as most (liberal) democratic theory would have it, but an expression of egoistic and self-interested behaviour with detrimental effects on community life and well-being.

This critique of human agency (in general) and self-interested behaviour (in particular) as a corruption of divine laws was not only directed against institutions of the state, but also against religious authorities. As one respondent remarked: 'there are some un-Islamic Imams [in this country]. They make decisions based only on their own interests' (RB-m-047). This line of argument was also frequently used to criticize certain kinds of *fatwa*. When I asked a local elected politician in Sylhet Division about the incidents of *fatwa* that had severely violated fundamental rights of women in this area, he told me that:

> In Bangladesh, some people are only Muslim by name. They claim to speak for Islam—but in fact, they only speak for their own self-interest. This is not the proper use of Islam; this is propaganda Islam. But if people followed the real Islam, the Islam laid out in the Holy Qur'an, Hadith Isma, and Kias, then peace would come! (RB-m-046)

Again, the 'real Islam' as revealed through fixed and unchanging laws was contrasted with intervening human agency, based on selfish motivations that caused conflict and disorder. Although the interviews quoted above all come from Chittagong and Sylhet Division, and thus from the historically more conservative eastern part of the country, the importance of Islam as a moral resource prevails across the Muslim citizens of rural Bangladesh as a whole, albeit to varying degrees. This prevalence of Islam as a moral resource to think about the normatively desirable resolution of conflict is somehow puzzling. On the one hand, Islamic laws are considered to be perfect, flawless, and a legitimate point of moral orientation that transcends the petty self-interests that guide worldly politics. On the other hand, as shown above, the Muslim family laws that are backed and formalized by the state are frequently not enforced in rural Bangladesh. There are two reasons for this paradoxical attitude towards Islam and Islamic state-backed laws in rural Bangladesh.

Firstly, as shown above, my respondents distinguished between 'the real Islam', on the one hand, and the manipulation of Islamic principles of political self-interest, on the other. As the state-backed courts are perceived to be highly corrupt, they cannot constitute a legitimate forum for the appropriate interpretation and realization of divine principles. Instead, the courts become a locale for intervening human agency, in which laws are made and enforced not to promote divine principles, but to further individual interests. Secondly, the enforcement or non-enforcement of religious principles, whether codified in state-backed law or not, is closely tied to the maintenance of patriarchal structures in rural Bangladesh. Thus, as argued above, it is precisely those aspects of religious family law, which undermine patriarchal privilege, that are systematically not enforced. Whereas those aspects of Islamic law that are backed by the state but threaten to undermine established patriarchal practices are not enforced, the extra-judicial—and thus illegal—policing of women's freedoms is occasionally justified in the language of Islam. Since the early 1990s, an average of thirty-five to sixty *fatwa* cases have been reported annually (Siddiqi 2011a, 47; see also Chapter 3). In the vast majority of these cases, the disputes involve women and, more precisely, women's sexualities. As Dina Siddiqi has shown for various cases of violence against women that have been justified in the name of *fatwa*, the language of Islam and Islamic law can be instrumentalized by rural elites to police and sanction the transgression of gendered hierarchies within village communities. In most of these cases the transgressions are not simply reducible to women standing up against men. Instead, they generally involve a multiplicity of intersecting registers of domination, including gender, but also class and generational hierarchies (Siddiqi 2011a). The hierarchies also figure prominently in the second justification narrative in which the logic of non-enforcement is embedded: the notion of harmony.

The Notion of Harmony

The second point that can be distilled from the *shalish* case described at the outset of this chapter is a prioritization of peace and social harmony over justice. Importantly, both are conceptually distinguished in rural Bangladesh and the former is not collapsed into the latter so that justice would simply mean the recreation of social harmony. Instead, the conceptual distinction between justice, on the one hand, and social harmony, on the other, as well as a clear preference for the latter over the former is a reoccurring pattern of reasoning I encountered in all of the five regions where I conducted my field research. Having asked respondents in all four divisions about their preferences through the use of a hypothetical thought experiment, 82 per cent expressed a clear preference for social harmony over social justice. This preference has also been confirmed in a number of group discussions, in which I used a similar thought experiment based on a fictitious conflict and asked the participants which of the following two options they would prefer: (1) a full but non-consensual compensation of the victim, which leaves the originator of the offence seriously dissatisfied, or (2) only a partial compensation of the victim, to which the perpetrator could also agree.

This clear distaste for non-consensual compensatory justice was also clearly linked with a strong rejection of the state-backed judiciary. My respondents generally presented two sets of arguments for their rejection of state-backed conflict-resolution mechanisms. The first set revolves around the notorious problems of corruption and inefficiency within the state-backed courts: as argued above, in all five regions, engaging the formal judiciary was univocally considered to be 'a waste of time, money, and energy' (RB-gd-107) as 'the courts are too corrupt, there is no justice there for common people but only for the rich and powerful' (RB-m-094). This is the first of two quite different sets of reasons for what Nader has called 'the harmony ideology' (see also Chapter 2), i.e. efficiency: non-state or ADR mechanisms are generally faster and cheaper than the resolution of conflicts in state-backed judiciaries. The reasons cited above clearly point in that direction. Besides the pressing issue of corruption, which has been attested by my respondents as well as by reports of international NGOs (Transparency International 2012), however, a second set of arguments was brought forward against the resolution of conflicts in the state-backed courts: 'the state courts will not sit and discuss your case thoroughly. There are too many cases in the courts; they have to decide quickly. It's much better to have a *shalish* with good representatives, who know both parties and can discuss the case fully!' (RB-m-026). This is a different argument than the critique of corruption and the overall inefficiency that haunts the state courts. This second argument highlights a different kind of limitation of the state-backed judiciary: the formal courts can, by definition, only pass binding verdicts instead of engaging both parties in a process of reconciliation. However, processes of reconciliation are an essential means to the recreation of peace and social harmony, which is the normative order underpinning the logic of non-enforcement.

The divergent normative foundations of state-backed courts and community-based mediation were very clearly expressed by one UP chairman in Chittagong Division, who told me: 'the goal of the courts is to make one party happy, the other unhappy. Our goal, however, is to make both parties happy!' (RB-m-070). Thus, my respondents argued that 'the traditional *shalish* is always based on the specific context, in which a conflict emerged and tries to re-create the harmony between the parties involved. The arbitration council, on the other hand, is based on laws. Sometimes, the decisions of the arbitration council leave one party dissatisfied' (RB-m-064). Again, the logic of conflict resolution in the state-backed courts, based on nationally binding laws and thus always—by definition—decontextualized, is contrasted with a logic of non-state mediation, which tries to recreate peace and harmony within a specific community. The prioritization of non-state fora over state-backed courts is thus based on a justification narrative woven around the notion of 'harmony'. This notion of harmony is not reducible to efficiency; instead, it constitutes a different narrative of justification than the one that prevails in the state-backed courts: it prioritizes community integrity over individual satisfaction. The appreciation of harmony and the integrity of one's immediate community are, therefore, deeply engrained in the living law of rural Bangladesh. As Sumaiya Khair, a long-time observer of informal conflict-resolution mechanisms in Bangladesh, argued:

> when mediation arrived first in this country, all the NGOs were really sceptical. But people in the rural areas loved it: they would keep on settling for mediation rather than justice. Although this might be counter-intuitive for us, for them justice is really not so important: it's a matter of priorities. The NGOs actually showed them lists, highlighting how much they could gain in a formal court case, and how much less they would get in mediation—but still people kept preferring mediation! (CSO-f-084)

The preference for non-state conflict-resolution mechanisms over the state-backed courts is, however, further qualified by people in rural Bangladesh. This further differentiation might be captured by analytically distinguishing between the authority of the *shalish* and its legitimacy.

The Unavoidable Authority of Social Harmony

Despite their prioritization of non-state harmony over state-backed justice, many of my respondents also highlighted the dangers and potential drawbacks of *shalish* decisions. In different ways, all these reservations against *shalish* revolved around the potential of perpetuating unequal relations of power within and through *shalish* decisions. As I argued in Chapter 3, *shalish* are often inaccessible for women, they frequently discriminate against otherwise marginalized people within a community, for example landless peasants or day labourers, to get a satisfying decision in a *shalish* (Siddiqi 2003, 9–11), and their decisions are often biased and informed not only by the matter of the conflict but also by overall power dynamics and, increasingly, political influences (Lewis and Hossain 2008b, 43). Finally, some of my respondents argued that *shalish* can be (almost) as corrupt as the state-backed courts: 'the *shalish* is like a vehicle: if you give it fuel, it runs' (RB-m-110), a student told me during a group discussion.

The critique of *shalish* as a vehicle for the reproduction of power imbalances, either in the form of financial bribes or the exercise of political influence, points to the underside of peace and harmony as guiding principles within *shalish* decisions. The recreation of peace and harmony within a community that is characterized by structural inequalities is very likely to perpetuate those inequalities, which might even have been considered to be foundational to the social order of a specific community in the first place. For example, landless labourers have little alternative but to accept the recreation of 'harmony' on unequal terms if they face a conflict with the owner of the land where they work, as a legal anthropologist and barrister at the Supreme Court of Bangladesh argued:

> So if you are a landlord and I work on your field, and we have a conflict, I cannot get justice, because the day after tomorrow, I have to go to your field again. People cannot avoid the people they are living with, so that's why they want harmonious relationships at all costs! (CSO-m-105)

Pursuing a similar line of argument, Dina Siddiqi has argued that 'the language of consensus—when the consensus is not reached democratically—becomes a powerful tool for suppressing dissent. The ideal of consensus and the restoration of social harmony frequently translate into the imposition of judgements that may be far from neutral' (Siddiqi 2003, 11). This unavoidability of one's own social context was also voiced by some of my respondents, who attested that they were satisfied with the decisions they received in a *shalish* or in a village court, but also added comments like: 'we all have to live in this society; so it's better if we live in it peacefully' (NGO-f-081). Thus, the preference for social harmony needs to be understood against the horizon of possibilities against which it is articulated. This, however, does not mean that the prioritization of harmony over justice is not genuine. Instead, it imposes a further question: from the point of view of people in rural Bangladesh, under which conditions is the reconstruction of peace and social harmony desirable?

The Fragile Legitimacy of Social Harmony

The critique of *shalish* as the perpetuation of power relations was paralleled by accounts of what constituted a 'good', i.e. a normatively desirable, *shalish* in the eyes of my interlocutors. In Sylhet, a small group of young men said that a good *shalish* is one 'in which the whole village participates. There is one particular person who presides over the *shalish*, but it is not a political figure or anything like that. It must be a neutral person who is respected by everyone—in this way, you can get a good decision' (RB-m-053). Asked about the danger of perpetuating power relations in *shalish*, another man from a village close to the one where the *shalish* described at the beginning of the chapter occurred told me: 'Only if professors, doctors, or other honourable persons are present in a *shalish* this *shalish* can produce a just decision based not only on power' (RB-m-028).

According to these criteria, the *shalish* described above was a good one. There was a high degree of community participation in the hearing of the statements as well as a broad base of people, almost two dozen, who negotiated the actual case and designed the compromise, which resulted in the reconstruction of social peace in the UP. Importantly, during these negotiations, the various participants were not treated equally in a formal sense but were, instead, understood within their very specific social contexts. This was one of the decisive factors for rendering this *shalish* a good one in the eyes of the community members involved. However, as I also showed in this case study, the 'good *shalish*' could only be produced through the involvement of the law-enforcement agencies and the formal judiciary, which put significant pressure on the chairman as well as the local elites to facilitate a *shalish* that would be acceptable to all parties involved. Thus, the logic of non-enforcement and the normative presupposition of community-based mediation in a *shalish* are inseparably intertwined: whereas the logic of non-enforcement is based on a preference for social harmony, the latter might need to use the former to actually facilitate a *shalish* that is considered not only authoritative but also legitimate by all the parties involved.

4.4. CONCLUSION

This chapter has complicated the relationship between state and non-state legal institutions. Both are not only legislatively integrated through carefully crafted collision regimes. Instead, as my evidence from rural Bangladesh as well as further studies in Pakistan (Nelson 2011) and Sudan (Salomon 2011) have shown, state and non-state institutions can become entangled in the logic of non-enforcement. In rural Bangladesh, this logic of non-enforcement is decisively mediated by the symbols of the state, like uniforms or official paperwork. While being mediated by the state, the logic of non-enforcement is also intricately imbricated with normative vocabularies of community harmony as well as of Islam and Islamic law. Both are inseparably intertwined with relations of power so that the restoration of community harmony as much as the application of Islamic principles becomes highly selective and deeply shaped by the patriarchal order of things in rural Bangladesh. Taken together, this interplay of state and non-state institutions, the symbols that facilitate it, and the normative orders in which it is justified constitute the living law in rural Bangladesh. This is the background knowledge with which arriving norms have to resonate if they are going to have any impact on the dynamics of conflict resolution within village communities. As I have theoretically explicated in Chapter 2, it is the complex task of the translators to make these norms resonate in ways congruent with the established background knowledges of the people inhabiting a specific social and political context. Part II turns to this task. It starts with an analysis of the contemporary efforts of the EU, UNDP, and four local NGOs to promote 'the rule of law' through village courts in rural Bangladesh.

Part II

5

The Project 'Activating the Village Courts'

Although a key international donor, UNDP's actual office for the activation of village courts in Bangladesh is a rather peculiar international space. Located in Dhaka's diplomatic quarter, it completely blends in with all the other international representations and embassies in the surrounding streets. Like all the embassies, it is hidden behind barb-wired walls, its entrance is cautiously protected by a private security guard, and its territory is clearly demarked and carefully signposted by the blue flag of the UN. The flag is omnipresent; it is on the buildings, the cars, and even the pencil with which the security guard records the movement of people as they step from the streets of Dhaka into the realm of 'the international' and vice versa. Yet, as one enters the compound and moves behind the façade of the international, a different picture emerges. Everybody working in the UN building that houses the staff for AVCB is actually a Bangladeshi citizen; and most of the senior personnel had long and distinguished careers as judges in the state's judiciary before being seconded to the UN.

Just like the project team of the UN, the village courts themselves are neither exclusively international nor completely local. Instead, as I have shown in Chapter 3, the village courts emerge out of a long historical trajectory in which transnational norms about the rule of law and local logics of conflict resolution have influenced each other as they became entangled in recursive processes of translation. This complex intertwining between 'the global' and 'the local' also continues today as the first section of this chapter shows. It analyses the genesis of the contemporary project that aims at activating the village courts in Bangladesh and reconstructs the ways in which Bangladeshi and international experts co-constructed the village courts as institutional sites suitable for the promotion of the rule of law, broadly conceived. Following the reconstruction of the project genesis, in the second section I turn to the actual project design and introduce the key actors currently involved in the project. Located in very different contexts, the EU, UNDP, and the four local NGOs are all linked in an official project narrative that is spun around the village courts as a normatively desirable institution that ought to be activated in rural Bangladesh. Although connected through this narrative, the different actors involved in the project nonetheless make sense of the village courts in rather different ways. Whereas the EU conceptualizes the village courts as an extension of the state-backed rule of law, UNDP's national experts understand them as institutions of democratic governance. The four local NGOs, finally, conceptualize the village courts as institutions for the promotion of community-based justice. Before turning to the analysis of these translations within the official project narrative, however, the next section turns to the ways in which the initial idea for the project was developed in the first place.

5.1. THE PROJECT GENESIS

Introduced by the colonial administration in the early twentieth century and then later reinvigorated through post-colonial legislation in the 1970s, the village courts have never fully taken hold in the practices of conflict resolution in rural Bangladesh. They have existed on paper, i.e. in the law books of the state, but not in practice (Rahamāna 2010, iv). Largely unknown in rural Bangladesh, the village courts started to attract the attention of international donor agencies only in the early 2000s. This interest was sparked primarily by arguments advanced by several Bangladeshi legal experts in the upper echelons of the judiciary, including a justice and a lawyer at the Supreme Court and a professor of law at Dhaka University. Building on their reflections on grassroots-level initiatives with non-state courts as a tool for enhancing access to justice for the poor, the EU commissioned a substantive study on the topic. This study culminated in an initial report, which argued that the poor 'had been priced out of the justice system', that 'legal complexities, costs, delays, corruption, and too much emphasis on the normative aspect of law' have turned accessing justice through the state's courts into 'a daunting task for the poor'. At the same time, 'recourse to the informal sector has proved no panacea either because of bias and corruption' within non-state justice institutions (Jahan and Stapleton 2013, 4). In conclusion, the report recommended the experimental shift towards non-state justice institutions as a way of promoting the rule of law in general and access to justice in particular.

This recommendation resonated with developments within transnational policy paradigms. Increasingly dissatisfied with the outcomes of formal rule of law reforms pursued through state-backed judiciaries, international donor agencies have been increasingly targeting non-state justice institutions throughout the past decade. At the forefront of this shift towards non-state institutions is the World Bank's Justice for the Poor Program. Having worked in twenty countries since 2002, the Program has investigated various alternatives to 'orthodox' or 'mainstream' rule of law interventions. These alternatives ranged from the training of paralegals to enhance accountability and hence service delivery of the health-care sector in Sierra Leone to the reform of state-backed land-management systems in Vanuatu or community-based legal empowerment schemes in Indonesia's West Java.[1] In the words of two if its key protagonists, Michael Woolcock and Deval Desai, the single characteristic that defines this turn towards non-orthodox rule of law promotion that is at the heart of the 'Justice for the Poor' programme is an:

> emphasis on taking context and the rules of the game seriously [and] doing so by adopting an experimental approach to 'finding and fitting' solutions that respond to locally nominated and prioritized problems. Such an approach is juxtaposed and legitimated against orthodox approaches in which universal best-practice solutions (i.e., the legal texts, procedures, and institutional structures that prevail in developed countries) are imported in response to problems determined by external experts. (Desai and Woolcock 2015, 162)

Departing from the promotion of the state-backed rule of law thus leads to experiments in justice of various kinds, including the experimental engagement of non-state justice institutions.

The human rights-based engagement of non-state institutions is also the central theme of an almost 400-page report commissioned by various UN organizations. Published in 2013 by UNDP, UNICEF, and UN Women, the comprehensive study of 'Informal Justice Mechanisms: Charting a Course for Human Rights-Based Engagement' starts with the 'recognition that Informal Justice Systems are an empirical reality, albeit a complicated one' (UNDP et al. 2013, 7). They are a complicated reality precisely because they are so popular in the Global South. According to the report, several reasons account for this popularity. The two most prominent reasons concern the efficiency and legitimacy of non-state justice institutions vis-à-vis their state-backed counterparts. As the report argues, for many people in the Global South, the state-backed courts are often geographically distant, generally inaccessible, and frequently marred by corruption and inefficiency. Non-state justice institutions not only offer faster, cheaper, and generally more accessible alternatives; they are also likely to be more in sync with local normative orders. This combination of efficient conflict resolution and the resonance with local belief systems accounts for the popularity of non-state institutions. At the same time, these institutions are frequently criticized by national as well as international human rights organizations for their patriarchal biases, the reproduction of local power relationships, and continuous marginalization of the concerns of women, children, and other vulnerable members of village communities. The key question for international donor agencies is thus how to evacuate the

[1] For an up-to-date list of project activities, see the Program's website: http://web.worldbank.org/WBSITE/EXTERNAL/TOPICS/EXTLAWJUSTICE/EXTJUSFORPOOR/0,,contentMDK:22906721~menuPK:7914193~pagePK:148956~piPK:216618~theSitePK:3282787,00.html, accessed 2 March 2016.

advantages of non-state justice institutions from these attested weaknesses (Berger 2017).

Like Deval Desai and Michael Woolcock (2015), the UN report highlights the importance of context-sensitive interventions that start from a careful analysis of both state and non-state legal systems, the ways they are linked, and their respective strengths and weaknesses from a human rights perspective (UNDP et al. 2013, 137–57). Again, the emphasis is on experimental programming that starts with the identification of people's legal preference through 'testing' and 'pilot schemes' (UNDP et al. 2013, 145). Although published after the project to activate the village court in Bangladesh had already started, the report's logic also played out in rural Bangladesh. On the basis of the fact-finding mission commissioned by the EU, a first piloting scheme with village courts was launched in cooperation with a local NGO, MLAA (Jahan and Stapleton 2013, 4). MLAA has been working in different kinds of ADR since 1978 and is a nationally and internationally recognized authority in the field of non-state justice delivery. MLAA has developed its own model of community mediation, the so-called Madaripur Mediation Model. Over the last couple of years, this model has been adopted and is now being used in modified forms in Malawi, Sierra Leone, Nigeria, and South Sudan. It is also currently being piloted in southern Portugal (Jahan and Stapleton 2013, 41). Besides working with their own model of conflict resolution, MLAA has also been working with the village courts and arbitration councils. These experiences have been a crucial influence on the design of the AVCB project, as a World Bank report states and a high-ranking EU official has confirmed (Das and Maru 2009, 20; EU-m-069). Thus, the project is neither purely European nor exclusively Bangladeshi. It emerges out of recurring interactions between Bangladeshi activists, members of the judiciary, transnational policy experts, and international bureaucrats.

These interactions unfold as part of a larger historical trajectory, which I have analysed in greater detail in Chapter 3. This trajectory stretches back over a century and throughout its course some striking similarities persist. In 1919 and 2010, the introduction of village courts was anticipated by the increasing production of knowledge about what Europeans perceived to be the local dynamics of conflict resolution in rural Bangladesh. In both cases, this empirical material was used to modify European ideas about 'the rule of law'. This line of reasoning precedes even the actual introduction of the village courts in 1919; and it has persisted until today. Whereas Bentham argued at the beginning of the nineteenth century that the universally valid norm of the rule of law needed to be modified in order to fit the local realities of Bengal, the EU follows a similar logic almost two centuries later. Again, the rule of law that is conceptualized as a universally valid norm across the globe is modified in light of what are perceived to be the local realities 'on the ground'.

Yet this ground is always considered to be shaky and the deviation from authoritative Western models is considered to be fraught with uncertainty. The introduction of village courts therefore proceeded as large-scale social experiments, in the early twentieth as much as in the early twenty-first century. The contemporaneous experiment has two dimensions. On the one hand, the entire project is conceptualized as a large-scale experiment in justice. Its aim is to probe the possibility of creating functional equivalents to the state-backed legal system through the targeted engagement of non-state institutions. On the other hand, a further experiment is built into the project design; and this experiment pertains to the respective roles of different actors within the promotion of the rule of law and human rights through village courts in Bangladesh. Whereas the project is implemented in four regions of the country through local NGOs, in a fifth region it is implemented directly by UNDP's Dhaka-based experts. This experiment bears clear results, as I show in Chapter 6. It shows how the village courts only materialize within the landscape of rural conflict resolution if transnational notions of 'the rule of law' that ought to be promoted through these courts are translated by the grassroots-level staff of local NGOs. The following section introduces these NGOs as well as the other key actors involved in the activation of village courts—and especially the different ways in which they make sense of the village courts—in greater detail.

5.2. THE PROJECT DESIGN

Three key actors are involved in the project. The EU has been a driving force behind the initial project design and continues acting as its main funder, contributing a sum total of 10 million euro for the activation of 350 village courts between 2009 and 2015. The EU sits on all Project Committee meetings where budgetary issues and future activities are discussed, commissions annual independent results-oriented monitoring reports, and is much more involved in project monitoring than implementation. Implementation has been outsourced to UNDP. As described at the outset of this chapter, UNDP's project team for the activation of village courts is exclusively staffed by Bangladeshi experts, and these experts work in one of four project components (UNDP 2008, 71). As part of the first component, UNDP's team has (1) reviewed the legal framework of the village courts, drafted a new village court Act, and ushered it through the legislative process until the Act became nationally binding law in 2013. They have (2) also designed training materials and modules for UP chairmen, village court staff, and local police. This was (3) supported by an outreach campaign that included radio and television programmes on the village courts as well as the design and distribution of wooden courtrooms (called *eljas*), supplementary files for recording village court sessions, posters, stickers, calendars, flipcharts, and brochures providing information on the village courts. A final part of UNDP's project team has been charged with (4) the monitoring and evaluation of all project activities, including village court cases filed, heard, and resolved in the individual UP. Through these four components, UNDP becomes the central actor within the overall project architecture. UNDP is also the nodal point where communications between the EU, governmental authorities, and the four local NGOs that implement the project at the grassroots level intersect.

The four local NGOs are internally the most diverse actors within the project. The members of their executive boards tend to be highly educated and are part of the national intellectual elite. Two of the executive directors—Sara Hossain and Fazlul Hoque—are both nationally and internationally respected legal experts, scholars, and activists. In contrast, the fieldworkers and court assistants that implement the project at the grassroots level are usually recruited from the immediate vicinity of the villages where the courts ought to be activated. They have usually completed primary schooling, received training and attended several workshops facilitated by the project. There is thus a wide gap between the urban elites presiding over the four local NGOs and the rural implementers that work with the village courts at the grassroots level. This gap reflects a wider rift that runs through Bangladesh's non-governmental sector. Historically exceptionally vibrant, Bangladesh's civil society has been radically altered through a rapid influx of foreign donations that led to what Lamia Karim (2011) has called 'the Structural Transformation of the NGO Sphere'. This structural transformation has not only blurred the boundaries between state and civil society (Ahasan and Gardner 2016; Lewis 2004); it has also produced non-governmental elites highly experienced in the interaction with international donor agencies. Whereas the upper echelons of Bangladesh's non-governmental sector are therefore well versed in the policy speak of international donor agencies, those who implement the projects on the ground tend to be much closer to the lives of people in rural Bangladesh.

At the grassroots level, the AVCB project employs one fieldworker and one court assistant in each of the 338 UPs where the project aims at activating a village court. The task of the fieldworker is to conduct courtyard meetings and explain the roles and functioning of the village courts to the rural population. Until December 2012, the project counted that more than 930,000 people had attended these courtyard meetings (Asaduzzaman 2013a, 59). Furthermore, the fieldworkers support the community-based organizations (CBOs) that have been formed by the project. The CBOs are supposed to assist the village population with all proceedings in the village courts; they are also supposed to ensure the sustainability of the activated village courts beyond the lifeline of the actual project. Besides the CBOs, court assistants help people to file their applications with the village court. They are also responsible for maintaining the village court records in the UP and prepare the case statistics for the project's monitoring and evaluation apparatus (see also Chapter 8).

UP staff members are supervised by an upazila (sub-district) supervisor who generally has one further support staff. The upazila supervisors, in turn, report back to the district offices of the local NGOs. In these offices, several people are employed for accounting, monitoring, and training. The district-level trainers conduct workshops both with the project's fieldworkers and court assistants as well as specific target groups like the UP chairmen or religious leaders. All district-level staff are trained and supervised by the respective departments of the UNDP branch of the AVCB project (UNDP-AVCB). They are also supervised by and have to report to the headquarters of their respective NGOs. Thus, in total the four local NGOs alone employ approximately 1,000 members of staff for the activation of the village courts in Bangladesh. Although this strict organizational hierarchy tries to maximize the accountability within the project, all three actors nonetheless have very different ideas about what kind of institution the village courts in rural Bangladesh actually ought to be.

5.3. TRANSLATIONS WITHIN THE OFFICIAL PROJECT NARRATIVE

All three actors that compose AVCB—the EU, UNDP, and the local NGOs—inhabit different contexts. At times, the boundaries between these contexts are rather fuzzy, for example in the case of the top-tier administrators of the local NGOs and the Bangladeshi staff of UNDP. Both of these groups belong to Bangladesh's intellectual elite and have similar histories of socialization. Yet, throughout the following analysis, when I speak of local NGOs I focus primarily on the activities of village fieldworkers and court assistants at the grassroots level. Thus, at least schematically, the various protagonists of the project navigate very different contexts, i.e. the world of European diplomats and aid workers, the intellectual elites of Dhaka, and the villages in rural Bangladesh. Each of these contexts is constituted by a different background knowledge—and 'the rule of law' is translated against these different background knowledges in interactions between the EU, UNDP, and the four local NGOs.

These translations are enabled by an underspecified global liberal script of which 'the rule of law' is a central part. Within this script, 'the rule of law' is inseparably tied to adjacent notions of democracy and human rights (Ehm 2010, 3). This triad is further supported by peripheral concepts like social justice, equality, accountability, and participation. The precise meaning of the rule of law now depends on the ways in which these core and peripheral concepts are organized (Freeden 1998, 2–54). As any other concept, 'the rule of law' therefore carries what Paul Ricœur has called a 'surplus of meaning' (Ricœur 1976). This surplus of meaning allows for some room for manoeuvre within contemporary transnational liberal scripts. It allows subtle shifts in the meaning of 'the rule of law' (discussed below); yet it does not allow moving beyond the confines of transnational liberalism as a whole. Within these confines, the EU, UNDP, and the four local NGOs can make sense of the village courts in rather different ways.

EU Delegation in Dhaka: The Rule of Law as Access to Justice

The first instance of contextualizing the overall attempts of the EU to promote democracy, human rights, and the rule of law through its development cooperation in Bangladesh is at the level of the EU delegation in Dhaka that is speaking to two different audiences: the administration of the Directorate-General for International Cooperation and Development in Brussels and UNDP in Bangladesh. According to several representatives of the delegation, Brussels 'grills them' primarily at the beginning of a project and then supervises project implementation via results-oriented monitoring reports. Whereas the administration in Brussels puts pressure on their colleagues in Dhaka, the Dhaka delegation in turn is responsible for pressuring UNDP. Thus, the EU's Dhaka delegation is itself a translator that mediates between the overall objectives of the Brussels headquarters and the implementing agencies.

In Brussels, the village courts are firmly understood in terms of the rule of law. The project is filed as 'legal and judicial development'; and at the outset of the project, the desk officers in Brussels repeatedly inquire about the link between the village courts and state-backed judiciary. In Brussels, the village courts are therefore understood as an extension of the state-backed rule of law. Similarly, in Dhaka, the project is described as 'support to the justice system'. The brief project description on the EU delegation's website reads:

> Support to the Justice System: Activating Village Courts:
>
> The overall programme objective is to improve access to justice and human rights in Bangladesh particularly among disadvantaged and marginalised groups, and thus contribute to good governance, and poverty alleviation.
>
> The project purpose is to empower and enable the poor, women and vulnerable groups to access a fair and effective justice system at the local level by activating 500 village courts so that disputes may be resolved in an expeditious, transparent and affordable manner.[2]

[2] http://delbgd.ec.europa.eu/en/projects/gov_humanrights_projects2.htm, accessed 25 June 2012.

Here, no direct emphasis to the concept of 'the rule of law' is made. Instead, the project heading refers to its institutional referent: the justice *system*. Improving the functioning of the institutional referent is the purpose of the project, which aims at facilitating 'access [to] a fair and effective justice system at local levels' for marginalized people in Bangladesh. Although the purpose of the project is to facilitate fair and effective institutions, the overall objective of the project is to 'improve access to justice and human rights'. As Jürgen Habermas has argued, human rights are Janus-faced in the sense that they refer to both moral and legal rights (Habermas 2010). The same holds for justice, which is both a normative ideal and an assemblage of institutions designed to realize this ideal (however defined). Within the project, both aspects are implicitly linked and differentiated only as 'overall objective' (promotion of justice and human rights) and 'project purpose' (facilitation of fair and efficient local institutions). Thus, the EU conceptually links the institution of a village court with a particular normative order, i.e. with a specific notion of justice. But which kind of justice ought to be facilitated by the village courts?

The kind of justice that ought to become accessible through the village courts is further decontested through two adjacent concepts: fairness and human rights. The concept of fairness is a complex but very popular one in academic debates over justice (e.g. Rawls 1985). As the EU understands it, 'fairness' means the adherence to procedural criteria that ensure the transparent, effective, expeditious, and efficient resolution of conflict. These are the procedural criteria which ought to be embodied in the state-backed judiciary. However, given the high levels of corruption and inefficiency, the state-backed courts fall short of their own procedural aspiration—and the village courts should therefore become their functional equivalent. Access to justice through the village courts consequently amounts to access to the kind of justice that is enshrined as an ideal in the state-backed laws. Furthermore, the notion of fairness also includes a strong component of equality, as it is paired with the simultaneous emphasis on human rights.

Since the overall objective of the project is to improve access to both justice and human rights at the same time, the latter fills the former with more substantial content: justice is thus the realization of human rights, in particular for 'the poor, women, and vulnerable groups'. However, at least academically, the precise content of human rights is also debated. Finding a way between 'contextualist particularism' and 'indifferent globalism', Rainer Forst, for example, has argued for the right to justification as the most basic human right (Forst 1999, 56). Importantly, he also argues that not all other rights can be universally derived from this basic right to justification. Thus, '[t]he basic right does not determine from the outset which substantial reasons are adequate, which rights can be demanded, or which institutions and social relationships can be justified . . . the right to justification leaves this to members' specific cultural or social context' (Forst 1999, 42). In contrast, the conceptualization of human rights within the justification narrative of the EU does not follow this participatory approach of deliberating about the specific content of human rights. Although no direct reference is made within the project, the European Instrument for Democracy and Human Rights frequently refers to the 1948 Universal Declaration of Human Rights. Thus, the content of justice within the project description is filled by a notion of human rights, which, in turn, is defined through the UN's Universal Declaration.

The emphasis on the village courts as an extension of the state-backed laws coincides with an understanding of the village courts as an institution of local governance. This, however, creates a tension in the spatial imagination of the project. On the one hand, EU representatives in Dhaka stressed that AVCB was not a 'pure' rule of law project. Instead, it was more of a hybrid between a rule of law and a local governance project. As the village courts centre on a local elected politician (the UP chairman) the separation of powers dissolves within the project. Thus, EU officials argued that the project itself should be more broadly understood as local governance rather than as a rule of law project. On the other hand, however, they also highlighted the importance of a uniform implementation of the project across different regions of Bangladesh, where the project currently unfolds. As one representative of the EU argued, 'the initial idea of the project was to build up the village courts as the lowest tier of the formal judiciary in Bangladesh. Therefore, it is essential that we pay close attention to the uniform implementation of the project across all four regions [where the project is currently implemented]' (EU-m-069). Again, this emphasis on uniform implementation across different regions highlights the extent to which the EU conceptualizes the village courts as an extension of the national state-backed judiciary: as this judiciary is at least supposed to work in a uniform way across the whole country, the village courts must do the same. Furthermore, in the ongoing deliberations to extend the project beyond the first funding phase, this is one of the key arguments: as the village courts are the lowest tier of the national state-backed judiciary, they cannot be limited to 10 per cent of the country's UPs but need to be introduced more widely (EU-m-108, EU-gd-123).

This overall line of argument shows how the EU conceptualizes the village courts as an institution of the state-backed rule of law: it is a rule of law-based ADR. In Chapter 2, I introduced two ways of conceptualizing ADR. On the one hand, ADR can be thought of as an effective and cost-efficient extension of the normative order that is embedded in state-backed laws. This kind of ADR allows people to participate in functional equivalents to the state-backed courts in case the state-backed courts do not operate as they ought to, for example by imposing unduly high costs for litigation or significant delays in the articulation of enforceable verdicts. In essence, then, this conceptualization does not substantially alter the meaning of 'justice': in ADR, people simply get what they ought to have got from the state-backed courts to begin with. On the other hand, ADR can also be conceptualized in terms of alternative normative orders than the ones that are inscribed in the state-backed laws. In these cases, the kind of justice that is facilitated by ADR is not desired because it reproduces the justice principles of the state-backed courts, but because it does exactly the opposite: in these cases, ADR becomes a matter of identity, belonging, and resistance. The EU conceptualizes the village courts in the first sense, not the second.

UNDP: the Rule of Law through Democratic Governance

Within the processes of project implementation, the EU delegation in Dhaka exclusively communicates with UNDP and abstains from direct engagement with the involved NGOs or direct negotiations with the respective ministries (EU-m-092). In contrast, UNDP functions as the nodal point of the project where representatives of the four local NGOs as well as from the MLGRD intersect. Thus, UNDP caters for diverse audiences and unavoidably speaks to multiple publics at the same time. Addressing different publics than the EU's delegation in Dhaka also changes the meaning of the village court as an institution to be activated. The cooperation with the MLGRD rather than with the Ministry of Law softens the EU's emphasis on the rule of law. Although the emphasis on the justice system continues, it is now saturated with an emphasis on democracy. As the chief legal advisor of the project, himself a former high-ranking official in the Bangladeshi judiciary who has been a magistrate judge for two decades, pointed out:

> the village courts fall under the supervision of the Ministry of Local Governance, and not the Ministry of Law... We treat it [the village court] as local justice: although it is backed by the law, it really is a mixture of formal and informal justice delivery systems. By law, the village court is a formal institution—but the ways in which it conducts trials is very much informal... The law entrusts the Union Parishad Chairman, an elected institution, with the trial of civil and criminal cases. This is why it is directly related to the democratic process.
>
> (UNDP-m-003)

Here, the shift from an emphasis on the rule of law towards a redefinition of village courts as democratic institutions which deliver local justice, is immediately linked to the addressed official audience, i.e. the Ministry of Local Governance and not the Ministry of Law. Furthermore, this shift is also driven by the different background knowledge against which the village courts are understood: as Bangladeshi citizens with long-lasting experience in the state-backed judiciary, the members of staff of UNDP-AVCB must be acutely aware of the local political dynamics surrounding non-state justice institutions.

Thus, the emphasis on adherence to procedural criteria of the state-backed rule of law is complemented with a more distinctly political notion of democratic governance that tries to accommodate the political dynamics that are likely to surround the village courts. Knowing that the state-backed courts only constitute a rather imperfect collision regime, and that the judiciary is therefore unlikely to be able to hold the village courts fully accountable, UNDP-AVCB adds a further layer of democratic accountability.

The shift from the emphasis on the rule of law to a broader notion of democratic governance is also formally inscribed in the project through the project document.[3] The project document constitutes the legal basis for the project as a whole and is thus the key text of the project. Signed by UNDP and MLGRD, the document 'provide[s] the baseline for the Project Management. It will be used as a reference point for all major decisions to be taken about the programme in the future and used at the conclusion of the programme to measure whether it was managed successfully and delivered acceptable results' (UNDP 2008, 69). Thus, the project document is both the basis and the benchmark for all activities officially unfolding within the process of project implementation. Here, the focus area of the project is defined as 'democratic governance' with the intended 'key results: participation, responsive institutions, engagement by the poor, serving the needs, concerns, and interests of people' (p. 68). Participation is linked to responsive institutions and the project document recommends a 'pedagogical approach that can meet the real need of people living in poverty and create pressure from below for institutional reforms' (p. 70). The project document also highlights the direction of institutional reform, whose aim should be to 'strengthen local government institutions to be responsive to local needs and offer appropriate legal service' (p. 71). Here, a particular conceptualization of participation surfaces. Participation is implicitly equated with the creation of accountability. It is geared towards the responsiveness of local institutions, which are understood as service providers. Thus, the people participating in local political processes are, first and foremost, consumers; and their participation is aimed at the efficient delivery of the services they would like to consume.

Besides the addition of 'democracy' as an efficient system of accountable service delivery, the project document also saturates the notion of promoting the rule of law in Bangladesh with a historical perspective. As the report (p. 69) states:

> There is a tradition of local justice in Bangladesh that goes back to the practices developed in ancient South Asian village communities. From time immemorial, the local authorities have performed mediation and arbitration functions (*shalish*) and

[3] For the AVCB project, two project documents have been signed—the first in 2008 and an altered version in 2013. Unless otherwise indicated, I focus on the initial document.

have exercised the power to administer civil and criminal justice. The institutional form of this local justice is the provision of village courts—an institution of formal justice at the lowest tier of local government.

Here, the provision of village courts is further justified through a historical narrative that links local dispute-resolution mechanisms to the lowest tier of the state-backed judiciary. Thus, in this paragraph an allegedly authentic local practice is integrated into the state. This reverses the line of argument advanced by the EU. Whereas the EU aims at extending the existing state-backed justice system through the village courts into rural areas, UNDP departs from existing non-state justice mechanisms and aims at formalizing these mechanisms in ways compatible with the state's legal system.

In the bottom-up approach of UNDP, distinctly modern categorizations (like the specification of civil and criminal law as distinct legal cases) are read back into past socio-legal practices in rural Bangladesh. The project document does not mention disputes related to family law, which are governed by religious laws in Bangladesh and do not fall into the jurisdiction of the village court. Therefore, a very modern reading of traditional socio-legal practices in Bangladesh serves as a supporting narrative for the project as a whole. However, the legitimizing power of tradition is not wholeheartedly endorsed but finds itself in a rather ambivalent position: on the one hand, the existence of local arbitration and mediation since 'time immemorial' serves to justify the current activation of village courts. On the other hand, the project document also lists the 'socio-cultural environment' as Risk No. 4 in its risk assessment. The Risk Log states that 'the socio-cultural environment may affect access to justice for women [and thus] gender inequality may occur' (p. 81). This tension between local practices as a resource and threat to the village courts also figures prominently in the further translation of the local NGOs that substitutes the emphases on the rule of law and democratic governance with the notion of *samaj* justice.

Local NGOs: the Rule of Law as *Samaj* Justice

In the project narrative that emerges in the communication between UNDP and the four local NGOs the language of communication switches from English to Bengali. All participants in this communication are Bangladeshi citizens—and besides meetings and workshops, the most important product of this communication is the training materials that are produced by UNDP and used by the local NGOs to facilitate the activation of village courts in the four regions in which they are operating. In the training materials—and thus in the project narrative as a whole—the notion of 'the rule of law' dissolves and is replaced by an emphasis on *samaj* justice. There is an ambiguity of translations here. Most straightforwardly, *samaj* means 'community'. This, however, has two connotations: on the one hand, *samaj* justice encompasses local justice, i.e. justice that is created within the confines of the village community or even smaller sub-unit of social organization in rural Bangladesh. On the other hand, however, it also refers to a form of social justice as the notion of *samaj* includes a sense of the ways in which these community relationships ought to be organized (Devine and White 2009, 15). Thus, the notion of *samaj* justice tries to mediate between the unavoidable authority of the *shalish* and its fragile legitimacy outlined in Chapter 4. While maintaining the insistence on the recreation of community harmony, the notion of *samaj* justice simultaneously stresses the importance for this community to be inclusive.

Table 5.1 indicates three further departures from the ways in which the EU conceptualizes the village courts: it changes both the geography and the content of justice as well as the meaning of human rights. The shift in the meaning of human rights is a rather subtle and nuanced one. At the international level, human rights are defined through references to the Universal

Table 5.1. Formal justice and *samaj* justice

Subject	Formal justice (State courts)	*Samaj* justice (Village courts)
System	Written system of laws	Social system (community)
Field	Definite laws and court system	Bigger than the formal justice system
Framework	Managed within the framework of laws	Managed within the framework of human rights
Control	Controlled by laws	Controlled by social practices and morality
Process	Take action against people who break the law	Change the reasons for breaking the law
Motivation	Fight against crime and injustice through judgments	Establish equality and non-discrimination Rebuild the social system and context
Morality	Demand that everybody is equal only in the eyes of the law Give punishment to a person who commits a crime	Morality of human rights, such as equality, non-discrimination, participation, and universality is prioritized over formal justice Try to solve the problems and the circumstances in which the crime happened
Remedy	Give punishment to the person who commits a crime Give compensation to the victim	Eliminate the causes of the crime within the social context where the crime happened Repair and rebuild the social system
Larger aim	Formal justice aimed at establishing a law-governed society	Change social dynamics and create friendly relations between all members of a society Stay equally side by side in a society (comradeship)

Declaration of Human Rights, adopted by the UN in 1948. These rights are, first and foremost, rights against the state. Within the Universal Declaration, individual autonomy is defended against illegitimate interference from—or even violation by—state authorities. However, the local NGOs reconceptualize human rights as claims against one's own social context. Although the addressee of rights-claims changes, their basic function remains intact: *samaj* justice is 'managed within the framework of human rights', i.e. neither the procedures nor the outcomes of *samaj* justice must, under any circumstances, violate the human rights of the participants. Thus, the function of human rights as a protection of individual autonomy against illegitimate outside interference is maintained at the local level in Bangladesh. Only the definition of 'outside interference' changes: from the state to society.

The change of the addressee of rights claims coincides with changes in the content of human rights. Whereas the Universal Declaration defines a bundle of inalienable rights every human being is entitled to, the local NGO's conceptualization of human rights is more deliberative in a Habermasian sense. Thus, the morality of human rights encompasses equality, non-discrimination, participation, and universality. This amounts to a discursive notion of human rights where the most basic right is the right to participate as an equal member in non-discriminatory processes of deliberation, where only the unforced force of the better argument prevails, whereby 'the better argument' is established through the criterion of universality: the better argument is the one that should, in principle, be acceptable to all participants in a discourse. This is a different kind of universality than the one embodied in the liberal notion of 'the rule of law'. For the latter, universality refers to the nationwide application of existing state-backed laws through uniform procedures that do not vary regionally or in any other way. Within the context of a discursive notion of human rights, universality refers to inclusiveness: all those affected by the decision of the village court should have an equal right to have their voice heard, and the final decision should, at least in principle, be acceptable to each and every participant in the discursive negotiation of village court justice. The specific content of any further human rights is not philosophically prescribed but can only be established through processes of deliberation. This is much closer to Forst's notion of the right to justification than to the moral and legal principles enshrined in the 1948 Declaration. This, however, is a big shift in the meaning and content of human rights: whereas the Universal Declaration establishes pre-political guarantees, which protect individuals (generally against the state), the discursive approach to human rights deployed by the four local NGOs tries to use the emancipatory potential of human rights to create spaces of participation, in which the principles of *samaj* justice can be negotiated.

These two shifts in the content of human rights—from the state to society as primary addressee of rights claims as well as from a positivist to a discursive notion of human rights—are rather nuanced compared to the changing geography of justice. Instead of promoting the village courts as an extension of the state-backed judiciary, the four local NGOs conceptualize the village courts as a substantial alternative to state institutions. Whereas the state is portrayed as cold, distant, and incapable of delivering any kind of justice whatsoever as it insists on the universal application of state-backed laws, the village courts are an institution of community harmony. As I have shown in Chapter 4, the vast majority of people in rural Bangladesh prioritize harmony and the integrity of the community over the resolution of conflict through the uniform and context-independent application of nationally binding state-backed laws. In accordance to this normative order, which is deeply engrained in the background knowledge of people in rural Bangladesh, the four local NGOs consequently change the geography of justice: from the state and the national community to the level of the village community. This also quite substantially changes the idea of the village courts. It substitutes the village courts as an extension of the normative order of the state-backed laws to an institution that proactively resists this normative order and defends an alternative one (see also Chapter 2). Thus, the changed geography of justice significantly transforms the ways in which the village courts are understood in relation to state institutions.

This changed geography of justice also alters its content: it changes from a retributive to a restorative notion of justice. Whereas retributive justice emphasizes the need to punish violations of both formal laws and recognized informal rules, restorative justice aims at reconciliation and the prevention of crime through the elimination of its cause rather than through the threat of punishment. Thus, the concept of *samaj* justice tries to 'solve the problems and the circumstances in which the crime happened... eliminate their causes [and] repair & rebuild the social system'. Thus, *samaj* justice is 'much bigger than the formal justice system'. It is much bigger as the shift from a retributive to a restorative notion of justice introduces a redistributive dimension into the EU's conception of justice. The redistributive dimension of the village court becomes obvious in the following example, given by a high-ranking UNDP staff within the project:

> Imagine a person in a village steals something from his neighbour, maybe a goat or some rice. The neighbour then files a case in the village court and there is a trial. In the trial, it emerges that the person who stole the goat is very, very poor; he needed the goat to feed his family. The neighbour, on the other hand, has enough food for his family. Then, it is the obligation of the chairman to make sure that the reason for which the crime happened is eliminated. He has to talk to both parties and then they have to find a solution. Maybe the village can find a job for the poor person. Or they can support him and his family so that they have enough to eat. (UNDP-m-057)

This redistributive logic of the village courts highlights the *social* justice component. This social justice component, however, is also paired with an insistence on local justice, which, as argued above, distances the village courts from the state-backed laws of Bangladesh. This combination of social and local justice constitutes an intricate dilemma of the local NGOs: how can the deeply contextualized resolution of conflict at the community level—and without recourse to the state-backed laws—be facilitated without, at the same time, simply reproducing local hierarchies and relationships of power? As I have shown in Chapter 3, there is only a very fine line that separates the unavoidable authority of the *shalish* and its fragile legitimacy; and by de facto approximating the notion of *samaj* justice closer to the *shalish* than to the state-backed laws, the local NGOs have to find a way to navigate this tension.

The tension is a very serious one: how can peace and harmony in a community be restored without, at the same time, restoring the social hierarchies that have defined the content of harmony to begin with? This tension is even further accelerated as the procedural guarantees that the EU associates with the village courts are severed: instead of being controlled by a 'written system of law', the village courts are controlled through 'social practice and morality' (see Table 5.1, 'control'). Nonetheless, the interactions between staff members of local NGOs and the responsible project managers at UNDP have produced an understanding of the Village Court Act as 'a unique law; [it] is the only law in Bangladesh, probably the only law on the sub-continent, which empowers people—the only law!' (UNDP-m-057). It is empowering as it allows people to define the content of *samaj* justice. The key to this empowering component of *samaj* justice is an altered notion of participation: as argued above, the reconceptualization of human rights from externally defined pre-political guarantees into a basic 'right to justification' tries to carve out participatory spaces within the village courts and to thereby allow villagers to define what exactly the content of *samaj* justice actually is. Thus, there is still a human rights-based safeguard against the bare reproduction of power relations built into the NGOs' conceptualization of the village courts—but it is an increasingly thin one; and it does open the door to the possibility that the kind of *samaj* justice that is articulated in the village courts might start to look rather different from the justice that is imagined by the EU and UNDP.

The emphasis on *samaj* justice also alters the notion of participation within the project. While the EU interprets the village courts as an institution that allows poor and marginalized people to participate in the state-backed justice system, broadly conceived, UNDP understands participation primarily as a local democratic pressure that holds the village courts accountable to deliver justice. The local NGOs, in turn, go one step further and argue that participation actually refers to the articulation of justice principles themselves. Nonetheless, these three different translations of the village courts in terms of the rule of law, local democracy, and *samaj* justice are not mutually exclusive but constitute different interpretations of the village courts within the broad confines of the liberal script that informs the EU's development cooperation. These three translations within the normative order of global liberalism also maintain a fine layer of seeming continuity—a concern with accountable institutions: whereas the EU insists on the accountability of the village courts to the state-backed laws of Bangladesh, UNDP saturates this with a further component of local democratic accountability. The four local NGOs, in turn, argue that the village courts ought to be accountable to the village community and a form of *samaj* justice, which tries to define this community in inclusive terms.

5.4. CONCLUSION

These different understandings of the village courts as institutions of the state-backed rule of law, democratic governance, or *samaj* justice indicate the underspecification of transnational liberal scripts. Linking democracy, human rights, and the rule of law loosely together, these scripts are both enabling and constraining. Their underspecification enables different actors to make sense of an institution like the village courts in rather different ways and thereby allows them to integrate them into their specific vision of social transformation. At the same time, the scripts are constraining. Both the staff of local NGOs and the Bangladeshi legal experts working for UNDP depend on the continuous flow of transnational project resources for the maintenance of their own livelihoods; and they cannot challenge transnational liberal scripts in ways that would threaten these flows. These dependencies notwithstanding, the overall underspecification of transnational notions of the rule of law, and especially the ways in which these notions relate to non-state courts, opens some room for manoeuvre in which different actors can translate the rule of law differently. This chapter has shown how the key actors involved in the activation of village courts use this room for manoeuvre in rather different ways. Regardless of their differences though, all translations documented in this chapter have had to stay within the confines of transnational liberalism. Chapters 6 and 7 now turn to the analysis of how 'the rule of law' is translated beyond these confines as the flipcharts, posters, billboards, project-sponsored wooden courtrooms travel on to rural Bangladesh.

6

Translating Institutions

In rural Bangladesh, the AVCB project unfolds as a large-scale social experiment. Whereas in four regions it is implemented by a local NGO, in a fifth region, it is directly put into operation through UNDP's Dhaka-based project team. This chapter compares two of these regions where the project is implemented—one with the help of a local NGO, and one without. Through this comparison, I show how the project simply fails to alter the dynamics of conflict resolution in rural Bangladesh if it is not assisted by a local actor at the grassroots level. After having shown the importance of local NGOs as translators in the first section of this chapter, the following two sections analyse which effects the project actually has if it is implemented through local NGOs. I argue that the fieldworker and court assistants of the local NGOs firmly integrate the village courts in the universe of non-state justice institutions rather than approximating them to the state-backed judiciary. I illustrate this argument with a thick description of a village court session that turned into a *shalish* in Section 6.2. The following section then complements this case study with further evidence from the four divisions where local NGOs are activating the village courts. In the final section of this chapter, I show how the translation of the village courts into a de facto non-state institution helps to facilitate access to the UP chairmen as widely respected (and generally obeyed) arbiters of conflict in rural Bangladesh for those people for whom this access has been previously blocked. Although access to the UP chairman does not amount to the promotion of the rule of law, democratic governance, or *samaj* justice, I argue in the conclusion of this chapter that it is nonetheless important: it opens a further avenue for marginalized people to struggle for their own empowerment. In order to develop this argument, however, I first turn to the crucial importance of local NGOs as translators of 'the rule of law' in rural Bangladesh.

6.1. COMPARING AREAS OF INTERVENTION: THE ROLE OF TRANSLATORS

Just like the introduction of village courts by the colonial administration in 1919, the 'activation' of these village courts almost a century later was set up as a large-scale social experiment. This time, the experiment started with twelve trial village courts in Sylhet Division. As the results-oriented monitoring report of 2010 attests, for these trial courts, 'training modules and communication materials have been produced' and 'good communication materials have been disseminated in many UPs; the billboards have been set-up in strategically visible places; a number of UP chairs have been trained in the project' (Jahan 2010, 3). The same materials were used all over Bangladesh. In four divisions, they were used by local NGOs in charge of implementing the project at the grassroots level. Yet, in Sylhet UNDP decided to follow a different approach and 'to use the [UNDP] project team as a proxy state entity to equip the UPs, recruit the staff and train them . . . and directly supervise the staff, without reference to NGOs' (Jahan and Stapleton 2013, 12).

Although workshops had been given, training materials provided, and billboards set up, the twelve pilot village courts were introduced without the help of a local NGO. Instead, UNDP sent its experts from Dhaka to train UP chairmen and other stakeholders in Sylhet. As I visited Sylhet almost exactly one year after submission of the results-oriented monitoring report, the only sign of the project were the wooden courtroom furniture provided by the project and the billboards. Talking to one UP chairman outside his office in Sylhet Division, I pointed to the large billboard advertising the village courts and asked him what this project was about. 'That's a good question!' he told me, and continued:

> About one year ago, a man from Dhaka came and put up this billboard. I had to sign that I received it, and the next day someone else from Dhaka called to check if I really had received it. But that's all I know about this project, I have not heard from them ever since. Do you, by any chance, know what it's all about? (RB-m-045)

Similarly, as I talked to a high-ranking official within the district administration, she told me that she was not aware of the village courts, or any related activities by UNDP. As I pointed to the large billboard that advertises the village courts just outside her window, she asked her assistant to get a file. As he returned, she read the file and told me: 'yes, one year ago, there was a workshop, the project manager of UNDP was there—and we got . . . this signboard!' (ST-f-043). The irony in her voice could hardly be missed. Thus, in a very clear way both statements quoted above highlight the experience of the project in Sylhet Division. Although all the artefacts of the project, i.e. the village courtroom furniture, the large information billboards, and the training materials, have been transported to Sylhet, they have not been integrated into the local context in any meaningful way—at all.

In Sylhet, there was simply nothing which could bridge the artefacts of the project with the logic of conflict resolution in rural Bangladesh. Consequently, the artefacts remained meaningless, standing as alien and somehow abandoned ruins in the landscape of rural conflict-resolution mechanisms. In the project's Annual Reports from 2011 onwards, the twelve unions in Sylhet are not even listed anymore in the overall statistical breakdown of cases filed, resolved, and implemented. Instead, all village court-related statistics that are officially communicated by the project through its various reports exclusively focus on those UPs where the project has been implemented through the four local NGOs. The 2014 Annual Report states that between the end of 2009 and December 2012 a total of 67,770 cases were reported to the village courts, 53,330 of the cases had been resolved, and 45,421 of these resolved cases had already been enforced in the four divisions where the project is implemented through local NGOs (Asaduzzaman 2015, 2). At the same time, these detailed statistics that break the aggregate numbers down to districts as well as sex of applicants remain conspicuously silent about the activities of the village courts in those twelve unions where no local NGOs work with the village courts (Asaduzzaman 2013a). Here, the absence of published numbers is probably more telling than any statistic could possibly be: excluding the number of village court cases facilitated without the help of local NGOs quite clearly indicates that the experiment with non-NGO-mediated village court activation has not been very successful.[1] The 2013 Mid-Term Review compares the 338 UPs where the project works through local NGOs with the situation in the one division where it does not and concludes that '[t]he situation is not so positive in Sylhet where a different implementation approach was decided on in 12 UPs, namely to activate the [village courts] directly through the Project Management Team rather than through NGOs' (Jahan and Stapleton 2013, 12). Similarly, throughout my research in Sylhet, I could not find any traces of the village courts—except the billboards and courtrooms that had been placed in the twelve pilot unions. However, as argued above, none of these artefacts could carry any meaning, which would alter the local dynamics of local conflict resolution.

The artefacts provided by the project remained meaningless, as they were not connected in any intelligible way to the background knowledge reconstructed in Chapter 4. This changed with the integration of local NGOs into

[1] I have tried to access some case-related data for the village courts at AVCB-UNDP. However, people in general were quite reluctant to talk about the experience in Sylhet. They also refused to provide any data. My suspicion is that there simply are no data: as I argue in Chapter 7, one of the key tasks of the local NGOs is the maintenance of village court registers and thus also the production of case-related data. Without the help of intervening NGOs, there are also no case-related data—even if there were at least some village court sessions.

the project, as the following two brief case studies illustrate. The first is taken from Sylhet Division, where UNDP tried to work without the help of a local NGO. The second is from Hathazari district in Chittagong Division, where the project is implemented through a local NGO, the Bangladesh Legal Aid and Services Trust. In many ways, Chittagong and Sylhet Division are structurally very similar: both are located on the eastern border of Bangladesh, both constitute the economically more affluent parts of the country, and in both cases this affluence is closely connected to the flows of remittances from the Bangladeshi diaspora in the Gulf States and the UK (Lewis 2011, 160–1, 187–8). Furthermore, as World Bank data from 2013 show, both have had similar trends in poverty reduction over the past decade: the poverty headcount in Sylhet decreased from 42.4 per cent in 2000 to 28.1 per cent in 2010. During the same time, the poverty headcount in Chittagong decreased from 45.7 per cent in 2000 to 26.2 per cent in 2010 (Gimenez et al. 2013, xiii). In 2010, the poverty headcounts in Sylhet and Chittagong were less than 2 per cent apart so the potential constituencies for the village courts are roughly of the same relative size to the overall population of these two divisions. Finally, both Chittagong and Sylhet have historically been strongholds of the development of Islam in its various syncretized forms in Bangladesh, and both are today generally considered to be religiously more conservative than the rest of the country (van Schendel 2009, 252–7). Thus, for the purpose of this research project, Sylhet and Chittagong are the most similar cases, with the only difference being that in Chittagong the AVCB project is implemented through the help of a local NGO whereas in Sylhet it is not. This difference is highly significant—as the following two case studies show.

Talking to a villager who only owns a very small plot of land in Sylhet Division, he told me that his neighbours, endowed with capital from their relatives in the United Kingdom, opened a small dairy farm. This farm now pollutes his land and causes a serious health hazard for his children as his neighbours dispose all the waste on his property. After having unsuccessfully tried to resolve this conflict with his neighbours directly, he told me that he approached various local elected politicians, including his ward member and the UP chairman, multiple times. However, each and every time the chairman told him that his neighbours were too powerful, so he could not help him. Not persuaded by this excuse, the man concluded that the chairman did not actually want to help him, as he maintained good relations with them. Highly frustrated, my interviewee eventually gave up trying to solve this conflict and simply tried to come to terms with the fact that no help whatsoever was available (RB-m-040).

In contrast to this example, I also interviewed a Hindu woman in a UP where the AVCB project is active in Chittagong: sitting in her house with her brother and two of her children, Karuna told me that her neighbour's son, maybe fifteen or sixteen years old, had severely beaten her pregnant cow.

The cow had lost her calf afterwards. As it was their only cow, this was a significant financial loss for the family. After having unsuccessfully tried to solve the conflict directly with the neighbours, she called her local ward member for help. However, the ward member repeatedly refused to help her. Eventually, she filed a formal complaint with the village court. After discovering that the incident had been reported to the village court, and thus also to the UP chairman, the ward member changed course and went to see Karuna. Instead of having to see the ward member for an appointment, he went to her house to talk to her, as Karuna repeatedly stressed. Together with the boy's family, the ward member asked her to withdraw the case and accept a compensation payment for the lost calf. Although the payment did not amount to the full value of the calf, Karuna accepted their offer and signed a Compromise Sheet (Rule 33) at the village court. I asked her if she thought that she got justice through the village courts. She answered that no, she didn't—but she was still very satisfied with the outcome. Without the village court, her conflict would not have received the attention of the local authorities at all. Neither would she have received at least some money as compensation (RB-f-074).

Located in Chittagong Division, this incident happened in a part of Bangladesh that regularly suffers intercommunal violence and attacks on Hindu and Buddhist minorities; at the time of our conversation, the latest round of violence was just about to end. Eight months earlier, fourteen Hindu temples and about fifty houses of Hindus had been destroyed in an escalation of violence which could only be stopped after the imposition of emergency laws and the dispatch of 500 police and four platoons of the Border Guards Bangladesh.[2] In this context, Karuna as a poor Hindu woman is suffering from intersecting class, gender, and religious discriminations. However, through the intervention of one of the four local NGOs that helped her to file a formal case with the village court, she could gain access to the UP chairman. This, in turn, forced the ward member to act and consequently helped her to ensure at least a partial compensation of her financial loss. Thus, in Karuna's case, the village courts did not simply perpetuate power relations but significantly challenged them and therefore also supported her empowerment. Importantly, however, this empowerment did not amount to access to justice as either the EU or the local NGOs understand it: Karuna did not get access to either the functional equivalent of state-backed or to *samaj* justice. Instead, the outcome was more nuanced: Karuna was recognized as a member of her village community, and therefore the UP chairman also had to attend to her concerns. This included her in a community from which she had been previously excluded. It did not, however, include her necessarily as an equal member. Nonetheless, Karuna firmly endorsed the outcome of the village court case. Although it

[2] A summary of the events with references to relevant news reports has been published by the Country of Origin Research and Information Bangladesh Country Report (CORI 2012, 82).

did not amount to *samaj* justice, it at least approximated it and therefore significantly improved her position in the resolution of the conflict. Approximating *samaj* justice in cases like Karuna's is a significant achievement of the local NGOs—as the difference between my case studies from Sylhet and Chittagong clearly shows.

This difference confirms the importance of translators as the central scope condition for translations of the rule of law that I have theoretically developed in Chapter 2. In the experimental set up of the project, all factors were held constant: the training materials, the artefacts provided, and the institutional set up of the village courts. The only difference was the involvement of local NGOs—and whereas the project failed without their intervention, it changed the dynamics of conflict resolution in favour of poor and marginalized people in those areas where the field staff of local NGOs acted as translators. However, the translators significantly altered the meaning of the rule of law; and only this substantially changed meaning of the rule of law allows translators to have an impact on the dynamics of conflict resolution in rural Bangladesh. Although this impact neither fully realizes the proclaimed intentions of the EU nor the proclaimed ones of the four local NGOs, it is still much closer to what the fieldworkers and court assistants conceptualize as *samaj* justice. The remainder of this chapter analyses the impact of the local NGOs in greater detail; it begins with a thick description of what actually happens when the local NGOs activate the village courts in Bangladesh.

6.2. THICK DESCRIPTION: THE VILLAGE COURT-TURNED-*SHALISH*

Around midday, my colleague and I arrive at a small village some two and a half hours north of Jessore to attend a village court session scheduled for 12 p.m. It is the first formal hearing. A formal case has been filed with the village court and both parties have been summoned to appear before the UP chairman to state their case and then either agree to a compromise ('Rule 33') or nominate representatives for a second and possible third village court hearing, after which the jury will pass a judgment. As we arrive at the administrative building where the village court sessions are usually held, a few men are sitting in the courtyard. They welcome us and invite us for tea, while the court assistant, employed by one of the four local NGOs and thus indirectly on the payroll of the EU, is already busy preparing the forthcoming trial: he carries the heavy wooden chairs for the judges and the conflicting parties, all paid for by the project, from the courtroom to the courtyard. Integrated with about two dozen other chairs, the judges' chairs as well as the seats for the conflicting parties who confront each other in the AVCB-decorated courtroom start to form a circle in the courtyard of the UP complex.

As I observe the literal transformation of a village court into a *shalish* by replacing and rearranging the artefacts (i.e. the chairs) that endow the village court with an air of formality, a woman arrives at the courtyard, holding a letter in her hands. She is the defendant of the forthcoming village court session. Her name is Nafisa, and she tells me: 'My neighbour accused me of having killed his hens, three of them, by poisoning them. But the day the hens died, I was not even at home.' She is really angry and complains about her neighbour: 'this is a fraud case! My neighbour harasses me, time and again. He swears at me and insults me badly. I think he just harasses me because he wants us to leave the place where we live right now. We don't own the land where we live—and he now wants us to leave.' I ask her if she has tried to talk to her neighbour already. 'Yes, many times,' she replies, 'many times I told him that I did not kills his hens—but he just insulted me! And now he even dragged me to this court, just to insult my honour.' As she says this, she again shows me the letter that summoned her to attend the first hearing of the village court. Nafisa leaves to look for her husband who is late although he was supposed to support her throughout the trial. In the meantime, the applicant arrives. He also holds the letter in his hand that summoned him to the first hearing. We start talking: his name is Mohsin, and he tells me: 'I was not at home when the hens died, but my mother and sister saw how Nafisa killed the hens. And yes, it's true, my mother swears a lot and insulted her [Nafisa]—but so did she.' At this moment, Nafisa returns with her husband. Now, both parties start arguing with each other. Eventually, the chairman arrives at the courtyard where about twenty-five people have gathered by now. He takes his seat on the judge's chair. The court assistant hands him a file, which he studies carefully. Then, he opens the session and suggests: 'This should not be a village court session but more like a primary hearing. Maybe, we can solve this problem here and now and don't have to do a village court.' He asks Mohsin to explain his problem, and why he filed a case with the village court. Mohsin stands up and reiterates the story he had told me before: his mother and sister have seen how Nafisa poisoned his hens. The chairman listens to what is a quite repetitive but very emotional statement and then asks Nafisa to explain herself. She tries to get up, but the chairman orders her to remain seated. She does so, and says: 'I did not poison the hens, I am innocent, but he always harasses me and accuses me; he also uses very bad language and insults me'. Her statement is interrupted as the chairman receives a phone call and discusses another matter for some time. As he hangs up, he says: 'okay, it really might be the case that the hens died without being poisoned, maybe they were sick. This can happen very easily in winter.' At this point, he is interrupted by Mohsin's sister, who complains that 'we are the only Muslims living in our neighbourhood. And they just want to harass us.' Nafisa answers immediately by arguing that 'they are Muslims and only want to expel us from our house so that they do not have to live with Hindus'. While both parties continue arguing, turning the conflict over dead hens into an inter-communal dispute, the chairman is on the phone again. He then silences the fierce discussion and states: 'I have called for another ward member [i.e. the elected representative of the village where both parties live]. But the statements of both parties have been taken. Now, we will take a decision on what should happen. But we wait for the ward member first.'

As we are waiting, the chairman is in high demand: a number of people approach him and ask for his help in various conflicts: one man has a land dispute, another a family conflict, a third has been the victim of theft. The chairman listens to the cases and asks the court assistant to file appointments for further village court trials in the future. He also looks at me, shakes his head, and says, rather puzzled: 'this is only a conflict over six dead hens. How much can six hens cost?' He sighs, and shakes his head again. Eventually, the ward member arrives and talks to the chairman. Both whisper and nobody can hear what they are saying. Then, the ward member addresses both Nafisa and her husband as well as Mohsin and his sister: 'Nobody came and talked to me! Why did you not talk to me? Now, this is a very complicated case, and there are no witnesses.' Mohsin's sister interrupts and disagrees, saying that she clearly saw, with her own eyes, how Nafisa poisoned the hens. Nafisa interrupts her and says that she, Mohsin's sister, always complains about her and spreads these malicious rumours. Both women now talk at the same time while the chairman and the ward member, looking rather distressed, put their heads together again and whisper. Then, the chairman addresses the audience: 'We will take a decision now—and both parties will have to agree to this decision!'

There is a moment of silence, both parties hesitate. But then, Nafisa starts again: 'She abuses us, again and again; she insults us, spreads rumours, and uses very bad language against us'. Her husband now supports her: 'Very insulting language, really bad words, always against us, all these harassments'. And Nafisa continues: 'She has insulted us so many times; now she says that she has seen everything! What has she seen? She should put her hand on her head [gesture of swearing]; or she should touch the Holy Qur'an and swear again what she has seen!' Nafisa is standing now; she speaks in a loud voice, almost crying. The chairman interrupts her: 'Slowly, slowly. Maybe you should swear, swear that if you have killed the hens, God should take away your three daughters!' Mohsin's sister immediately picks up on this: 'the hens were poisoned, in her house, I'm sure!' The chairman is not so sure, and asks—again—if anybody else saw the incident. Nobody responds. He then calls for the court assistant, who has disappeared. She comes running, the file under her arm. The chairman, visibly angry, scolds her: 'there is a trial going on, where were you?' He grabs the file and reads again. In the meantime, the ward member complains again that the incident has happened in his ward and nobody consulted him. Why did nobody come and talk to him? Again, an awkward silence, both parties look to the floor. It is the chairman who breaks the silence.

He looks up from the file and addresses Nafisa:

> Woman, you talk too much! You interrupt me all the time—now, listen to me: there is a Muslim family living in your neighbourhood. Please be kind with them. Now, we have to forget this conflict and leave it behind; we also have to leave behind all the injuries this conflict has caused. But in the future, if Nafisa's family harms Mohsin's family again, they will be punished. For now, you have to live happily together and do not fight.

Now, Nafisa's husband jumps off his chair and shouts at the chairman: 'Fine, we can try to live happily and peacefully together. But if another hen just dies, why should we be responsible for this? We did not do anything!' The chairman tries to calm him: 'This time, there are no witnesses, there is no proof. In the future, incidents like this must not happen again, you must try to live side by side, as good neighbours.' This is too much for Mohsin, who now jumps up from his seat as well and starts marching off, barely turning around to order his sister to follow him. The chairman is visibly angry: 'you cannot leave yet, sit down and wait!' he tells Mohsin, quite firmly. Mohsin sits down again and the chairman continues: 'So I settle this case: no compensation has to be paid. No village court session is necessary, both parties mutually agree to a compromise. The case finishes here and now—go and sign the papers!' The whole circle starts to mumble, people start moving. Some men drag Mohsin and Nafisa's husband into the middle of the circle and talk to them, urging them to shake hands.

The two men don't look at each other. Nafisa's husband stares at the floor, angry, disgusted. Mohsin looks away—and both quickly turn away, their hands have barely touched. Then, it's the women's turn: Nafisa and Mohsin's sister enter the middle of the circle, surrounded by the audience; everybody is standing now, talking to them. The women's hands touch, equally quickly, both looking away. Mohsin's sister immediately walks away, following her brother. Nafisa remains in the circle, visibly upset, repeatedly proclaiming: 'I have not done anything—and they drag me here, in front of this court, without any reasons. They insult me . . . by bringing me to this court!' While Nafisa is complaining, the chairman is surrounded by members of the village communities who ask him to sign birth certificates, nationality proofs, and other administrative documents. The village court session is over—and I sneak away and go to the room of the court assistant, who is employed by the local NGO. As I approach the building, Mohsin's sister just exits the office. She does not look at me but to the floor, and rushes away.

The office of the court assistant, who is employed by the local NGO through the funds of the project, is located within the UP complex. It is a small room, next to what was supposed to be the village courtroom. As I slowly enter the office, Nafisa is still signing the paper, she is visibly upset. She also leaves, without saying a word. Now, the court assistant and I are alone in the room. We look at each other—there is still tension in the room. She hands me the 'Rule 33: Compromise Sheet'. This is a government-prescribed form, printed by UNDP, paid for by the EU, and delivered by the local NGO that employs her. The form is empty; nothing is filled in—except two carefully crafted signatures, one of Nafisa and the other one of Mohsin's sister. *Carte blanche* for the court assistant. I ask her what happens to the rest of the file. She looks surprised, and tells me that she will fill it in, of course. She does—and we wait. As she finishes, she hands the completed form to us. It reads:

> Content of the Compromise:
>
> 1. The Accused has confessed the crime and understood that it was a mistake. She has apologised
> 2. The complainer has accepted the apology and forgiven the accused
> 3. Both sides have been reconciled
> 4. They promise that they will never do that again in the future
> 5. Both sides sign on the compromise sheet.

I look at the 'Content of the Compromise' again—still a bit puzzled: the record of the village court session bears hardly any resemblance to what I have just seen. This document clearly departs from the kind of 'bureaucratic rationality' that Max Weber associated with official paperwork, and that I introduced in Chapter 2. Instead of neutrally recording social and legal facts, the compromise sheet radically transforms the legal interpretation of the dispute resolution. So I ask the court assistant if it happens often that conflicts are solved through such a compromise, and not a trial, and if she always has to fill in the forms like this. She smiles and says 'yes, most conflicts are settled through a compromise as we sit outside and discuss the matter. Only the very difficult cases are actually trialled in the courtroom. I always have to write the paperwork like this, it is my job!' I also ask her why she filed Mohsin's sister, and not Mohsin, as applicant of the village court trial. 'Because it's important that women go to the village court'. As she is speaking, a man enters the room and tells me that the chairman wants to speak to me, now, in his office. I have to leave.

6.3. RESISTANCE OF THE CHAIRMEN

This thick description of a village court session highlights the ambiguity of the recreation of community harmony that I have discussed at greater length in

Chapter 2. In this village court session, harmony was not the result of deliberative processes leading to reconciliation and forgiveness; instead, it was imposed by the political authority of the UP chairman. This imposition not only undermined the local NGOs' promotion of *samaj* justice (Section 5.3) but also the procedural standards of the 2006 Village Court Act (analysed in Section 3.3). According to these standards, a first village court session that fails to generate a genuine compromise between the conflicting parties would lead to the constitution of a village court jury that passes a final judgment by majority vote. However, in the case described above, the conflicting parties were made to sign a compromise sheet by the UP chairman, although no real compromise had been found and both parties had left the court session dissatisfied. Signing a compromise sheet according to Rule 33 means that the case is considered to be closed and no further legal action in the village courts or the state-backed judiciary are possible. By undermining the procedural requirements of the 2006 Village Court Act, the legislative integration of the village courts into the state-backed judiciary is broken. This integration, as shown in Chapter 3, consists of (a) the imposition of procedural requirements, and (b) the possibility of appeal. Both provisions have been undermined in the hearing described above. Therefore, the UP chairman de facto approximated the village court much closer to the non-state rather than the state-backed justice institutions in rural Bangladesh. This approximation is, at least in part, an act of resistance by the chairmen.

Resisting the Formalization of Non-State Conflict Resolution

The village court session described above ended with the imposition of a verdict by the UP chairman, which clearly left both parties unsatisfied. In contrast to the official project narrative (at the NGO level), which portrays village courts as mediation fora based on the ideal of mutual understanding and *samaj* justice, this particular case was closed by the uncontested authority of the chairman. Despite this authority, the role of the chairman in this case was ambiguous: although having the power to settle the case by himself, he called for a person of lower rank and significantly less administrative powers—the local ward member—and consulted him before passing his verdict. The chairman consulted the ward member as he was not used to dealing with such apparently trivial matters like the death of hens. At the same time, the ward member on numerous occasions articulated his anger about not having been consulted by the conflicting parties before they addressed the village court, and thus the UP chairman. Thus, it is very likely that the village court session described above negotiated a conflict which, without the AVCB project, would not have reached the attention of the chairman at all. As the chairman told me after the court session, in the beginning he was opposed to the idea of the village courts, which negotiated only what seemed to him very trivial matters. However, after more and more people filed cases with the court assistant, he realized that 'village courts are quite useful for poor people who only have conflicts over a couple of hens or some damaged crops'. Although the chairman conceded that he still preferred to chair those *shalish* sessions that negotiated cases significantly above the 25,000 thaka ceiling of the village courts, he has now turned his attention also to the concerns of the poorer people of his UP.

Although the UP chairmen assume a key role in the village courts and are, de facto, elevated into the position of state-recognized judges, they have been the strongest source of resistance against the project. At first sight, this resistance seems paradoxical as the formal powers of the UP chairmen are significantly increased through the project. Despite the formal increase in power, the chairmen have rejected the activation of village courts for two reasons: on the one hand, the activation of village courts forced them to turn their attention, and thus also their time and resources, to what they considered to be marginal and trivial conflicts. On the other hand, their enhanced judicial powers in the village courts are circumscribed in a very narrow jurisdiction, which is limited to minor criminal and civil cases up to a value of 25,000 thaka. Compared to the informality of the *shalish*, where chairmen can negotiate anything from land conflicts involving millions of thaka to rape and murder cases, this is a severe limitation of the chairmen's powers. Thus, virtually all field staff of the four implementing NGOs I asked about contestations of the project mentioned resistance from the UP chairmen. Even if some staff of the local NGOs stressed that the chairman in their own UP was very supportive of the project, they all agreed on the overall resistance of these locally elected politicians to the project as a whole. The resistance of the chairmen has been expressed in a number of ways, which can be analytically disentangled into (a) modifications of the village courts, and (b) the continuation of non-state conflict resolution beyond the village courts. The modification of the village courts through the UP chairmen unfolds, in turn, through two strategies: the outright refusal to hold village court sessions and the manipulation of the parties' representatives and thus the monopolization of decision-making powers within the hands of the chairmen alone. As one fieldworker in Chittagong Division told me about the chairman's refusal to hold village court sessions: 'until today, [the village court] does not really work fully: for example, sometimes the chairman just does not come to the village court sessions' (NGO-f-077). This is congruent with my own observations as it happened to me frequently throughout my field research in Bangladesh that I wanted to attend village court sessions but ended up waiting for hours with both conflicting parties for the chairman to arrive at the village court—which he never did. The refusal to hold village court sessions is often caused by the chairman's disregard of the importance of a particular conflict. Thus, in the case study presented above, it seems very unlikely that the chairman would have called a *shalish* over six dead hens. Without the possibility of formally filing an application with the village court, the case most probably would have never appeared on the radar of the UP chairman. Thus, the activation of village courts and the motivation of the chairmen to hold village court sessions are inseparably intertwined. As one fieldworker concluded: 'you cannot activate the village courts if you cannot activate the UP chairman!' (NGO-m-087).

One of the most important argumentative strategies employed by the four local NGOs to persuade the chairmen to hold village court sessions was to highlight their new powers as judge within the village court. Thus, the NGOs highlighted that the chairman is 'the main judge in the village court' (NGO-m-085), that he is 'the chief justice' (NGO-m-087), and that he now has 'powers like a Magistrate' (NGO-f-062). This argumentative strategy employed by local NGOs, which stresses the role of UP chairmen as judges in village courts, however, leads to the second modification mentioned above: the manipulation of the representatives. Throughout my field research, 78 per cent of the people asked about the role of representatives within the village court stated that the representatives, in their experience, either followed closely the advice of the UP chairman or were simply not nominated by the conflicting parties in the first place. In these cases, the chairmen nominated representatives at their will. Thus, people across all four divisions in which the project takes place told me that: 'the chairman only chooses people [representatives] according to his will' (RB-m-048), 'the representatives only follow the chairman's advice' (NGO-f-080), or 'the representatives were simply not present [in the village court trial]' (RB-f-082). This failure of nominating representatives that actually represent the interests of the conflicting parties was also confirmed in my observation of various village court sessions in all four divisions where AVCB is operating. In one instance, I witnessed eight consecutive village court sessions in which the representatives did not change between different cases at all. Furthermore, there was little, and often even no consultation between the chairman and the representatives before the judgment was passed by the village court. After another village court session that I observed in Chittagong Division, and which ended with the imposition of a verdict by the chairman without consultation of the representatives who were his close associates and did not talk at all throughout the entire court session or the subsequent decision-making process, the court assistant of the AVCB complained: 'this was not done in the proper way; this was like a *shalish*, not like a village court' (NGO-f-080).

Doing village courts like *shalish* is one strategy of UP chairmen to resist the formalization of, and thus the external control over, non-state dispute-resolution mechanisms. According to the distinction between the authority of the *shalish* and its legitimacy outlined in Chapter 4, these were generally 'bad' *shalish*: they did not allow for significant degrees of community participation but, instead, monopolized the decision-making powers in the hands of the UP chairmen. Thus, many of the village court sessions that I observed did not actually circumscribe but enhanced the powers of the UP chairmen, albeit in cases that did not really interest the chairmen. Paradoxically, precisely because they involved cases that did not really interest the chairmen, these court sessions still had an empowering effect on poor and marginalized people who could not have otherwise attracted the attention of the chairman at all: once they had access to the UP chairman, this access generally also meant that their conflicts were taken seriously and it was widely considered that some kind of compromise needed to be found. As the case of Karuna introduced at the beginning of this chapter shows, these compromises are not necessarily forged on equal terms; but for poor and marginalized people, they are still significantly better than no compromise at all.

Besides the transformation of village court hearings into *shalish* sessions, a second strategy to resist the formalization of non-state justice institutions is employed by the UP chairmen: this strategy is to hold a *shalish* after a village court session. In December 2011, I attended seven consecutive village court cases in Chittagong Division. The representatives did not change between individual cases and were hardly, if at all, involved in the decision-making processes. As the series of village court cases came to an end, the people on the judges' bench stood up, closed the series of trials, and walked into another room—to hold a *shalish*. In both the *shalish* and the village court sessions, the chairman acted very authoritatively and imposed his decision on the conflicting parties. This blurring of the lines between village courts and *shalish*, whether in the form of 'village courts-as-*shalish*' or 'village court-before-*shalish*', is not limited to Chittagong Division as I could observe similar processes in Madaripur as well as Rangpur and Khulna Divisions. Thus, across all four divisions, the village courts are firmly integrated into the universe of non-state justice mechanisms in Bangladesh. This is a clear departure from the institutional ambitions of the EU, which supports the activation of village courts in the hope that they might form the lowest tier of the state's judiciary. Whereas the EU focuses on the incipient formality of the village courts as quasi-formal institutions, the four local NGOs integrate the village courts within the legal and political worlds beyond the state in rural Bangladesh.

Expanding the Toolkit

By integrating the village courts within the universe of non-state conflict-resolution mechanisms in rural Bangladesh, the four local NGOs unavoidably further blur the line that separates state and non-state justice institutions. Being aware of this blurring line between state and non-state institutions, the NGOs also expand their institutional repertoire and promote not only village courts. Instead, they also include another quasi-formal institution—the arbitration council—as well as discussions about *shalish* in their field activities. The set-up of the arbitration council is very similar to that of the village court, with the main difference being the focus of the village court on civil and minor criminal disputes whereas the arbitration council deals with three aspects of Muslim family law: divorce, maintenance, and multi-marriages (see also Chapter 3). The engagement of the arbitration council also extends to the court assistants: although not formally part of the project, several court assistants have told me that they help especially women with filing the necessary documents to apply to the arbitration council for the dissolution of marriage, maintenance, and the acceptance or rejection of multi-marriages (NGO-m-104; RB-gd-117; NGO-m-087).

Whereas, from an institutional perspective, the inclusion of the arbitration council is comparatively easy because of the very similar set up of arbitration councils and village courts, the inclusion of *shalish* within the training materials and programmes of the four local NGOs is more challenging. The NGOs explicitly 'try to improve the decision of a *shalish*' by arguing that a *shalish* should follow the same values as the village courts and thus allow for more participation of women and other marginalized members of the village community (NGO-m-031). This inclusion of the arbitration council and *shalish* techniques is endorsed by UNDP and is thus included in the official training materials. As the head of the training section of UNDP who is responsible for the design of all training materials as well as the training of trainers explained: 'We focus on the needs of the people. That's why we have included *shalish* and Arbitration Councils in the training materials [on the village court]. Because if you want to build a medicine box, you cannot only include Paracetamol and nothing else' (UNDP-m-057). As I have argued in Chapter 5, all the staff of UNDP-AVCB are Bangladeshi citizens; they have long-standing experience with state and non-state legal systems and are therefore acutely aware of the complexities of the latter. Presumably, this awareness also underpins their toleration of the expanded toolkit: they know that the 'activation' of village courts cannot be hermetically sealed off from *shalish* and the arbitration councils. This integration of the village courts into the universe of non-state justice institutions, however, is not without consequences.

Consequences of the Approximation to Non-State Justice Mechanisms

Three consequences emerged from my conversations with people in rural Bangladesh. Firstly, many people criticized the increasing influence of local elites on the outcomes of non-state justice institutions, including the village courts. As one interviewee told me in Chittagong Division: 'the village court should represent different sections of society: educated people, religious people, political leaders, etc. But it is not like this, the committee only represents the interests of the ward members and the elites they represent' (RB-m-048). Another interlocutor in Khulna Division told me that 'most cases [in *shalish* and village courts] are decided by local musclemen' (RB-m-094). Secondly, the influence of local elites coincides with high levels of corruption and bribery. As one interviewee told me:

> the Union Parishad chairman takes bribes from everybody. Whenever there is a conflict, he tries to profit himself. Often, he even accelerates conflicts and then takes bribes from both parties. As he is the chairman, he is also the judge. He can just take bribe from everybody by promising to speak in his or her favour as a judge. (RB-m-038)

Finally, besides these monetary influences on the village courts, most of my interviewees also stressed the increasing politicization of non-state conflict resolution mechanisms along party lines. This is part of a broader politicization of local institutions that has been identified by David Lewis and Abul Hossain in their study of the local power structure in Bangladesh (Lewis and Hossain 2008b, 43).

These qualitative results that I gained from the analysis of my interviews are also confirmed by the overall findings of a survey commissioned by UNDP: in 2012, UNDP-AVCB commissioned a *Review of Social Barriers and Limitations of the Village Courts*. Out of the 1,409 respondents across the country, 49.6 per cent mentioned 'Bias/Nepotism/Political influence/Bribe/Misjudgment of village court officials' as one of the key obstacles to the functioning of village courts. This was only topped by 55.7 per cent who argued that 'Lack of awareness of mass people' was the key obstacle. Other obstacles for the activation of village courts did not generate more than 17.8 per cent or less of all responses (Barkat 2012, 80). Thus, in my investigation as well as in the larger survey-based report of UNDP, people in rural Bangladesh confirmed that the village courts had started to reproduce some of the characteristics associated with *shalish*: the influence of powerful elites, corruption, and the increasing politicization of local institutions along party lines. In fact, the importance of the UP chairmen in the village courts has often turned them into 'bad *shalishes*' as the authority of the chairmen undermined more participatory processes that characterize what my respondents considered to be a 'good *shalish*'. Ironically, however, a 'bad' *shalish* can be very good for marginalized people: at the end of the day, it is significantly better than no *shalish* at all. As I have argued in Chapter 4, a bad *shalish* is characterized by a low degree of community participation—and in most village court sessions that I have observed, the decision was made by the chairman alone. However, precisely because larger community participation is hindered, in the village courts, two rather unlikely participants can meet quite directly: the UP chairman and a person who is marginalized within his or her village community. By participating in the village courts—even if it is run as a 'bad' *shalish*—marginalized people become visible members of their village communities and can thus also lay claims upon this community. These claims do not constitute demands for the strict adherence to procedural standards, including the nominal equality before the law. They do, however, demand social harmony and the integrity of the community, of which poor and marginalized people can become a part through village courts-turned-*shalish*.

6.4. CONCLUSION

Whether in the form of good or bad *shalish*, the village courts have been approximated to non-state justice mechanisms rather than the state-backed judiciary. This approximation undermines the impartiality of village court decisions and consequently departs from a key aspiration of the liberal notion of the rule of law: the impartial adjudication of conflicts through the application of legal principles alone. Whereas the liberal notion of the rule of law insists on the impersonal application of legal principles to any given conflict, the village courts activated by AVCB promote the context-dependent negotiations of disputes. In these negotiations, interpersonal relationships play a fundamental role. Thus, the village courts are not a functional equivalent to the rule of law, if the latter is understood as the impartial and universal application of laws within a given territory. However, the project nonetheless succeeds in providing access to the UP chairmen for poor and marginalized people. Consequently, the project neither promotes the rule of law, as intended by the EU, nor necessarily facilitates access to *samaj* justice, as envisaged by the four local NGOs. Instead the fieldworker and court assistants at the grassroots level integrate poor and marginalized people more into the universe of non-state justice mechanisms that are based on the authority of the UP chairman. Although neither access to the state-backed judiciary nor a functional equivalent thereof is extended to the rural poor, the facilitation of access to the UP chairman as the most efficient institution of conflict resolution in rural Bangladesh is undoubtedly a success of the AVCB project. As I have shown in this chapter, this success decisively depends on the activities of the four local NGOs. Without their intervention, the project simply fails and produces hardly anything but alien billboards standing like abandoned ruins in the landscape of non-state conflict resolution in rural Bangladesh. Chapter 7 explains how the four local NGOs manage to facilitate this access to the UP chairmen—and why this success cannot amount to a promotion of 'the rule of law' as it is envisioned by the EU.

7

Translating Practices and Normative Orders

In this chapter, I analyse how the four local NGOs translate the rule of law in order to have an impact on the dynamics of conflict resolution in rural Bangladesh—and why this impact cannot amount to the outcomes envisioned by the EU and UNDP. To anticipate my argument: the local NGOs integrate the village courts into the landscape of non-state conflict resolution in rural Bangladesh by translating both the practices and the normative order that (together with the institution of the village court) constitute the EU's notion of the rule of law within the context of the project; they thus translate the village courts against the background knowledge that I have reconstructed in Chapter 4. The first part of this chapter is concerned with the translation of practices, and in particular with the practice of documenting institutionalized conflict resolution in writing. The four local NGOs make use of the official forms and formats provided by UNDP within the context of AVCB. However, they do not use these documents as neutral carriers of information that render the messy complexities of particular conflicts transparent and intelligible in the eyes of the state-backed judiciary. Instead, the fieldworkers and court assistants who are employed by the project use the official documents as a symbolic capital, which allows them to replicate the logic of non-enforcement for those people in rural Bangladesh who do not have access to the state-backed courts—and can consequently also not use these courts as a tool to alter the dynamics of non-state institutions. Thus, through the use of official documents as symbolic capital, the field staff of the local NGOs succeed in generating access to the UP chairmen. Although this access improves the lives of vulnerable, poor, and marginalized people in rural Bangladesh, it is not identical to the access to justice that the EU seeks to promote.

The second section of this chapter subsequently shows that the translation of practices is paralleled by the translation of the *liberal* rule of law into a normative vocabulary that is intelligible in rural Bangladesh. Thus, the four local NGOs translate the ostensibly secular vocabulary that informs the EU's ideas about the rule of law into explicitly religious narratives of justification. More precisely, the local NGOs try to improve the situation of women in rural Bangladesh through frequent reference to Islam and Islamic law. They use this vocabulary of Islam and Islamic law both to prevent violence against women and to carve out participatory spaces in which women can influence the social contexts they are navigating on a day-to-day basis. However, as argued in Chapter 4, the interpretation of Islamic principles in rural Bangladesh closely interacts with the maintenance of patriarchal social structures. Consequently, the promotion of women's rights through reference to Islam and Islamic law is fiercely contested. These contestations revolve around the question: who has the right to interpret Islam and Islamic law in rural Bangladesh? In the final section of this chapter, I therefore show how the local NGOs respond to this contestation through a dual strategy: on the one hand, they use theological arguments to support their interpretation of Islam. On the other hand, they argue that *their* interpretation is congruent with the interpretation of Islam and Islamic law that informs the state-backed Muslim family laws. Before turning to the translation of the normative vocabularies of the rule of law, however, I turn to the translation of practices by starting with my observations of one of the training sessions that has been facilitated by a local NGO for their fieldworkers and court assistants.

7.1. DOCUMENTING THE VILLAGE COURTS AND THE SYMBOLIC POWER OF PAPERWORK

In November 2012, I joined a training session by one of the local NGOs for their fieldworkers and court assistants in Rangpur. At that point, the project had been running for almost two years and it was a refresher training for the documentation of village court cases. Within the project, the court assistants are explicitly employed to facilitate the proper documentation of all village court sessions held within the context of the project. They file the application sheets, send the notification letters to all parties involved, protocol the actual sessions, and write the verdicts (see also Chapter 5). In every union where the project is operating, the local NGO employs one court assistant and one fieldworker. Whereas the fieldworker's task is to spread information about the village courts, the court assistants quite literally write the village courts into the landscape of non-state conflict resolution of rural Bangladesh. As the project was implemented in thirteen UPs in the district where the refresher training took place, twenty-six court assistants and fieldworkers (thirteen men and thirteen women) assembled in the training centre of the local NGO to rehearse the documentation of village court sessions.

It was a two-day workshop and I joined on the second day. During the first day, the participants had studied, again, the rules and regulations of the 2006 Village Court Act, i.e. the composition and jurisdiction of the village court. On the second day, the revision of the actual documentation of village court sessions was scheduled. In order to rehearse the correct ways of filing court sessions, i.e. writing the application, invitation letters for the jury and both conflicting parties, documenting the trial, and filing the verdict, UNDP has designed training materials that use the following hypothetical case:

> Kader Sheikh one day was taking tea in his village while Shiaz M. came along and asked him for a loan. Kader gave him 8000 Thaka in the presence of a witness. Shiaz told him that he would return the money after the harvest. But three, four, five months passed—and Kader did not get his money back. Kader frequently went to Shiaz's home to ask for the money, but Shiaz did not answer. After some time, Shiaz said that he would just not return the money, never. Shiaz used bad language and insulted him; he even told Kader that he was a fisherman [a person of low status]. Kader told Shiaz: 'please treat me politely and don't use bad language against me'. Later, Shiaz even threw a sandal to Kader and hurt him. Kader now became demoralized and insulted; so he went to the village authorities and asked for their help to get justice. But he did not get any justice. Without any other option left, Kader decided to go to the Village Court and filed a case to get his money back, and to get compensation for the insults. A village court session is opened and both Shiaz and Kader nominate two representatives. They hear the case and discuss the matter. In the end, Shiaz understands his mistake and apologizes to Kader. He has to give the money back and also pay 1000 Thaka compensation for the insults. (Fieldnotes, November 2012)

The twenty-six fieldworkers and court assistants worked with this hypothetical case in four groups, preparing all the pre-trial, trial, and post-trial documentation of the case. The documentation of this case is very comprehensive and includes not less than twenty-one different forms that need to be filled in, including the formal application of Kader with the village court, the invitation letters to the UP chairmen, the representatives, and Shiaz, the documentation of the trial, the verdict sheet, and the registration of the case in the village court case register. After the group work had finished, the groups swapped their documentation and had it double-checked by another group. The results were subsequently discussed in open plenum. What emerged in the plenary discussion was that not a single documentation of the case was complete. The most common omissions included:

- Description of the case in the application was not done properly as crucial information, like the amount of money owed by Shiaz, was missing.
- The notification sheet for the defendant, i.e. Shiaz, was missing.
- The names of the nominated representatives were missing. This was the case for each of the four groups.

- The verdict documentation was incorrect.
- The signature of the chairman on the verdict was missing.
- The dates were incorrect. In one case the date of the verdict preceded the date of the actual application for a village court session.
- The name of the applicant was missing.
- The copies of application, trial documentation, and verdict for the court registry were missing.

As the plenary discussion proceeded, both the trainer and the district supervisor of the local NGO got increasingly upset: 'so many mistakes! How is it possible that, after two years, you make still so many mistakes?' The trainer added: 'this is serious, very serious! It is a big problem if you do not fill the forms in correctly... In the future, we cannot tolerate these mistakes anymore!' As their complaints continued, the atmosphere in the room was deteriorating—and the participants were as puzzled about the trainer's anger as the trainer and district supervisor were about the participants' difficulties with the seemingly endless paper trail of village court documentation.

These apparent difficulties of the fieldworkers and court assistants to use the official documents in the ways intended by the EU and UNDP are surprising. Rangpur is regarded as the most successful of all four divisions where the project is implemented (EU-m-069). It is also the 'showcase' of the project and the only field site frequently presented to representatives of the EU and the country directors of UNDP. Just six weeks before the workshop, the 'Ambassador and Head of Delegations of the European Union to Bangladesh Mr. William Hanna highly appreciated the ongoing activities of the Village Courts in bringing justice to the doorsteps of the rural people while visiting Bhangni Union Parishad of Mithapukur Upazila in Rangpur District on October 4, 2012'.[1] Mr William Hanna's applause for the activities of the local NGO in Rangpur is not unjustified: between September 2010 and October 2012 the twenty-six fieldworkers and court assistants who participated in the workshop had helped to file a total of 2,246 cases with the village courts in Rangpur District, out of which a total of 1,627 cases had been resolved either through a village court session or through a formal pre-trial settlement in accordance with Rule 33 (ESDO 2012).

As only 452 cases have been dismissed for default, 80 per cent of the over 2,000 cases that the twenty-six fieldworkers and court assistants had filed over the course of the past two years have been (or are still being) dealt with by the village courts. Thus, there is a clear discrepancy between the court assistants' ability to comply with the formal requirements for case documentation and

[1] 'EU Ambassador Applauds Village Courts', at http://www.villagecourts.org, accessed 6 June 2013.

the actual number of cases they do file. But why is there such a discrepancy? The fieldworkers and court assistants are clearly very motivated; otherwise, there would be no (or at least fewer) cases that are actually filed. Is it because the official formats, up to twenty-one for a single case, are intellectually too demanding for the court assistants who have generally only received a rudimentary level of formal education? The notion of 'capacity building' that informs the kinds of training activity described above implicitly seems to suggest this: it presupposes a lack of knowledge. However, as Timothy Mitchell has argued, learning something new *always* presupposes delearning something old, something which is familiar, known, and deeply engrained in embodied background knowledge (Mitchell 2002). This background knowledge can hardly ever be fully superseded and replaced. Instead, it leaves its traces on everything new that is entering the social worlds we inhabit. Thus, new information can only be absorbed against our background knowledge—and new information as well as new capacities are always unavoidably filtered through it. Thus, something new is only learned in light of the already-known. But what is this 'already-known' in the context of this workshop and for the fieldworkers and court assistants throughout Bangladesh more broadly? In the next section, I argue that it is the logic of non-enforcement—analysed in Chapter 4—which influences the ways in which the field staff of the four local NGOs do (and do not) understand the use of official documents, formats, and templates that are used within the AVCB project.

The Symbolic Power of Official Documents

As seen above, the fieldworkers and court assistants struggle to fill out the forms and documents provided within the context of AVCB as prescribed by their NGOs' internal supervisors as well as the staff members of UNDP. This thick description as well as evidence provided in Chapter 6 shows how the production of legal documents within the context of the AVCB project does not amount to the creation of a legal rationality in a Weberian sense. The documentation of village court sessions does not close the gap between abstract and nationally applicable legal principles and particular instances of conflict. Although UNDP provides a total of twenty-four different forms and formats—eleven prescribed by the government and a further thirteen developed by UNDP—these documents do not render the messy realities of local conflicts legally transparent. This was also more than apparent in the thick description of the village court session in Chapter 6: the way in which the case was filed had hardly any resemblance to the ways in which the dynamics of the conflict resolution had unfolded. This, in turn, seems to suggest that the substantial production of written documents in the village courts is rather useless and informed primarily by a (somehow unfitting) Weberian fantasy about the rule of law as bureaucratic paperwork. On the one hand, the written records do not actually record what happened in a process of conflict resolution; on the other hand, even if the documents did accurately depict social and legal facts, these facts could not be acted upon as the state lacks substantial enforcement capacities. In the village courts, these enforcement capacities are even further diminished as the oversight mechanisms of the village courts through the MLGRD are weak, at best: no uniform reporting mechanisms exist, and the UP chairmen do not have to provide detailed information about the village courts to their respective superiors (Asaduzzaman 2012, 50–1). All of this seems to suggest that the paperwork produced in the village courts is nothing but an administrative burden. But are the files and formats written by the court assistants really that meaningless for people in rural Bangladesh?

In contrast to my own initial suspicion, most of my respondents in rural Bangladesh have singled out the production of written documents as *the* distinguishing feature of the village court. As one of them has argued very clearly: 'the only difference is that in the village courts, you get written documents, in *shalish*, it is all verbal' (RB-m-099). Using a total of twenty-four different files and formats, the fieldworkers and court assistants write the application for a village court case, the letter summoning the contestant as well as potential witnesses to the village court sessions, and the final judgment. Thus, virtually everybody who is somehow involved in a village court case, either as applicant, contestant, witness, or jury member, is equipped with at least one official document, written on official paper. These official papers were considered to be very important by most of my respondents in rural Bangladesh. Thus, through the official paperwork, the approximately 650 fieldworkers and court assistants employed within the project quite literally write the village courts into the universe of non-state justice institutions in rural Bangladesh. Within this context, where roughly 40 per cent of the rural population are illiterate (UNDP 2013, 120), writing these documents was almost univocally considered to be an essential service that the field staff of the four local NGOs provide to their constituencies. But why is this service so important?

Understanding the importance of providing written documents to extremely poor people requires a change in perspective, away from the content of these documents and towards a more careful analysis of what these documents actually do. This implies understanding documents as material artefacts whose meaning is unstable, context-dependent, and open to renegotiation, quite independently of the discourses that these documents are thought to carry. Such a change in perspective also sheds further light on the logic of non-enforcement that I theoretically introduced in Chapter 2 and empirically reconstructed in Chapter 4. According to the logic of non-enforcement, people file cases with the state-backed courts not in order to get binding and enforceable verdicts, but to alter the dynamics of non-state justice institutions like the *shalish*. This logic of non-enforcement works in complex and complicated ways: it allows people to either access non-state institutions to begin with; or, in case they already have access to a *shalish*, it allows them to alter its dynamics in their favour. Paradoxically, this is possible in spite of the fact that most people in rural Bangladesh do not consider the state to have any significant enforcement capacity. Through this logic of non-enforcement, state and non-state justice institutions are linked; and this link is constituted by trails of official documents and bureaucratic paperwork. Through documents, the state is brought into non-state courts and starts to operate there. Although it does not impose its order, the state—mediated by its artefacts—therefore changes non-state justice.

Take the *shalish* outlined in Chapter 4 as an example: throughout the entire case, various kinds of official paperwork were present. As the police dispersed the crowd that had gathered after Yafi had been injured, the officers took testimonies from the conflicting parties, the chairman, and various witnesses. Scribbled in notebooks, these testimonies were subsequently transposed into an official report filed at the police station. This report, then, was passed on to the magistrate court and the prosecutor in charge who opened a case against Khairul. At the same time, medical reports were filed in Chittagong Medical College where Yafi was treated for his injuries. These reports became forensic evidence and travelled into the police file stored at the station and copied in the prosecutor's office. A first court hearing had been scheduled for the week following the *shalish*; and Yafi's brother had just received an official invitation as a key witness. This invitation, the medical report from the hospital, and further documentary evidence are lying on the desk, in front of the chairman who presides over the *shalish*. In the *shalish*, they are enacted in a particular way: in his introductory speech the chairman points out that this is the third *shalish* session; the previous two have failed to bear results and now this session has to succeed, otherwise, the state's court gets involved. As he makes his case, he holds the court letter in both his hands, moving it up and down to the rhythm of his speech. The document is present, visible, part of the *shalish*. It is laid to rest on the table again as the conflicting parties give their statements. The invitation letter appears again in the *en camera* negotiations between the conflicting parties. Together with the medical reports and hospital bills, the court letter and police reports circulate around the table. So do land titles and other documents indicating the financial situation of the involved parties. In the end, a compromise is reached. This compromise is public and pronounced at the end of the *shalish*. But before this, it has been written down and all parties have signed it.

What this example shows is an intricate interplay between the written and the verbal (Gupta 2012, 198–208). Written documents mattered; but they only mattered in the ways in which they were verbally enacted and thereby 'reinscribed', i.e. in the ways in which the meaning of these documents was discursively presented (often quite independent of the information they actually carried). In the case of the document produced at the end of the *shalish*, the one signed by all parties, this was a process of validation. The chairman publicly announced that a compromise had been found and written down. Then, the victim's brother openly pardoned the perpetrators. He allowed them to rise again as they asked for forgiveness; and thereby he virtually enacted the reconciliatory outcome of the *shalish*. The document that fixed the terms of this reconciliation was thereby validated. In contrast, the documents of the state that circulated throughout the *shalish* were verbalized in a different way. The court letter that summoned the victim's brother as key witness to a first hearing, for example, was read by the chairman as a call to find a solution in this *shalish*. Here, the document acquired a function quite different from its apparent content; the content aimed at bringing witness testimony into the state's courtrooms to pass justice. But as it was read out by the chairman and subsequently discussed in the *shalish*, this document served the acceleration of non-state justice. What these two documents and the ways in which they were used in the *shalish* show is that the written and the verbal cannot be easily separated. Instead, they interact. And in these interactions, the state's documents do not further the enforcement of the state's laws; but they change the dynamics of the *shalish* nonetheless. In other words, as state documents are discursively enacted, they exercise a power that is incongruent with the state's enforcement capacities.

There are two ways of accounting for the power of state documents. The first is the rational fear of getting involved with the state. Although the enforcement capacities of the state are limited, getting involved with state agencies can turn out to be costly and burdensome. For example, prolonged cases in the state courts do consume money, time, and energy, as most of my interviewees in rural Bangladesh frequently stressed. Being involved in a court case requires a significant amount of paperwork. Yet official documents like birth certificates, identity cards, driving licences, land titles, tax records, death and burial certificates, police, court, and prison records, or the necessary paperwork sanctioning marriage and divorce are often difficult to obtain; and at least some of these are always necessary when involving the state. Acquiring these documents often requires travelling to the offices of the relevant authorities, additional paperwork, and 'a little money for tea' (Shehabuddin 2008) for the bureaucrat in charge. Despite limited enforcement capacities, the state therefore still has a certain degree of 'disturbance capacity'. This means that although its laws and rules are frequently not enforced, the state nonetheless exercises a tangible power in people's lives; and this power is mediated by bureaucratic paperwork. Besides this rational fear of getting involved with the state, however, there is also what Akhil Gupta has described as an 'irrational reverence for documents' (Gupta 2012, 208–14).

As Gupta has shown in his ethnographic study of the working of the bureaucracy in India, many people treated documents produced by the state as if they were 'magical' or 'sacred objects'. And 'although subaltern and illiterate people were especially likely to treat written documents as objects with inherent powers, to some degree that view was held by all subjects of the state' (Gupta 2012, 212). Gupta discerns the ways in which official documents are treated almost as sacred objects by the ways in which they are kept, especially though not exclusively among poor villagers. Official documents are carefully wrapped in paper, the paper is then again wrapped in cloth, the cloth is placed in a metal container and, if available, the metal container is then stored within a glass cupboard (Gupta 2012, 212). In rural Bangladesh, documents are kept in similar ways and treated with the same degree of reverence. Often when I asked people about their village court experiences, and whether they would allow me to have a look at the documents, solemn ceremonies followed. Boxes were taken out of cupboards, cloth was removed, layers of protective paper carefully opened, and village court files were produced, often with an air of pride. This was the case among literate and illiterate people alike. In general, people who could not read documents would still recognize them; they would recognize how official they were, see whether they were signed, and how sophisticated this signature was. Was it one of those signatures of a poor and barely literate person; or was it an authoritative signature, complex, complicated, maybe even artistic, and designed in a way to make forgeries all the more difficult?

These recognitions are crucial. They are deeply engrained in people's background knowledge and therefore operate almost pre-reflectively (cf. Bourdieu 1990). In Bourdieusian terms, official documents constitute a symbolic capital that is tightly linked to other forms of capital. As argued above, the access to documents depends first and foremost on money. In order to file a case with the state-backed courts, for example, people from remote villages first have to travel to the city where the nearest court is located. This requires not only taking the bus and paying for the fare, it also means losing income for one day, which is especially difficult for landless day labourers who depend on a daily cash income to sustain their livelihoods. In the city, further money has to be spent to get to the court premises. A lawyer has to be employed in order to navigate the complex ways of justice within the state's judiciary. And if a lawyer cannot be hired, extremely poor and illiterate or barely literate people need to pay at least one of the professional case writers who runs their offices on the pavements outside of court premises and other governmental offices. For a small fee, these case writers help people to produce the filled-out forms necessary for the acquisition of further documents like court records, police reports, or any kind of certificate. Besides money, access to state documents also depends on personal relationships and, increasingly, political affiliations (Lewis and Hossain 2008b, 43–50).

Personal relationships and political affiliations constitute a social capital that aids access to key figures in control of documents, like bureaucrats, police officers, or UP chairman whose signature is a necessary first step in the acquisition of identity cards, marriage certificates, or documents facilitating access to special governmental schemes.

Very poor and marginalized people with little money and not much social capital therefore have only highly limited access to official paperwork. This is where the fieldworkers and court assistants become decisive. They equip poor and marginalized people with official paperwork they could not otherwise access. The eleven different government forms are all highly official. They all include a cover page that displays the emblem of the MLGRD. They also display the flag of the EU and the logo of UNDP. Virtually everybody involved in a village court case is equipped with at least one of these forms. I encountered these forms as I talked, for example, with Karuna who had lost a calf in a conflict with her neighbour's son (see Chapter 6). Having unsuccessfully tried to receive compensation for her financial loss, it was literally the act of filing a village court case which brought the conflict to the attention of the chairman. This, in turn, facilitated the resolution of the conflict. Only the pressure of the chairman made the opposing party agree to a *shalish* that resulted in a compromise acceptable to all parties. Similarly, the village court-turned-*shalish* discussed in Chapter 6 was to a significant part facilitated by the presence of official paperwork. The chairman would usually not attend mediation sessions over what he termed 'such a trifling matter as six dead hens'. Yet, as an official village court case had been filed, and the applicants of the case arrived at the village court premises with their official invitation letter, the chairman felt compelled to hold a village court session.

The fieldworkers and court assistants therefore translate one of the key practices of the rule of law: the production of official paperwork. Instead of using the official forms and templates for the neutral and orderly keeping of village court records, they deploy these documents as a symbolic capital. By equipping poor and marginalized people with official paperwork these people could not otherwise access, the fieldworkers and especially the court assistants change not only the meaning of 'the rule of law', they also intervene in established power hierarchies in rural Bangladesh. This works only because the fieldworkers and court assistants translate the paperwork provided by UNDP into established patterns of conflict resolution in rural Bangladesh. More precisely, they translate bureaucratic paperwork as key artefacts of the project into the logic of non-enforcement. According to this logic, inhabitants of rural Bangladesh can use the insignia of the state-backed judiciary to alter the dynamics of non-state justice mechanisms—and this is exactly what happens to the official forms and formats that are deployed within the context of the AVCB project. Therefore, the local NGOs fulfil one of the central additional conditions for succesful translations outlined in Chapter 2.

By enacting documents in practice, they transalte minimal material resources (literally only paper) into a symbolic captial that has a significant impact on local dynamics of conflict resolution.

This translation of paperwork is also apparent in the very high number of cases that are settled through a Rule 33 compromise that follows a formal appeal to the village court but precedes the jury judgment in an actual court session. Both the cases of Nafisa and Karuna described in Chapter 6 were settled by such a compromise. However, even if the village courts are formally constituted and pass a jury verdict in the second or third hearing, the overwhelming majority of these verdicts are passed either unanimously or with a 4:1 majority. As I argued in Chapter 6, this does not mean that a consensus is always reached. Often, it might simply be the case that the representatives follow closely the opinion of the UP chairman. Nonetheless, it means (a) that conflict resolution stays at the UP level as hardly any of the village court sessions are appealable, and (b) that the village courts are therefore one further avenue to circumvent the enforcement of state-backed laws. In that respect, they are very similar to the *shalish*. The key difference for poor and marginalized people is, as I have argued above, that they can make use of the official forms and formats provided by the project to gain access to the UP chairman in the first place, as also the case of Karuna in Chapter 6 clearly highlighted.

The translation of bureaucratic paperwork into a symbolic capital that follows the logic of non-enforcement is therefore decisive. It significantly improves the situation of poor and marginalized people in processes of conflict resolution. Yet it simultaneously undermines the aspiration of international donor agencies to activate the village courts as the lowest tier to the state's judiciary. Besides this translation of a key practice of 'the rule of law', the fieldworkers and court assistants also translate the normative vocabulary in which international donor agencies conceptualize it—from transnational liberalism into the normative vocabularies of community harmony and Islamic law.

7.2. TRANSLATIONS OF NORMATIVE ORDERS

Translating Human Rights

During a group discussion with the governing board of MLAA, a pioneering legal aid organization, source of inspiration for the AVCB project, and one of the four local NGOs that implement the project in rural Bangladesh, I asked how they explain the concept of human rights to the people in rural Bangladesh with whom they are working. In response, one senior member of the organization said:

> so this is a very difficult question. And also motivating people about human rights is not that easy. But for that you have got to talk to them. What is a human right? What is the definition of a human right? The right one needs to be human, without which a man cannot be, you know, himself as a member of the community or a citizen of the state. That's simple but very difficult! (NGO-gd-112)

Here, human rights indicate the right to membership in a community, or, as Hannah Arendt has argued, 'the right to have rights' (Arendt 1973, 295–6), though in this case, this right is not granted by the state in the form of citizenship but by the village in the form of community membership. This right to have rights is never discussed in abstract terms but always contextualized and applied to concrete problems, conflicts, and challenges the participants of courtyard meetings or other NGO activities are facing.

These challenges are also discussed in interactions between the fieldworkers of the local NGOs and the CBOs that have been formed in the course of the project. CBOs assemble widely respected representatives from village communities who ought to function as multipliers of village court-related information. They are a cornerstone in the project's sustainability strategy as they remain embedded in local communities even after the project has formally ended. CBOs are therefore a key channel of communication between the fieldworker and various constituencies in rural Bangladesh. In a long discussion with twelve representatives of CBOs in Madaripur, the notion of the right to have rights was further specified.

We are sitting in a community centre close to where Tapathi, introduced at the beginning of Chapter 1, had facilitated her courtyard meeting. Initially, the five women and seven men report different conflicts that had occurred in the vicinities, in which they were working. They discuss these conflicts as well as possible solution strategies involving village court proceedings as much as resolutions via *shalish* courts. I involve them in a prolonged discussion about the fundamental principles that ought to guide decisions in both *shalish* and village court proceedings, a topic they also frequently raise with members of their respective CBOs. They point to five fundamental rights everybody should enjoy—the right to food, shelter, health, education, and clothing. It is these five things, they argue, that are necessary in order to be part of a community, and to be able to participate in community-based processes of conflict resolution.

This right to participation is not abstract. It departs from the abstract universalism of contemporary transnational human rights discourse and, instead, always starts from the specific context, and—probably even more importantly—the social relations in which a person is embedded (Siddiqi 2011d). Not all of these relations, and the hierarchies they imply, are questioned though. Take generational hierarchies as an example. Talking to a community-based women's organization in a rather remote village where

MLAA has been working for decades, one of the women clearly approved of the outcomes of different kinds of human rights-based training programmes that the NGOs had been running for the past two decades. As she argued, 'these rights are wonderful, you know. Because previously, our husband simply decided to whom to marry our daughters; but now, through human rights, they know that they have to consult us and that we make this decision together' (RB-gd-107). Here, the notion of human rights is employed to widen the participatory spaces for married women (though not necessarily for unmarried ones).[2] This widening of participatory spaces was not limited to marital politics, but also included increased participation in decisions about which crops to seed and which investments to make as a household. This notion of human rights does not explicitly point back to the Universal Declaration of Human Rights or the various sets of rights anchored in international treaties.[3] It neither reproduces the abstract universalism that underpins contemporary transnational human rights discourses. Instead, human rights as they are translated by the fieldworkers and court assistants at the grassroots level in rural Bangladesh start from existing social relationships and seek to develop social traction by enhancing spaces for participation within these relationships.

This strong emphasis on the right to participate in decision-making processes which significantly affect one's life is part of the broader argumentative strategy pursued by MLAA. As an organization, MLAA facilitates conflict resolution in *shalish*, village courts, or other ADR mechanisms through community participation. This was highlighted in particular by a gender specialist who has worked for many years with the organization. She argued that 'community participation can solve any kind of conflicts', including those

[2] Whether this is actually compatible with the Universal Declaration of Human Rights has to remain an open question: Article 16(2) of the Declaration only states that 'Marriage should be entered into only with the free and full consent of the intending spouses'. This does not preclude that daughters fully consent to their mother's choice of husband; and I would assume that in many cases her mother's participation in the decision-making process increases rather than decreases the likelihood of the daughter's consent to her future husband. At the same time, however, it is equally implausible to assume that this always happens; in rural Bangladesh, as much as anywhere else in the world, mothers and daughters do have, at times, fierce disagreements. Again, in this particular example it is important to note how the translation of human rights unfolds against the backdrop of intersecting power relations: in the example just quoted, married women are empowered vis-à-vis their husbands as much as vis-à-vis their unmarried daughters, For an analysis of the complexities of marital politics in rural Bangladesh, see White (2010, 2012).

[3] This is not to say that the 'thicker' notion of human rights as they are articulated in international human rights treaties are not important for the work of local NGOs in Bangladesh: thus, the local NGO makes frequent references to CEDAW to combat domestic violence, for example, and protect the bodily integrity of human beings. In this chapter, however, I am more concerned with the ways in which fieldworkers make the human rights language of international treaties available in rural Bangladesh by translating it into local discourse. These are also translations, but translations that maintain a strong line of recognizability as they preserve, at least most of the time, the normative cores of international human rights treaties.

that the state-backed laws cannot solve, for example the divorce of Hindu marriages, which is not provided for in Hindu family law. It is thus only that 'people's participation makes the decision, the MLAA fieldworker only observes that this decision is made in accordance with the law' (NGO-gd-112). However, here 'the law' refers not only to the state-backed laws of Bangladesh but to a diverse set of legal and normative resources, including the state-backed laws as well as international human rights discourse and religious principles (NGO-f-056). Thus, the local NGOs operate in a context where multiple legal and normative codes govern the lives of poor and marginalized people (Shehabuddin 2008, 27).

In order to navigate this complex context, the local NGOs use a wide repertoire of normative vocabularies to carve out and increase the existing participatory spaces for poor and marginalized people, and in particular women. One of these resources is the language of human rights, which is, as I have shown above, translated into a basic claim for enhanced participation, which is often expressed in terms of *samaj* justice (see Chapter 6). In this way, the local NGOs do not necessarily contradict global human rights treaties, but make them accessible to people in rural Bangladesh by including them in prevailing logics of community harmony, with all the complexities and complications this entails. Besides this translation of human rights into participatory spaces within non-state conflict-resolution mechanisms, Islam and Islamic law constitute a powerful normative order in rural Bangladesh. The next section shows how local NGOs use the language of Islam and Islamic law to improve the situation of women, the kinds of contestation this provokes, and the ways in which local NGOs in rural Bangladesh respond to these contestations.

Promoting Women's Rights through the Language of Islam and Islamic Law

As argued in Chapter 6, addressing the concerns of women is only possible if the local NGOs expand their institutional toolkit and thus abandon the exclusive focus on the civil and criminal cases that can be negotiated in the village courts. As they are expanding the institutional toolkit, the local NGOs not only focus on the village courts but also include the arbitration councils in their field activities. They thus add another quasi-formal institution that deals explicitly with Muslim family law. However, including the arbitration council unavoidably expands the normative vocabulary through which matters of social and local justice are communicated as the promotion of women's rights is only possible through the language of Islam and Islamic law. As I talked to a senior gender specialist at UNDP, who has worked for many years as a fieldworker, and later as a trainer of trainers for one of the local NGOs involved in the AVCB project, the importance of the language of

Islam and Islamic law for the improvement of the situation for women in rural Bangladesh became very apparent. As she argued:

> It is our duty to make the connection between Islam and what the [state-backed] laws say. Our [Muslim family law] comes from the Qur'an; so if you follow the law, you are following Islam. Bangladesh is a Muslim country—and without respecting religion, without showing the connections between the law and the Qur'an, nobody will listen to you! This is my experience as a trainer, as a social activist... In my trainings, I always show: there is a law—and this law comes from the Qur'an. The inheritance law comes from the Qur'an, the divorce law comes from the Qur'an, every Muslim [family] law comes from the Qur'an. But in the villages, there are many illiterate people. They might recite the Qur'an in Arabic, but they do not know what's written in the Qur'an. So it is my duty to translate the Qur'an into their language. (NGO-f-056)

Literally translating the Qur'an into the language of people in rural Bangladesh is in some instances identical to the promotion of the state-backed family laws, which are based on religious law (see also Chapter 3).

Although the state-backed Muslim family laws have been heavily criticized by international human rights organizations for discriminating against women and for violating Bangladesh's obligations under international human rights law (see for example Human Rights Watch 2012), the state-backed Muslim family laws nonetheless carry an emancipatory potential for women in rural Bangladesh: as I have argued in Chapter 4, precisely those aspects of Muslim family law that threaten the established patriarchal order in Bangladesh are systematically not enforced.[4] Thus, women do not get their legally granted shares of inheritance, divorces are frequently not registered with the state, due maintenance payments are withheld, and multiple marriages are entered without the written consent of the first wife or wives (Human Rights Watch 2012, 3). Consequently, the promotion of compliance with the state-backed Muslim family law has the potential to improve the situation of women in rural Bangladesh. The four local NGOs I worked with throughout my field research thus promote the state-backed Muslim family law—and do so through the normative orders of Islam and Islamic law.

Take the question of divorce as an example. Most fieldworkers and court assistants in all four divisions of Bangladesh where local NGOs are in charge of activating the village courts have reported experiences with women approaching them with questions pertaining to divorce and the dissolution of marriage.

[4] This argument is inspired by and heavily indebted to Matthew Nelson's (2011) work on the effects (or lack thereof) of state-backed Islamic laws on inheritance practices in Punjab, Pakistan. The parallels between Pakistan and Bangladesh are striking, especially in light of Bangladesh's political history, which is, at least to a large extent, a history of trying to carve out a secular Muslim identity for Bangladesh *in contrast to* Pakistan.

Under the MFLO of 1961 (discussed in more detail in Chapter 3), the possibility of verbal divorce through the man by uttering the word '*talaq*' three consecutive times is foreclosed. Instead, the MFLO formalizes divorce proceedings and prescribes a ninety-day mediation phase after the application for divorce has been formally filed by the husband with the chairman. Although the precise legal implications of the provisions of the MFLO have been fiercely contested since its inception, the fieldworkers and court assistants defend the imperative of a prolonged mediation phase, and the resulting impossibility of spontaneous divorce. Yet they do so less in the terminology of the state-backed courts, which, as argued above, have seen intense litigation on questions such as what happens if a husband fails to provide written notice to the UP chairman. Instead, they defend sustained efforts at restoring good relationships within a marriage as a Qur'anic requirement.

Similarly, the fieldworkers and court assistants defend women's right to initiate divorce (*talaq-i-tafwiz*), which can be granted by the husband to the wife on the marriage registration form, as a religious imperative rather than a legal possibility. In addition to the possibility of *talaq-i-tafwiz*, the staff members of local NGOs also disseminate information regarding the possibility of divorce in the case of mutual consent or if the wife relinquishes her claim to the dower that has been paid by her husband (*khula*). Dower (*mohrana*) is a central component of an Islamic marriage; it consists of a payment by a husband to his wife, usually in the form of money, jewellery, or other assets. Although at least an instalment of the dower is payable at the time of marriage, many women in rural Bangladesh do not claim its full amount out of fear of antagonizing their husbands (Shehabuddin 2008, 85–7). Similar fears also pertain to questions of polygamy, which is legally sanctioned in Bangladesh if specific conditions are met. Again, in questions relating to polygamy, the fieldworkers of local NGOs point to Islam as a normative order and highlight the Qur'anic requirement of maintaining all wives equally. They also argue that the prior consent of the wife or wives to further marriages is a religious imperative. It is also a legal one; and in many instances in which the fieldworkers and court assistants aim at enhancing participatory spaces for women, they at least implicitly draw on existing state-backed Muslim family laws in Bangladesh.

Yet the use of Islamic narratives of justification by the local NGOs is not limited to the promotion of state-backed Muslim family law. Thus, the gender specialist and former fieldworker quoted above also explained that she always uses the example of the wife of Mohammed to convince the male participants of her workshops to treat the female members of their family respectfully:

> Our Prophet, when he got the voice from Allah, at first he shared with his wife. When he came back from *Eid*, at first he shared with his wife. When he made a decision, he first consulted with his wife. I always provide this example to my

> communities: if you take any decision, please consult with your wife. You listen to your wife, because our Prophet did that as well. (NGO-f-056)

Similarly argumentative structures are used by local NGOs in rural Bangladesh (also beyond the AVCB project) to contest widespread dowry practices as well as violence against women as un-Islamic.[5] As Elora Shehabuddin has shown, arguments that 'it is said in the hadith that our Prophet never raised a hand against his wives' or that 'according to the hadith, men are not allowed to hit their wives' are used by both grassroots-level workers of local NGOs as well as villagers in rural Bangladesh to combat violence against women (Shehabuddin 2008, 102). In these cases as well as in the example cited above, references to the *hadith*, the collection of examples from the life of Mohammed, are used to combat violence against women as well as to enhance their possibility of participating in the social and political lives of their communities.

These references to Islam and Islamic law are persuasive because *both* villagers and fieldworkers firmly believe in them: as I asked a fieldworker of one of the four local NGOs if she thought that Islamic law was bad for women, she looked at me, laughed, and said: 'of course not! Islamic law is perfect, for everybody—also for women. The big problem is that Islamic law is not applied in rural Bangladesh' (NGO-f-063). In fact, most fieldworkers I talked to in rural Bangladesh shared this position and firmly argued that adherence to Islamic law (as they understood it in reference to the state-backed Muslim family laws) would be best for men and women alike. This is important as it fulfils one central pre-condition for translations outlined in Chapter 2. The translators understand, and at least partially share, the background knowledge of the people they are translating for. This is also the case in rural Bangladesh as all my evidence suggests that the translation of secular vocabularies into Islamic narratives of justification is not strategic in the sense that the translators would actually firmly believe in secular principles and then only deploy religious arguments instrumentally. Instead, my evidence suggests that the reverse is the case: the principled beliefs of the fieldworkers I met in rural Bangladesh are principled beliefs of Islamic law and the resources provided by international donor agencies can be used strategically to advocate exactly these beliefs. Consequently, the fieldworkers and court assistants in rural Bangladesh actually want to improve the situation of women through the interpretation of Islamic law that is codified by the state. The demand for the enforcement of the state-backed Muslim family laws is therefore both moral and political. It is, however, heavily contested.

[5] For a detailed discussion on dowry practices, see White (2013).

7.3. WHO HAS THE RIGHT TO SPEAK FOR ISLAM?

The local NGOs also address the *fatwa*-related violence discussed in Chapter 4. However, besides the references to the illegality of extra-judicial punishments that was confirmed by the Appellate Division of the Supreme Court in 2010, the local NGOs also deploy a second narrative of justification: they contest those *fatwa* that demand the physical punishment of women as un-Islamic. In response to the kind of *fatwa* that has attracted a high degree of national and international media attention as they policed women's sexualities through the exercise of physical violence, the local NGOs argue that the imam who issued these *fatwa* actually lacked the knowledge and required education to issue a *fatwa*. Thus, these *fatwa* were not in accordance with Islamic law at all. As one district supervisor of the local NGOs involved in the AVCB project told me:

> in the courtyard meetings where they discuss the village courts they emphasise a lot that these *fatwa* are, in fact, against the Qur'an and the principles of Islamic law. In order to be allowed to issue a *fatwa* you have to study for many years. You have to study not only the Qur'an and the Hadith, but also what is called *fiqh*. The Imam in your village is a pious man and he knows the Qur'an and Hadith—but he is not allowed to give *fatwa*. If he gives a *fatwa*, this is against Islam.
>
> (NGO-m-061)

However, this strategy of arguing that some *fatwa* issued by local religious leaders constitute violations of Islamic law as well as the promotion of women's rights through the language of Islam draw the local NGOs into fierce contestations that revolve around the question: who has the right to interpret Islamic law in rural Bangladesh?

In order to analyse this contestation, it is helpful to look at 'the hard case', i.e. at the region of Bangladesh where this contestation is the most intense. Within the context of my field research, this region is Chittagong and, more precisely, the District of Hathazari. In Hathazari, the Al-Jameatul Alia Darul Uloom Moinul Islam Madrasa, popularly referred to as 'Hathazari Madrasa' or 'Boro madrasa', is one of the top ten Islamic educational institutions in South Asia in terms of academic standards and reputation (Ahmad and Nelson 2009, 33). Established in 1896, it is the largest Deobandi madrasa in Bangladesh and supervises in cooperation with two other madrasas a network of 7,000 smaller educational institutions throughout Bangladesh (Riaz 2008, 149). These institutions are largely Qwomi madrasas, i.e. they are not regulated through the state's Madrasa Education Board. Since 2010, the political movement Hefazat-e-Islami, a loose grouping of smaller Islamic parties as well as up to 25,000 madrasas, has been coordinated through the Hathazari Madrasa (Mustafa 2013). The Hefazat movement started in response to the government's 2009 draft Women's Development Policy, which would have given men and women equal legal entitlements to inheritance. Mobilizing significant resistance, the Hefazat movement eventually pressured the government into abandoning the draft policy (Allchin 2013).

Four years later, in April 2013, the Hefazat-e-Islami reappeared on the political stage in Bangladesh, demanding stricter blasphemy laws and capital punishment for bloggers who allegedly had insulted the Prophet Mohammed. Gaining significant momentum, the movement organized mass rallies in April and May 2013 and presented its thirteen-point demands. Talking to a senior lecturer of *fiqh* (Islamic jurisprudence) in Hathazari madrasa in January 2012, I asked him what he considered to be the biggest problem in Bangladesh's contemporary legal system. He told me:

> The biggest problem is that the laws are written by humans. These laws cannot solve all human problems; as it has been amended time and again. These laws are not long-lasting. Long-lasting are only God's laws; only if they are implemented could the world live in peace... Every political party in Bangladesh is led by a Muslim. But an Islamic name does not mean that people really try to implement Islam. There is not a single party that seriously tries to implement Islamic law. (RB-m-014)

He explicitly referred to the Muslim family law, which he considered to be in clear violation of Islamic law. According to him, two aspects of the current Muslim family laws are in violations of Islamic principles: certain aspects of the laws of inheritance and the impossibility of immediate verbal divorce through *tin talaq* (discussed above).

A few days after this conversation, I attended a workshop of the AVCB project with religious leaders that took place in the immediate vicinity of Hathazari Madrasa. Halfway through the workshop, the trainer and the district supervisor of the local NGO were confronted with the following argument by one of the participating Islamic scholars: 'but in 1961, the government changed the laws of inheritance for Muslims—and now they are thinking about changing it even more! But the 1961 MFLO is against Islam—it must not be used; it is against the Qur'an'. In response, the district supervisor said:

> When the law was passed in 1961, the government consulted many religious scholars, who approved of the Ordinance. The Ordinance is in accordance with Islamic law. The government would never pass a law that violates Islamic law. All of you, you need to study the Qur'an and the Hadith, and the Sunna very carefully; then you will see that the government does not pass laws that are against Islam.

As the imam was not persuaded, the trainer and district supervisor eventually just ended the discussion and proceeded with the agenda of the workshop. Although unsuccessful in this instance, the contestation outlined above highlights two argumentative strategies employed by the local NGOs vis-à-vis established religious authorities: on the one hand, the local NGOs engage in substantial debates over the content of Islamic law and thus draw upon theological lines of reasoning to justify the content of the state-backed Islamic laws in Bangladesh. On the other hand, the local NGOs simultaneously refer to the state as the only institution that is entitled to articulate legitimate and therefore binding interpretations of Islamic law.

This particular debate over inheritance in the 1961 MFLO is rather scholastic. It only concerns cases in which a child's father dies before the paternal grandfather. Thus, commenting on the debate that took place within the workshop, one NGO district supervisor told me: 'in the villages, most people do not know about the 1961 Muslim Family Law Ordinance. They only know about *shalish* and how they solve conflicts within a *shalish*. Thus, we only get these kinds of debate [as the one that has been outlined above] in the trainings with learned Islamic scholars' (NGO-m-031). However, even less learned religious authorities, like the imams in the villages who have generally received only a rather basic training in Islamic jurisprudence, do know about the Islamic principles for divorce. As I have shown above, the fieldworkers and court assistants defend the registration of women's rights to initiate divorce, the imperative of prolonged mediation phases prior to divorce, and the illegitimacy of verbal divorce (*tin talaq*) as Islamic principles. Yet in contestations with religious authorities, the fieldworkers and court assistants expand their argumentative strategies. Like the trainer in the workshop quoted above, the fieldworkers and court assistants deploy a dual argument that aims at grounding the legitimacy of their interpretation of Islamic Law with, firstly, reference to religious sources and, secondly, the state-backed Muslim family laws. As a district supervisor of another local NGO in Dhaka Division explained:

> Sometimes, it happens that religious leaders don't agree with what we say about divorce. In these cases, we sit down with the Imam and discuss: we tell them that the question of divorce is not conclusively answered in the Qur'an. Thus, we have to look at the Hadith, Isma, and Kias as well. We show them the sources and argue that our interpretation of Islamic law is the correct one. It is also the same interpretation that we find in the [state-backed Muslim family] laws. For example: in the Qur'an it is written that when a husband says three times *talaq* [divorce], the divorce is valid. Then, the Imam might insist on an intervening Hilla marriage. But we show them that the right interpretation of Islamic law is the one in the [state-backed] Muslim Family Law, which always demands a 90 day mediation period, always. Thus, we tell the Imam that they need to register all divorces with the Union Parishad Chairman—otherwise, the divorce is not valid according to Islamic Law. (NGO-m-061)

Here again both lines of argument intersect: on the one hand, references to the religious sources are used to justify a particular interpretation of Islamic law.

In a second step, the local NGOs argue that this interpretation is the basis of the state-backed Muslim family law.

As any justification narrative, this line of argument combines arguments about normative validity with claims to political authority. In the case above, the district supervisor of the local NGO as well as his colleagues all argue that a three-month mediation period in potential divorce cases is normatively prescribed by Islamic principles. These principles, in turn, are enshrined in the state-backed laws. Thus, the failure to follow the state-backed procedures of divorce would render the divorce un-Islamic and thus invalid not only in a legal, but also in a moral sense. As I have shown above, the interwoven claims to normative validity and political authority are contested by religious authorities in rural Bangladesh. Their favoured interpretations of Islamic law also support the patriarchal structures of rural society and thus do have a high degree of social traction. Furthermore, as I have shown in Chapter 3, contestations over the questions of who has the right to speak for Islam are not new in rural Bangladesh—and the role of the state in the interpretation of Islam and Islamic law has been, and continues to be, the subject of long but ongoing debate. The fieldworkers and court assistants I interviewed in rural Bangladesh have clearly sided in these debates. They continuously argue that the state—and only the state—has the authority to interpret Islamic law. In this instance, the four local NGOs actually promote the rule of law; at least in the narrow sense of the enforcement of nationally applicable state-backed law, irrespective of the context in which any particular conflict emerged.[6]

7.4. CONCLUSION

These translations of normative vocabularies as well as of key practices of 'the rule of law' as it is understood by international donor agencies explains why the project only has an impact in those areas where it is implemented through the intervening help of local NGOs. As argued in Chapter 2, translations only occur if they are facilitated by translators who transform the meaning of travelling norms and ideas in ways that allow them to resonate in particular contexts. The fieldworkers and court assistants of the four local NGOs master this task of the translators. They skilfully use all the artefacts, including the official forms and files provided by the project. Instead of using these forms to render particular conflicts transparent and intelligible within the legal

[6] Of course, by promoting the village court, the local NGOs also advocate the implementation of the 2006 Village Court Act. However, as I argued in Chapter 3, this is a peculiar kind of law, as it demarcates the boundaries in which state-backed law can officially be suspended as long as certain procedural criteria are adhered to.

rationality of the state, they use them as a symbolic capital. This, in turn, allows them to replicate the logic of non-enforcement and thereby integrate poor and marginalized people in Bangladesh, who do not have any access to the state-backed courts, into the logic of non-enforcement. Thus, the four local NGOs facilitate access to the UP chairmen as respected arbiters of conflict in rural Bangladesh, but they do not promote the rule of law as imagined by the EU or other bi- and multilateral donor agencies more generally. Furthermore, the four local NGOs abandon secular discourses of women's empowerment, in which Islam is often understood as an obstacle rather than a resource. Instead, the local NGOs translate secular notions of human rights and the rule of law and improve the lives of women in rural Bangladesh explicitly *through* the language of Islam and Islamic law.

As I have shown in this chapter, translating the normative orders of secular liberalism into the vocabulary of Islamic law unavoidably leads to contestations over the question of who has the right to speak for Islam. In these contestations, the four local NGOs argue that the best interpretation of Islamic law is codified in the state-backed Muslim family laws. This narrative of justification for the enforcement of the state-backed Muslim family laws is the only instance in which the local NGOs promote the rule of law in the Razian sense that I introduced in Chapter 2 as the uniform and systematic application of substantial state-backed laws, regardless of the particular context in which a specific conflict has emerged. Raz deliberately dissociated this consistent application of law from any normative considerations. In contrast, the activation of the state-backed Muslim family laws by the local NGOs is explicitly motivated by strong normative aspirations: the fieldworkers and court assistants that I met in rural Bangladesh defended Islamic law precisely *because* of the enhanced participatory spaces for women that it prescribes. Thus, the local NGO's promotion of the Razian rule of law is not that far removed from the normative aspirations that the EU attaches to the rule of law by combining it with notions of democracy and human rights (see Chapter 5). Ironically, it is precisely this clearest instance of rule of law promotion by the four local NGOs that is systematically ignored and written out of the official project and monitoring apparatus. Chapter 8 will turn to this irony—and discuss what is lost in the retranslation of the NGO's field activities to the headquarters of the UN and the EU in Dhaka, Brussels, and New York.

8

Conclusion

All That's Lost in Retranslation

This book has brought to light two interrelated changes. On the one hand, the promotion of 'the rule of law' through the introduction of village courts changes the ways in which conflicts are resolved in rural Bangladesh. More precisely, it changes these ways to the advantage of poor and marginalized people whose access to non-state justice institutions has been previously impeded by gross inequalities of power. On the other hand, this happens only if the village courts are 'activated' by the fieldworkers and court assistants of local NGOs who translate—and thereby transform—transnational ideas about 'the rule of law' at the grassroots level in rural Bangladesh. As a consequence, both the ways in which conflicts are resolved in rural Bangladesh and the meaning of 'the rule of law' are altered considerably in processes of translation.

These translations do not follow unilinear trajectories from the global to the local. Instead, they occur in recursive interactions between various actors who are all located in different contexts. They unfold in long historical trajectories in which colonial officers have modified nineteenth-century understandings of the rule of law in light of the perceived empirical realties in the Province of Bengal. One century later, it was in the interactions between Bangladeshi activists and international legal experts that similar processes of translation started to emerge. Again, transnational notions of 'the rule of law' were modified in light of the seeming socio-legal realities in rural Bangladesh. In rural Bangladesh, as this book has shown, the rule of law is further translated. Yet what is still missing from the preceding analysis is an account of how the effects of the introduction of village courts in rural Bangladesh are retranslated into the world of transnational policy planners and development experts. How do translations of 'the rule of law' travel back from rural Bangladesh to the desks of international bureaucrats (and their consultants) in Dhaka, Brussels, and New York? And how do these international bureaucrats and their consultants make sense of the translations of 'the rule of law' in rural Bangladesh?

In the conclusion of this book, I address these questions through an analysis of the project's monitoring and evaluation apparatus. Following established global templates, this apparatus operates through a 'logical framework matrix' that measures project outcomes almost exclusively through pre-articulated targets that have to be matched. These targets include the total number of village court cases facilitated as well as the number of women involved in the cases. They also include the dispatch of so-called 'deliverables', i.e. the number of village courtrooms, posters, training sessions, and boxes of official paperwork provided. The monitoring and evaluation apparatus thus relies first and foremost on numbers; and I trace the ways in which numbers are produced and subsequently travel from the fieldworkers at the grassroots level to the upazila and district offices of their respective local NGOs, and on to UNDP's headquarters in Dhaka as well as the delegation of the EU right next door. As they travel, these numbers not only convey information—they also transform it; and in the second part of this chapter, I show how the logic of logical frameworks systematically eradicates the translations of 'the rule of law' that the previous chapters have documented. The following section revisits these translations of the rule of law and thereby prepares the ground for the subsequent examination of what is—and is not—retranslated into transnational policy paradigms through project monitoring and evaluation.

8.1. TRANSLATING INSTITUTIONS, PRACTICES, AND NORMATIVE ORDERS

The activation of village courts in rural Bangladesh is designed as a large-scale experiment—and it bears quite clear results. As I have shown in Chapter 6, the ways in which conflicts are resolved in rural Bangladesh change as the village courts are introduced. Through the village courts, poor and marginalized people can access local elites they could not have otherwise accessed. This access, in turn, enhances their possibility of participating in processes of conflict resolution. Yet the opening up of participatory spaces decisively depends on the ardent work of the fieldworkers and court assistants that are on the payrolls of local NGOs. These grassroots-level staff have taken part in a series of workshops and refresher training on different aspects of village court justice; they are usually hired from the surrounding areas in which they are working and have generally completed rudimentary formal education, typically in the form of primary schooling. Yet much more important than the primary schooling is their background knowledge about the ways in which conflicts are handled within the social world they have inhabited all their lives. Central to these is what I have called the logic of non-enforcement (see also Chapter 4).

Following this logic of non-enforcement, people in rural Bangladesh frequently file cases with the state-backed courts; but they do so not in order to get binding and enforceable verdicts, but in order to change the outcomes of non-state justice institutions in their favour. Take the *shalish* analysed in Chapter 4 as an example. Being involved in a land dispute with his older brother, the younger one initiated a *shalish*. As this *shalish* decided against him, he also filed a case with the state-backed courts, but he never expected a verdict from these courts. Knowing that settling land disputes in the state-backed courts is a lengthy and burdensome undertaking, the younger brother only wanted to get a second *shalish* with a better outcome. Filing a case in the state's court allowed him to initiate such a *shalish*, which decided that he should receive some financial compensation from his brother. Although still not in accordance with the state-backed laws, filing a case with the state courts—and physically taking this file to the *shalish*—allowed the younger brother to alter the outcome of non-state justice procedures to his advantage.

In general, this logic of non-enforcement works for two reasons. On the one hand, being engaged in the state-backed courts can be a costly and burdensome process. It requires not only hiring lawyers and paying administrative court fees but also obtaining official documents and the overall ability of navigating intricately complex bureaucratic processes. On the other hand, the state and its institutions also do have an everyday presence in the lives of people in rural Bangladesh—and symbols of the state like police uniforms or official paperwork are habitually recognized. The insignia of the state, like official stamps, ministerial logos, and carefully crafted signatures, are recognized even by people who cannot decipher the actual letters written onto the very documents they treat with so much respect and reverence. As Akhil Gupta has argued in the case of the villagers in rural India, documents are often treated as if they were 'objects invested with magical powers' (Gupta 2012, 212). These powers also work in rural Bangladesh so producing a piece of bureaucratic paperwork—for example one obtained at a police station or at the nearest district court—allows people to alter the dynamics of non-state justice institutions in their favour.

Importantly, this 'irrational reverence for documents' (Gupta 2012, 208) exists not only in South Asia but also in Western Europe and North America—and, as Gupta has powerfully argued, any ethnography of bureaucratic practices in South Asia needs to guard itself against the temptation of exceptionalizing or exoticizing what are actually quite quotidian responses to official paperwork almost everywhere in the world (Gupta 2013, 437). Bureaucratic paperwork can rarely be reduced to the information it carries. Instead, this information is, at least in the vast majority of circumstances, discursively enacted in interactions between bureaucrats, petitioners, and government officials. More generally, this points to the intricate ways in which the written and the oral become imbricated within specific social encounters. To give just two brief examples: firstly, in academia, PhD degrees are generally only conferred after examination in viva voce. The knowledge acquired cannot exist only in writing, it needs to be verified in a verbal encounter. Secondly, also in most state-based judiciaries around the world, witness testimony has to be presented verbally in order to be authenticated. This testimony is then turned into a written record, yet it is the verbal enactment that validates the testimony (Gupta 2012, 198–208; Vismann 2008). The written and the oral are therefore intimately linked, albeit in different ways, everywhere in the world.

In rural Bangladesh, the verbalization of official documents turns them into a symbolic capital, which is habitually recognized. This recognition is interwoven into a broader understanding about the ways in which conflicts ought to be resolved within village communities. These understandings, in turn, consolidate in normative orders, i.e. complex structures of values and normative aspirations that legitimize the exercise of political authority as well as the distribution of basic goods. In rural Bangladesh, two normative orders are tightly intertwined. Firstly, there is the openly articulated desire to live in harmonious relationships within a village community. Yet this idea of harmony is a complicated one. It encompasses a restorative ideal that is double-edged in the sense that the recreation of harmony, on the one hand, presupposes participatory processes in which all injured parties can take part while, on the other hand, also remaining vulnerable to the possibility of reaffirming established power hierarchies. In other words, the recreation of social harmony might reaffirm established hierarchies as much as it can challenge them. Secondly, at least among the majority Muslim population of Bangladesh, there is the equally openly articulated wish to live in accordance with Islam and Islamic law.

Like the idea of harmony, this normative order that informs processes of conflict resolution in rural Bangladesh unfolds against the backdrop of unequal power relations within rural communities. Although there was a univocal aspiration to live in accordance with the divine precepts of Islam and Islamic law amongst the vast majority of Muslims I talked to through my field research in rural Bangladesh, the actual application of Islamic principles was highly selective. Take female shares of inheritance in land as an example. Although Islamic law unambiguously establishes female rights of inheritance in immovable property (i.e. land), many women in rural Bangladesh forgo their rightful inheritance. Instead of claiming their inheritance, they swap the shares they would have inherited for the possibility of returning to their brothers' homes in case of need. Similarly, many women do not claim the dower to which they would be entitled under both classical Islamic law and the contemporary state-backed Muslim family laws. The application of Islamic law, whether backed by the state or not, is thus profoundly mediated by historically grown power relations so that only those principles that leave the patriarchal order of things in rural Bangladesh intact are systematically enforced.

The fieldworkers and court assistants have a profound knowledge of all of the above. They grasp the institutional legal landscape and the ways in which state and non-state institutions are entangled in practice; they see documents as a symbolic capital that can change the ways in which conflicts are negotiated in non-state fora; and they both understand and speak the normative vocabularies of community harmony and Islamic law. In short, they have an intimate knowledge of the living law in rural Bangladesh—and that is why their work is vital. Throughout the project, the fieldworkers and court assistants succeed in enhancing participatory spaces for poor and marginalized people. Yet they do so only because they do not promote the rule of law—at least not in the ways in which it is understood by international donors and development experts alike.

Rather than promoting 'the rule of law', the fieldworkers and court assistants ingeniously translate it in three interrelated ways. Firstly, instead of activating the village courts as the lowest tier to the state-backed judiciary, they integrate them firmly into the universe of non-state justice institutions. They tweak the jurisdiction of the village courts to encompass cases above the pecuniary limits of the Village Court Act. They also tolerate the non-adherence to procedural obligations imposed by the state on the village courts. Thereby, they approximate the village courts to the *shalish* rather than the state-backed courts; sometimes quite visibly, for example when the fieldworkers and court assistants move the heavy wooden furniture provided by the project from the courtroom to the courtyard and thereby physically reproduce the set-up of a *shalish* (Chapter 6).

Secondly, in addition to these institutional translations, the fieldworkers and court assistants also translate the normative vocabularies as well as some of the key practices associated with the liberal rule of law. Instead of following liberal secular scripts, they emphasize the importance of community harmony as well as Islam and Islamic law as guiding principles for the resolution of conflicts within villages. They argue, for example, that the restoration of friendly and cordial relationships between disputing parties is an imperative of the village courts and a feature that clearly distinguishes them from the anonymous application of nationally binding laws that would be facilitated in the state's courts. They also highlight the prescripts for divorce and maintenance under the Muslim family laws and detest any kind of violence against women through ceaseless references to Islam and Islamic law. Thirdly, instead of using the official files and documents provided by the project as neutral means for recording village court sessions, they turn official paperwork into a symbolic capital that allows poor and marginalized people to access local elected politicians they could not otherwise access. Through these three translations of institutions, normative vocabularies, and key practices, fieldworkers and court assistants allow transnational liberal notions of the rule of law to resonate in rural Bangladesh (Chapter 7). More precisely, they translate 'the rule of law' in ways that resonate with the background knowledge that informs all processes of conflict resolution in Bangladesh's villages. This point is also of theoretical significance.

A Theoretical Account of Norm Translations

As I have argued in Chapter 2, processes of norm translation have so far received scant attention within IR analyses. Whereas top-down approaches to norm diffusion have developed fairly dynamic models of the ways in which transnational norms affect the socio-political dynamics within receiving contexts, they have, at the same time, relied on overtly static accounts of norm content (Keck and Sikkink 1998; Risse et al. 1999, 2013). In contrast, bottom-up localization approaches have highlighted the multifaceted transformations that transnational norms undergo once they arrive in specific contexts. Yet they have underplayed the ways in which transnational norms alter, at times quite substantially, the political realities in precisely those locations where they are 'localized' (Acharya 2004, 2009). In contrast, the preceding chapters have empirically documented how changing notions of 'the rule of law' and changing socio-political dynamics in rural Bangladesh are intricately intertwined in what I have conceptualized as a process of norm translation. Theoretically, this notion of translation captures the transformation in the content of norms that occurs as they travel back and forth between one context and another. These changes, in turn, are driven by deeply embodied forms of background knowledge that are habitually taken for granted and implicitly relied on to navigate the complex social and political world they inhabit (Taylor 1997).

It is the task of translators to make arriving norms resonate within these worlds, to embed them in pre-existing institutional arrangements, render them intelligible in light of familiar normative vocabularies, and make them fit long-established patterns of social and political practices. This task for the translators is a complex one. It requires the innovative recreation of meaning within the arriving context. The ceaseless recreation of meaning, however, undermines the plausibility of an 'original' norm of which all subsequent translations would be mere derivates. Instead, each translation becomes its own original, as Walter Benjamin (1977) has already argued in his essay on 'The Task of the Translator'. Yet if every translation creates a new original, this poses an evaluative problem. How are we to judge the quality of a translation, if not by its fidelity to an alleged original? In the case of literary translations, this is an aesthetic question. In the case of the translation of norms, it becomes a normative one. Here, the quality of a translation depends on the degree to which the recreation of its meaning is conducive to the realization of its normative core. In the case of transnational liberal notions of 'the rule of law', this core is elusive. Yet as it is embedded within the liberal triad of democracy, human rights, and the rule of law, this core entails at least some kind of access to a liberal justice system. In translation, the transnational rule of law that materializes in rural Bangladesh maintains this core as the meaning of the rule of law changes. Instead of facilitating access to a liberal, state-backed justice system, the fieldworkers and court assistants facilitate access to complex legal landscapes in rural Bangladesh. They allow marginalized people to participate in non-state justice processes to which they would have had no access otherwise; and they do so precisely because they abandon 'the rule of law' as it is imagined by international donor agencies.

8.2. ALL THAT'S LOST IN RETRANSLATION

What happens to these ingenious translations of the liberal rule of law as they are fed back from rural Bangladesh into transnational policy paradigms?

Let's start at the grassroots level. Remember Tapathi, the fieldworker who disseminated information about the village courts in the courtyard meeting described at the outset of this book. At the end of the meeting described in the first pages of Chapter 1, Tapathi takes down the flipchart from the blue plastic chair on which it has been standing, rolls it up, and carefully places it back in the container. She then takes out a piece of paper and respectfully places it on the sitting surface of the chair, which is thereby transformed into a desk. She herself takes a seat on the mat on the floor behind the desk. On the other side, a queue, or at least something close to a queue, has been forming. The participants of the workshop stand in a semi-circle around Tapathi. One by one, they proceed to the desk and give their names, which Tapathi cautiously registers on the sheet. The sheet has been provided by the project; it is part of a whole set of forms through which the EU, UNDP, and four local NGOs constantly monitor all activities that unfold within the context of the activation of village courts.

From the individual fieldworkers and court assistants, these forms then start travelling. They are sent to the nearest upazila and district levels, where specialized staff are already employed for the facilitation of monitoring and evaluation, which is one of the four key pillars of the entire project (see also Chapter 5). At the district level the data arriving from the individual UPs and upazilas are checked, aggregated, and complemented with further data on activities facilitated directly by the district offices. These activities include the facilitation of workshops and training for the fieldworkers and court assistants of the NGOs as well as different additional target audiences like UP chairmen, religious leaders, or local village police. Saturated with further information, the reports are then passed on to the divisional headquarters of the respective NGO where further staff are employed for monitoring and evaluation. Tying all NGO-related project activities together, the team working at the divisional headquarters prepare monthly, quarterly, annual reports as well as mid-term reviews; all of which are sent directly to UNDP's project office in Dhaka.

What arrive from the villages in Dhaka are files that account for NGO activities. They do so by enumerating how many so-called 'deliverables' have actually been delivered to people in rural Bangladesh. They count how many courtyard meetings have been held, how many training and capacity-building workshops with different target audiences have been facilitated, and the respective number of participants that have attended each of these events. They also count the delivery of key artefacts, i.e. the number of billboards, posters, stickers, and courtrooms delivered to individual UPs as well as the amount of paperwork that has been dispensed in the course of project implementation. These reports therefore follow a general pattern in which the promotion of 'the rule of law' is quantified in the distribution of easily detectable deliverables. These deliverables, as Deval Desai and Michael Woolcock from the World Bank's 'Justice for the Poor' project have critically argued 'can be readily photographed, counted, tracked, aggregated, and compared. [They] raise few red flags and, after a time, enable senior managers to present a coherent (even compelling) narrative to sceptical politicians and voters of how public resources were spent in sensible ways in response to a clear and present development challenge' (Desai and Woolcock 2015, 163). What these deliverables do not detect is any qualitative change in specific dynamics of conflict resolution within a given context.

Within the AVCB project, the qualitative change ought to be measured through the enumeration of village court sessions. Besides accounting for the distribution of deliverables, the monthly, quarterly, and annual reports prepared by the local NGOs for the project administration in Dhaka also list village court case-related data. Case-related data are also numerical. Again, they distinguish between male and female inhabitants of rural Bangladesh. Besides the simple breakdown according to sex, the reports also distinguish between civil and criminal cases. For each category, they enumerate:

- number of total reported cases;
- total number of cases resolved;
- total number of cases implemented (i.e. of village court decisions that have been enforced);
- number of cases pending in the village courts;
- number of cases received from the higher courts;
- number of cases sent to the higher courts;
- total number of pending cases;

- number of representatives present on a village court panel;
- number of petitions to the village courts that have been dismissed for default.

It is through these numbers that the ceaseless work of the fieldworkers and court assistants at the grassroots level in rural Bangladesh becomes known to the monitoring and evaluation experts of UNDP in Dhaka and to the EU delegation next door.

In Dhaka, these numbers are matched against pre-defined targets. The EU and UNDP's project teams have developed a logical framework—or logframe—that is designed to measure the progress of the project through 'objectively verifiable indicators' (OVI). As an internal EU guideline on the design of logframes and OVI states, '[t]he meaning of an Objectively Verifiable Indicator is that the information collected should be the same if collected by different people. This is more easily done for quantitative measures than for those that aim at measuring qualitative change'. Quantification thus looms large in the logic of logical frameworks, which have increasingly infiltrated development discourses through the proliferation of new public management technologies and the move towards performance indicators, rankings, and efficiency assessment tools of various kinds that these have initiated (Desrosières 2015). In the case of the activation of the village courts in Bangladesh, quantification applies primarily to village court cases. As shown above, monthly, quarterly, and annual reports travelling from villages to upazila, district, and divisional offices contain data that are added up to the total numbers of village court cases filed, resolved, and enforced. Over time, changes can be detected; and the changed percentages of village court cases filed as well as the changes in the numbers of women participating in village court cases are taken as basic OVIs of the success (or failure) of the project. A further OVI is the reduction of the backlog of cases pending in the state courts. If this number decreases, so the argument of the logframe goes, the village courts will have been activated. This again highlights the intimate connection that the EU and UNDP forge between the village courts and the state-backed rule of law. If the village courts are successfully activated, they become a functional equivalent of the state courts.

Success or failure of the project thus seems very easily—and, more importantly, objectively—detectable. Yet, what is—and is not—measured in an objectively verifiable way has been constantly debated and revised within the project. Many of these revisions were instigated in response to external criticism. Every year, the project is evaluated through a results-oriented monitoring mission, which draws not only on numeric project data but also on information gathered through consultative meetings and field research. The annual results-oriented monitoring, as well as the mid-term reviews and the final evaluation are undertaken by external experts who operate in small teams. In the case of AVCB, both Bangladeshi scholars and foreign experts have been asked to produce these reports—and they have constantly disagreed about what should be measured, and how. Whereas the first results-oriented monitoring reports criticized the OVI for the simplicity and inability to capture the complex local dynamics that unfold around the village courts, the latter reports subsequently criticized the redefined, and more complex, OVI as 'overlong'. Thus, the mid-term review found in March 2013 that: '[t]he revised project logframe was described as "complex" in the last [results-oriented monitoring]. The [mid-term review] found it to be overlong and repetitive and quite unfit either as a planning or monitoring tool' (Jahan and Stapleton 2013, 13). In sum, then, the aspiration to assess the progress of the project through clear and objectively identifiable indicators is not immune to the influences of social processes and interactions. As different people tried to assess the project, they lay different emphases, and conceptualized different indicators in accordance with these emphases. Throughout the project, it was never entirely clear how the comprehensive monitoring and evaluation apparatus of the project was actually supposed to measure project outcomes. Thus, after more than three years of project activity, the mid-term review laconically states that '[t]he project has yet to define criteria for determining when a Village Court has been "activated"' (Jahan and Stapleton 2013, 44).

This is surprising. On the surface, the entire purpose of monitoring and evaluation is to (a) ensure that scarce resources are effectively deployed within project interventions, and (b) collect information on possible problems to initiate suitable corrective measures. Yet the numbers that are collected hardly ever seem to add up to a coherent picture of project success or failure—and the bureaucrats employed by the EU and the UN in Dhaka are painfully aware of this. As they have repeatedly told me, very different numbers on seemingly identical phenomena are constantly circulating on the floors of international bureaucracies in Dhaka, Brussels, and New York. For example the numbers of the actual backlogs of cases in both state and the village courts vary greatly, making it virtually impossible to say with any kind of certainty whether these backlogs have been reduced, and if so, by how much. Yet although people know that they cannot trust the numbers, they nonetheless highly depend on them. Numbers are therefore much more important than the information they superficially seem to convey. Instead of simply conveying information, numbers constitute a mathematical *lingua franca* through which very different actors in very different contexts can be connected. What is special about this lingua franca is, as Theordore Porter has argued, that 'quantification is a technology of distance. The language of mathematics is highly structured and rule-bound; [and] since the rules for collecting and manipulating numbers are widely shared, they can easily be transported across oceans and continents' (Porter 1995, ix).

This is the strength of numbers. They travel lightly because they seem independent of the people and circumstances that have produced them; and they thus do not carry the baggage of the contextual complexities of the places from which they emerge (Porter 1995; Hansen and Porter 2012). Yet this seeming neutrality of numbers is illusive. Just as paperwork needs to be enacted within specific social situations, numbers do not speak for themselves, not even within the world of transnational development experts. Instead, statistical data always need to be embedded in narratives (Espeland 2015); and the project has started to publish so-called 'Case Story Books'. The 2013 edition—titled 'Village Courts: Reflections on Stories from Real Life'—is a good example of the ways in which statistics and stories become intertwined as international organizations seek to communicate the outcomes of their activities to the wider world. It starts with hard data. Since 2010, a cumulative total of 43,593 cases have been reported to the village courts. Of these, 33,971 have been resolved within an average of twenty-eight days per case. A total of 27,406 village court decisions have already been implemented and the equivalent of US$1,163,214 has been recovered in compensation payments. 2,677 cases have been transferred from the district courts to the village courts and thereby reduced the backlog of cases in the state-backed judiciary. And 'in total 4,515 (32%) women obtained remedies through Village Courts [while the] representation of women in the [village court] decision making process has increased from 8% in 2012 to 11% in 2013' (Asaduzzaman 2013b, 6).

These hard data are then contextualized with twelve short case studies like the one of Pabrita Bala who is a poor widow living with her two disabled sons in Sreepur Upazila in Magura District. One day, her neighbour Subatra Kumar Mondol steals her bicycle, rickshaw-van, and fishing net. Although Pabrita was not at home at the time of the incident her son Nikhil witnessed it. After hearing his report, Pabrita tried to recover her belongings from the neighbour, unsuccessfully. She did not dare to approach the local police station or call for a *shalish* as her neighbour is an influential person within the village community. Yet, when she learned about the village courts from a local member of the UP council, she

> submitted a written complaint against Subarta Kumar Mondol in Nakole union parishad with BDT 2 court fee on 17th August 2012 claiming BDT 19,000 (USD 245.95) as compensation. Following the due procedure, the Village Courts session took the hearing on 29th August 2012 and openly declared its decision instructing Subrata Mondol to pay BDT 16,000 (USD 207.11) to the petitioner Pabitra Bala within 30 days. The respondent deposited BDT 16,000 (USD 207.11) within 04 days to Village Court for handing over to the applicant Pabitra Bala.
>
> (Asaduzzaman 2013b, 11)

The 'following [of] due procedure' is emphasized in most of the twelve case studies presented in the publication of the project. Here, the narrative of international donors about official paperwork as neutral carriers of information that allow for fair village court proceedings supersedes the narratives of the fieldworkers and court assistants. Seemingly objectively verifiable numbers therefore get embedded in the narratives of the international donors. In this case, numbers and donor narratives simply confirm ideas about the village courts as local and efficient extensions of the state-backed rule of law.

What gets lost in the retranslations of project outcomes into this narrative is the work of the translators—and the ways in which they transform transnational ideas about 'the rule of law' in ways that resonate with the background knowledge of people in rural Bangladesh. The integration of the village courts into the complex landscape of non-state justice intuitions is obscured. So are the ways in which participatory spaces for poor and marginalized people are enhanced in the names of community harmony or Islam and Islamic law. Instead of recording these normative vocabularies, the monitoring and evaluation apparatus transforms them into the familiar narratives of transnational liberalism that is woven around secular notions of democracy, the rule of law, and human rights. Finally, as I have shown above the monitoring and evaluation apparatus relies on a seemingly endless trail of paperwork that is produced in rural Bangladesh and then sent to Dhaka, Brussels, and New York. It is this trail of paperwork that allows international donor agencies to make authoritative claims to knowledge and expertise about processes of conflict resolution in rural Bangladesh (Berger 2017). These claims rely implicitly on the production of verifiable data about village court outcomes; and these data are unavoidably mediated by the written village court records. Yet, by only looking at the records, international donors miss the translation of official paperwork from seemingly neutral carriers of information to symbolic capital that enhances access to local elites for poor and marginalized people for whom this access has been previously blocked. Ironically, therefore, the monitoring and evaluation apparatus eradicates all those aspects that render the project successful in the first place.

8.3. TRANSLATIONS BEYOND 'THE RULE OF LAW' AND BANGLADESH

Instead of neutrally recording what happens 'on the ground', the monitoring and evaluation apparatus therefore fulfils a rather different purpose. It sanitizes project outcomes by eradicating all those translations that do not conform to the established parameters of transnational policy paradigms. The boundaries of these paradigms are therefore carefully policed; and the integrity of 'the international' as a space of technical expertise and moral superiority is meticulously guarded. Once they have been sanitized and cleansed of the translations that unfold in rural Bangladesh, the village courts start circulating within the world of international development experts, diplomats, and aid workers.

They already assume a privileged position within this world. A recent report by three UN agencies on 'Informal Justice Systems: Charting a Course for Human Rights-Based Engagement' cites them as the most comprehensive intervention of international donor agencies in non-state justice systems anywhere in the world today (UNDP et al. 2013, 220). This large-scale experiment in non-state justice is currently going into its second phase. As I am writing this conclusion, the EU has pledged another 25 million euro for the activation of 1,000 further village courts over the next five years (cf. Asaduzzaman 2015, 6). If anything, this is likely to further enhance the AVCB project as a reference point for future donor interventions in non-state justice systems. The village courts thereby become part of a much more global shift of international donor agencies towards increasing intervention in non-state courts, predominantly, though not exclusively, in the Global South. Highlighting persistent legal pluralism as an empirical reality in most of the world, the Word Bank, the UN, scholars, and practitioners therefore currently focus on non-state courts as possible sites for the promotion of transnational liberal scripts, broadly conceived (UNDP et al. 2013; Tamanaha et al. 2012; Desai and Woolcock 2015).

What I have shown in this book is that the global cannot simply overcome the local. Even if transnational scripts are adopted in light of the perceived empirical realities within a specific context, these realities only change if transnational norms are further translated, often in unexpected ways. These unexpected ways require further research, along at least two lines. The first line encompasses the more general investigation of which kinds of translation do occur under which conditions. This book has shown how—given the persistent work of translators who reinvent the meaning of norms in ways that resonate with people's tacitly held background knowledge—the emancipatory potentials of 'the rule of law' is translated into alternative normative languages and novel practices. Yet different translations are imaginable, for example when the same normative vocabulary is translated into a novel set of practices. One example of such translation is the increasing marginalization of Rohingya that live on Myanmar's western border with Bangladesh. As Elizabeth Shakman Hurd has shown, the increasingly assertive promotion of religious freedom by international donors has led to an international identification of the Rohingya as 'persecuted Muslims'; this identification has, in turn, further marginalized them from currently dominant imaginations of the Burmese nation as a multi-ethnic but overwhelmingly Buddhist community (Hurd 2015, 37–65). In this case, transnational human rights norms aimed at the protection of individual autonomy have been translated into exclusionary practices that actually have detrimental effects on the very autonomy they intended to enhance. In many ways, this is a mirror image of the kind of translation documented in this book; i.e. of the translation of similar normative aspirations into different normative vocabularies. Which kind of translation occurs under which conditions remains therefore an important line of further research.

The second line of research pertains to the provincialization of the international. As I have argued throughout this book, the international as the world of policy experts and diplomats is only a particular context with its own particularities. Yet the boundaries of this context are carefully policed; and any translation that challenges claims to either the technical expertise or the moral superiority of the international are systematically eradicated. Alternative normative vocabularies in which people try to imagine better worlds, unfamiliar practices, and institutional metamorphoses are all deleted in the monitoring and evaluation apparatuses of international donor interventions, also beyond the project that has been at the centre of this book, as David Mosse has shown. Mosse therefore concluded that development projects cannot fail in themselves; they can only be failed by wider networks and support and validation (Mosse 2005, 159; see also Mosse 2011). These networks also include scholars, for example in the case of a published dialogue between scholars and on non-state justice and development (Tamanaha et al. 2012). Provincializing the international as one among many different contexts therefore not only requires the anthropology of global institutions, diplomacy, and aid (Niezen and Sapignoli 2017; Neumann 2012; Mosse 2013). It also necessitates analytical vocabularies that decentre the Eurocentric underpinnings of much social science scholarship (Nicolaidis et al. 2014; Onar and Nicolaidis 2013).

This decentring agenda is important, especially for the defenders of contemporary global norms. If the argument of this book holds and the social and political dynamics of receiving contexts change only if transnationally diffused norms and ideas are translated in unexpected ways, then we need to familiarize ourselves more with the ways in which people in different contexts make sense of these arriving norms and ideas. This, in turn, highlights the need for a deeper genuflection towards the plurality of epistemologies that inform the ways in which people navigate the different social and political worlds they inhabit across the globe. It requires a greater appreciation for the multiplicity of normative orders, the array of practices that underpin them, and the myriad ways in which both might consolidate institutionally. This genuflection, therefore, requires two moves on behalf of the advocates of global norms: firstly, the recognition that they are situated within a particular context and, secondly, that therefore the ways in which they articulate universal norms is only one of many possible translations. This book has tried to support these moves by arguing that a bureaucrat in Brussels and a villager in Jolidpur are not that different, after all: they both translate the rule of law against their tacitly held background knowledges—and they both need translators that allow them to do so.

List of Interviews

No.	Position	Place	Date
001	Senior programme advisor, Asia Foundation	Dhaka	05.12.11
002	Senior programme officer, Danish Embassy	Dhaka	06.12.11
003	Senior legal advisor, AVCB/UNDP	Dhaka	07.12.11
004	Training and programme officer, GIZ	Dhaka	11.12.11
005	AL politician	Madaripur	12.12.11
006	Ward member	Madaripur	15.12.11
007	Upazila supervisor, AVCB/MLAA	Madaripur	16.12.11
008	Village member	Madaripur	16.12.11
009	Upazila supervisor, AVCB/MLAA	Madaripur	16.12.11
010	Dean, Faculty of Law, Dhaka University	Dhaka	20.12.11
011	Lecturer, Faculty of Law, Dhaka University	Dhaka	22.12.11
012	Senior legal advisor, AVCB/UNDP	Dhaka	28.12.11
013	Project coordinator AVCB/BLAST	Chittagong	05.01.12
014	Law lecturer, Boro Madrasa Hathazari	Hathazari	07.01.12
015	UP chairman	Hathazari	07.01.12
016	Ward member	Hathazari	07.01.12
017	UP secretary	Hathazari	07.01.12
018	Ward member	Hathazari	07.01.12
019	Imam	Hathazari	07.01.12
020	Local government official	Hathazari	08.01.12
021	ward member	Hathazari	09.01.12
022	Religious leaders, Hindu community	Chittagong	10.01.12
023	Ward member	Hathazari	11.01.12
024	Union chairman	Hathazari	11.01.12
025	Public prosecutor	Chittagong	12.01.12
026	Village member	Hathazari	14.01.12
027	Village member	Hathazari	14.01.12
028	Village member	Hathazari	14.01.12
029	Village member	Hathazari	14.01.12
030	Students	Hathazari	16.01.12
031	Upazila supervisor, AVCB/BLAST	Hathazari	16.01.12
032	Student	Hathazari	17.01.12
033	Student	Hathazari	17.01.12
034	Madrasa student	Hathazari	17.01.12
035	Barrister Supreme Court	Dhaka	23.01.12
036	Village member	Sylhet	27.01.12
037	Village member	Sylhet	27.01.12
038	Village member	Sylhet	28.01.12
039	Village member	Sylhet	28.01.12
040	Village member	Sylhet	28.01.12
041	Imam	Sylhet	28.01.12
042	Principle of Alia Madrasa	Sylhet	28.01.12
043	Deputy director local government	Sylhet	29.01.12

(continued)

No.	Position	Place	Date
044	UP secretary	Sylhet	29.01.12
045	*Shalish* facilitator	Sylhet	29.01.12
046	UP chairman	Sylhet	31.01.12
047	UP chairman	Sylhet	31.01.12
048	Village member	Hathazari	01.02.12
049	Student	Hathazari	01.02.12
050	Trainer, AVCB/BLAST	Hathazari	01.02.12
051	Professor, Political Science, Chittagong University	Chittagong	02.02.12
052	Imam	Hathazari	02.02.12
053	Member of AVCB-CBO committee	Hathazari	02.02.12
054	Village member	Hathazari	02.02.12
055	Professor Emeritus, University of Chittagong	Chittagong	03.02.12
056	Former MLAA staff and gender specialist, consultant for MLAA	Dhaka	05.02.12
057	Head of training, AVCB/UNDP	Dhaka	06.02.12
058	Head of legal aid and human rights, BRAC	Dhaka	07.02.12
059	Head of communications, AVCB/UNDP	Dhaka	08.02.12
060	Coordinator, AVCB/MLAA	Madaripur	13.02.12
061	District coordinator, AVCB/MLAA	Madaripur	16.02.12
062	District supervisor, AVCB/MLAA	Madaripur	16.02.12
063	Trainer, AVCB/MLAA	Madaripur	16.02.12
064	Fieldworker, AVCB/MLAA	Madaripur	16.02.12
065	UP chairman	Madaripur	17.02.12
066	Professor of Law, Law Faculty, Dhaka University	Dhaka	22.02.12
067	Barrister supreme court	Dhaka	22.02.12
068	Lawyer	Dhaka	22.02.12
069	Representative of EU delegation, Bangladesh	Dhaka	27.02.12
070	UP Chairman	Hathazari	01.11.12
071	Ward member	Hathazari	01.11.12
072	Member of AVCB-CBO committee	Hathazari	02.11.12
073	CBO member	Hathazari	02.11.12
074	VC claimant	Hathazari	02.11.12
075	VC claimant	Hathazari	02.11.12
076	Student	Hathazari	03.11.12
077	AVCB court assistant	Hathazari	03.11.12
078	AVCB court assistant	Hathazari	03.11.12
079	Participant in *shalish*	Hathazari	04.11.12
080	AVCB court assistant and AVCB fieldworker	Hathazari	04.11.12
081	AVCB court assistant	Hathazari	04.11.12
082	AVCB CBO and VC claimant	Hathazari	05.11.12
083	Former vice chancellor, Chittagong University	Chittagong	06.11.12
084	Professor of Law, Dhaka University	Dhaka	11.11.12
085	Project coordinator and monitoring officer, AVCB/ESDO	Rangpur	15.11.12
086	Project staff of citizens' initiative Bangladesh	Rangpur	15.11.12
087	District trainer, AVCB/ESDO	Rangpur	16.11.12
088	Upazila supervisor, AVCB/ESDO	Rangpur	18.11.12
089	Monitoring and evaluation officer, AVCB/ESDO	Rangpur	18.11.12
090	Imam and stakeholder in AVCB	Rangpur	18.11.12
091	Claimant and VC defendant	Rangpur	19.11.12
092	Representative of EU delegation, Bangladesh	Dhaka	28.11.12

093	External evaluator, AVCB	Dhaka	30.11.12
094	Advocate and assistant session judge	Khulna	03.12.12
095	District coordinator, AVCB/Wave Foundation and UNDP	Khulna	03.12.12
096	Ward member and three other community members	Khulna	05.12.12
097	VC claimant	Khulna	05.12.12
098	UP staff	Khulna	05.12.12
099	Secretary of UP chairman	Khulna	05.12.12
100	VC claimant	Khulna	05.12.12
101	High-ranking police officer	Khulna	05.12.12
102	VC defendant	Khulna	06.12.12
103	VC claimant	Khulna	06.12.12
104	UP chairman and AVCB court assistant	Khulna	06.12.12
105	Barrister of law, legal anthropologist, and consultant for BLAST	Dhaka	17.12.12
106	Head of National Human Rights Commission, Bangladesh	Dhaka	19.12.12
107	Rule of law expert	Berlin	09.01.14
108	Representative of EU delegation, Bangladesh	Dhaka	02.03.14
109	Senior legal expert, UNDP	Dhaka	28.02.16
110	Professor of Law, Dhaka University	Dhaka	06.03.16
111	Representative of EU delegation, Bangladesh	Dhaka	11.03.16

List of Group Discussions

No.	Participants	Place	Date
112	Women's group	Madaripur	17.12.11
113	Religious leaders	Hathazari	10.01.12
114	CBO	Hathazari	11.01.12
115	Students	Hathazari	16.01.12
116	AVCB fieldworkers and court assistants	Hathazari	17.01.12
117	Governing Board of MLAA	Madaripur	11.02.12
118	AVCB group of trainer of trainers	Madaripur	11.02.12
119	Union Council members during AVCB workshop	Madaripur	14.02.12
120	Group of students	Hathazari	03.11.12
121	Fieldworkers at mediation technique workshop	Rangpur	18.11.12
122	'Beneficiaries' of the project	Rangpur	19.11.12
123	EU delegation and UNDP, responsible for AVCB	Dhaka	02.03.16

References

Acharya, Amitav. 2004. 'How Ideas Spread: Whose Norms Matter? Norm Localization and Institutional Change in Asian Regionalism'. *International Organization*, 58 2: 239–75.

Acharya, Amitav. 2009. *Whose Ideas Matter? Agency and Power in Asian Regionalism*. Ithaca, NY: Cornell University Press.

Ahasan, Abu, and Katy Gardner. 2016. 'Dispossession by "Development": Corporations, Elites and NGOs in Bangladesh'. *SAMAJ: South Asia Multidisciplinary Academic Journal*, 13.

Ahmad, Khurshid. 2000. 'Islam and Democracy: Some Conceptual and Contemporary Dimensions'. *Muslim World*, 90 1–2: 1–21.

Ahmad, Mumtaz. 1993. 'The Muslim Family Law Ordinance of Pakistan'. *International Journal on World Peace*, 10 3: 37–46.

Ahmad, Mumtaz, and Matthew J. Nelson. 2009. 'Islamic Education in Bangladesh and Pakistan'. National Bureau of Asian Research, April.

Akmeemana, Saku, Naomi Hossain, Ferdous Jahan, and Erik Jensen. 2008. Survey: Citizens' Experiences of the Legal System in Bangladesh. Accessed 3 February 2017. http://microdata.worldbank.org/index.php/catalog/616/download/15824.

Alim, Abdul, and Tariq O. Ali. 2007. NGO-Shalish and Justice-Seeking Behaviour in Rural Bangladesh: BRAC Research Report. Dhaka: BRAC Research and Evaluation Division.

Allchin, Joseph. 2013. 'Germany Concerned by BNP's Support of Hefazat'. Accessed 9 June 2016. http://www.dhakatribune.com/politics/2013/may/09/germany-concerned-bnp%E2%80%99s-support-hefazat.

Amnesty International. 2001. 'Bangladesh: Landmark High Court Ruling against Fatwas'. Accessed 18 March 2016. https://www.amnesty.org/download/Documents/124000/asa130012001en.pdf.

Anderson, Michael R. 1993. 'Islamic Law and the Colonial Encounter in British India'. In *Institutions and Ideologies: A SOAS South Asia Reader*, edited by David Arnold and Peter Robb, 165–85. Richmond: Curzon Press.

An-Na'im, Abdullahi A. 2002. *Islamic Family Law in a Changing World: A Global Resource Book*. London: Zed Books.

Arendt, Hannah. 1973. *The Origins of Totalitarianism*. New York: Harcourt Brace Jovanovich.

Asaduzzaman, Sadar M. 2012. *Annual Report 2011: Activating the Village Courts in Bangladesh Project*. Dhaka: UNDP.

Asaduzzaman, Sadar M. 2013a. *Annual Report 2012. Activating the Village Courts in Bangladesh Project*. Dhaka: UNDP.

Asaduzzaman, Sadar M. 2013b. *Case Story Book: Reflections of Real Life Stories*. Dhaka: UNDP.

Asaduzzaman, Sadar M. 2015. *Annual Report 2014: Activating the Village Courts in Bangladesh Project*. Dhaka: UNDP.

Baderin, Mashood A. 2005. *International Human Rights and Islamic Law*. Oxford: Oxford University Press.

Bajpai, Rochana. 2011. *Debating Difference: Group Rights and Liberal Democracy in India*. New Delhi: Oxford University Press.

Banerjee, Sarmila. 1978. *Studies in Administrative History of Bengal, 1880–1898*. New Delhi: Rajesh Publications.

Barkat, Abul. 2012. *Review of Social Barriers and Limitations to Village Courts. Dhaka: Activating the Village Courts in Bangladesh Project*. Dhaka: UNDP.

Barry, Andrew 2013. 'The Translation Zone: Between Actor-Network Theory and International Relations'. *Millennium: Journal of International Studies*, 41 3: 413–29.

Bass, Gary J. 2013. *The Blood Telegram: Nixon, Kissinger, and a Forgotten Genocide*. New York: Knopf Publishing Group.

Benda-Beckmann, Franz von. 2002. 'Who's Afraid of Legal Pluralism?' *Journal of Legal Pluralism and Unofficial Law*, 47: 37–82.

Benda-Beckmann, Franz von, and Keebet von Benda-Beckmann. 1994. 'Texts in Contexts: Historical Documents as Political Commodity on Islamic Ambon'. *Ethnologica Bernesia*, 4: 223–43.

Benda-Beckmann, Franz von, and Keebet von Benda-Beckmann. 2007. *Gesellschaftliche Wirkung von Recht: Rechtsethnologische Perspektiven*. Berlin: Reimer.

Benhabib, Seyla. 2002. *The Claims of Culture: Equality and Diversity in the Global Era*. Princeton, NJ: Princeton University Press.

Benjamin, Walter. 1977. 'Die Aufgabe des Übersetzers'. In Illuminationen, edited by Siegfried Unseld, 56–70. Frankfurt am Main: Suhrkamp.

Bentham, Jeremy. 1843. Essay on the Influence of Time and Place in Matters of Legislation. Edinburgh: Stevenson and Co. http://www.laits.utexas.edu/poltheory/bentham/timeplace/timeplace.c01.html.

Benton, Lauren. 2002. *Law and Colonial Cultures: Legal Regiments in World History, 1400–1900*. Cambridge: Cambridge University Press.

Berger, Tobias. 2012. 'Mind the Gap! Political Ethnography and the Translation of Western Concepts in Non-Western Contexts'. In *Nichtwestliches Politisches Denken: Zwischen kultureller Differenz und Hybridisierung*, edited by Holger Zapf. Wiesbaden: Springer.

Berger, Tobias. 2016. 'Säkularismus, Islam, und die Grenzen der Toleranz in Bangladesch'. *Transit*, 49: 72–89.

Berger, Tobias. 2017. 'Global Village Courts: The United Nations and the Bureaucratization of Non-State Justice in the Global South'. In *Palaces of Hope: The Anthropology of International Organizations*, edited by Ronald Niezen and Maria Sapignoli. Cambridge: Cambridge University Press.

Best, Jacqueline, and William Walters. 2013. 'Translating the Sociology of Translation'. *International Political Sociology*, 7 3: 345–9.

Bliss, Frank, and Stefan Neumann. 2008. 'Participation in International Development Discourse and Practice: "State of the Art" and Challenges'. INEF-Report, 94/2008.

Boli, John. 1987. 'World Polity Sources of Expanding State Authority and Organization, 1870–1970'. In *Institutional Structure: Constituting State, Society, and the Individual*, edited by George M. Thomas, John W. Meyer, Francisco O. Ramirez, and John Boli, 71–91. Newbury Park: SAGE Publications.

Bonneuil, Christophe. 2000. 'Development as Experiment: Science and State Building in Late Colonial and Postcolonial Africa, 1930–1970'. *Osiris*, 15: 258–81.

Börzel, Tanja. 2010. 'European Governance: Negotiation and Competition in the Shadow of Hierarchy'. Journal of Common Market Studies, 48 2: 191–219.

Bose, Sarmila. 2010. *Dead Reckoning: Memories of the 1971 Bangladesh War*. London: C. Hurst.

Bose, Sugata, and Ayesha Jalal. 2004. *Modern South Asia: History, Culture, Political Economy*, 2nd ed. New York: Routledge.

Bourdieu, Pierre. 1984. *Distinction: A Social Critique of the Judgement of Taste*. Cambridge, MA: Harvard University Press.

Bourdieu, Pierre. 1990. *The Logic of Practice*. Cambridge: Polity.

Bourdieu, Pierre. 1991. *Language and Symbolic Power*. Cambridge: Polity.

Boyle, Elizabeth H., and John W. Meyer. 2002. 'Modern Law as a Secularized and Global Model: Implications for the Sociology of Law'. In *Global Prescriptions: The Production, Exportation, and Importation of a New Legal Orthodoxy*, edited by Yves Dezalay and Bryant G. Garth. Ann Arbor: University of Michigan Press.

Buhari-Gulmez, Didem. 2010. 'Stanford School on Sociological Institutionalism: A Global Cultural Approach'. *International Political Sociology*, 4 3: 253–70.

Callon, Michel. 1986. 'Some Elements of a Sociology of Translation: Domestication of the Scallops and the Fishermen of St Brieuc Bay'. In *Power, Action, and Belief: A New Sociology of Knowledge?* edited by John Law. London: Routledge and Kegan Paul.

Carothers, Thomas. 1998. 'The Rule of Law Revival'. *Foreign Affairs*, March/April: 95–106.

Carothers, Thomas. 2009. 'Rule of Law Temptations'. *Fletcher Forum of World Affairs*, 33 1: 49–61.

Chakrabarty, Dipesh. 2008. *Provincializing Europe: Postcolonial Thought and Historical Difference*. Princeton, NJ: Princeton University Press.

Chan, Stephen. 1997. 'Too Neat and Under-Thought A World Order: Huntington and Civilisations'. *Millennium: Journal of International Studies*, 26 1: 137–40.

Chan, Stephen. 2010. *The End of Certainty: Towards a New Internationalism*. London: Zed.

Chatterjee, Partha. 2011. *Lineages of Political Society*. New Delhi: Orient Blackswan.

Cody, Francis. 2009. 'Inscribing Subjects to Citizenship: Petitions, Literacy Activism, and the Performativity of Signature in Rural Tamil India'. *Cultural Anthropology*, 24 3: 347–80.

Cohen, Gerald A. 1990. 'Equality of What? On Welfare, Goods and Capabilities'. *Recherches Économiques de Louvain/Louvain Economic Review*, 56 3/4: 357–82.

Cohn, Bernard S. 1996. *Colonialism and Its Forms of Knowledge: The British in India*. Princeton, NJ: Princeton University Press.

Cook, Ian. 2004. 'Follow the Thing: Papaya'. *Antipode*, 36 4: 642–64.

CORI. 2012. 'Country of Origin Research and Information (CORI) Country Report Bangladesh March 2012'. Accessed 27 March 2017. http://www.refworld.org/pdfid/50618c6f2.pdf.

Cover, Robert. 1983. 'Foreword: Nomos and Narrative'. *Harvard Law Review*, 97.

Crozier, Michel. 1964. *The Bureaucratic Phenomenon*. Chicago: University of Chicago Press.

D'Costa, Bina. 2011. *Nationbuilding, Gender, and War Crimes in South Asia*. London: Routledge.

Daily Star. 2001. 'Fatwa Illegal, Declares HC'. 2 January.

Daily Star. 2004. 'Chittagong Court Building: A Landmark in Despair'. Daily Star, 18 October.

Das, Maiteyi, and Vivek Maru. 2009. Framing Local Justice in Bangladesh. Washington, DC: World Bank. Accessed 20 March 2013. http://web.worldbank.org/WBSITE/EXTERNAL/TOPICS/EXTLAWJUSTINST/0,,contentMDK:20813070~pagePK:210058~piPK:210062~theSitePK:1974062,00.html.

den Otter, Sandra. 2007. '"A Legislating Empire": Victorian Political Theorists, Codes of Law, and Empire'. In *Victorian Visions of Global Order: Empire and International Relations in Nineteenth-Century Political Thought*, edited by Duncan Bell, 89–112. Cambridge: Cambridge University Press.

Desai, Deval, and Michael Woolcock. 2015. 'Experimental Justice Reform: Justice for the Poor—Lessons from the World Bank and Beyond'. *Annual Review of Law and Social Science*, 11: 155–74.

Desrosières, Alain. 2015. 'Retroaction: How Indicators Feed Back onto Quantified Actors'. In *The World of Indicators: The Making of Governmental Knowledge through Quantification*, edited by Richard Rottenburg, Sally E. Merry, Sung-Joon Park, and Johanna Mugler. Cambridge: Cambridge University Press.

Devine, Joe, and Sarah White. 2009. 'Religion, Politics and the Everyday Moral Order in Bangladesh'. *Religions and Development Research Programme*, Working Paper, no. 40.

Dezalay, Yves, and Bryant G. Garth, eds. 2002a. *Global Prescriptions: The Production, Exportation, and Importation of a New Legal Orthodoxy*. Ann Arbor: University of Michigan Press.

Dezalay, Yves, and Bryant G. Garth. 2002b. 'Introduction'. In *Global Prescriptions: The Production, Exportation, and Importation of a New Legal Orthodoxy*, edited by Yves Dezalay and Bryant G. Garth. Ann Arbor: University of Michigan Press.

DiMaggio, Paul, and Walter W. Powell. 1983. 'The Iron Cage Revisited: Institutional Isomorphism and Collective Rationality in Organizational Fields'. *American Sociological Review*, 48 2: 147–60.

Draude, Anke, and Sonja Neuweiler. 2010. 'Die Herausforderung lokaler Vielfalt jenseits der westlichen Welt Governance in der postkolonialen Kritik'. SFB-Governance Working Paper Series, no. 24.

Drèze, Jean, and Amartya Sen. 2013. *An Uncertain Glory: India and Its Contradictions*. Princeton, NJ: Princeton University Press.

Dworkin, Ronald. 1986. *Law's Empire*. Oxford: Hart Publishing.

Eckert, Julia. 2009. 'Rechtsaneignung: Paradoxien von Pluralisierung und Entpluralisierung in rechtpluralen Situationen'. In *Normative Pluralität ordnen: Rechtsbegriffe, Normenkollisionen und Rule of Law in Kontexten dies—und jenseits des Staates*, edited by Matthias Kötter and Gunnar F. Schuppert. Baden-Baden: Nomos.

Eckert, Julia, Brian Donahoe, and Christian Strümpell, eds. 2012. *Law against the State: Ethnographic Forays into Law's Transformations*. Cambridge: Cambridge University Press.

Ehm, Frithjof. 2010. 'The Rule of Law: Concept, Guiding Principle, and Framework'. Trieste, 2010. Accessed 27 March 2017. http://www.venice.coe.int/webforms/documents/default.aspx?pdffile=CDL-UDT(2010)011-e.

Ehrlich, Eugen. 1986. *Gesetz und lebendes Recht: Vermischte kleinere Schriften*. Berlin: Duncker and Humblot.

Ehrlich, Eugen. 2002. *Fundamental Principles of the Sociology of Law*. New Brunswick, NJ: Transaction Publishers.

ESDO. 2012. *Annual Report: Activating the Village Courts in Bangladesh Project*. Dhaka: ESDO.

Espeland, Wendy. 2015. 'Narrating Numbers'. In *The World of Indicators: The Making of Governmental Knowledge through Quantification*, edited by Richard Rottenburg, Sally E. Merry, Sung-Joon Park, and Johanna Mugler. Cambridge: Cambridge University Press.

Faaland, Just, and John R. Parkinson. 1976. *Bangladesh: The Test Case of Development*. London: C. Hurst.

Finnemore, Martha, and Kathryn Sikkink. 1998. 'International Norm Dynamics and Political Change'. *International Organization*, 52 4: 887–917.

Forst, Rainer. 1999. 'The Basic Right to Justification: Towards a Constructivist Conception of Human Rights'. *Constellations*, 6 1: 35–60.

Forst, Rainer. 2013. 'Zum Begriff eines Rechtfertigungsnarrativs'. Normative Orders Working Paper Series, no. 03.

Forst, Rainer, and Klaus Günter. 2011. 'Die Herausbildung normativer Ordnungen: Zur Idee eines interdisziplinären Forschungsprogramms'. In *Die Herausbildung normativer Ordnungen: Interdisziplinäre Perspektiven*, edited by Rainer Forst. Frankfurt am Main: Campus.

Freeden, Michael. 1998. *Ideologies and Political Theory*. Oxford: Oxford University Press.

Freeden, Michael. 2008. 'Thinking Politically and Thinking about Politics: Language, Interpretation, and Ideology'. In *Political Theory: Methods and Approaches*, edited by David Leopold and Marc Stears. Oxford: Oxford University Press.

Freeman, Richard. 2009. 'What Is "Translation"?' *Evidence and Policy*, 5 4: 429–47.

Fung, Archon. 2004. *Empowered Participation: Reinventing Urban Democracy*. Princeton, NJ: Princeton University Press.

Galanter, Marc. 1989. *Law and Society in Modern India*. Delhi: Oxford University Press.

Gimenez, Lea, Faizuddin Ahmed, Iffath Sharif, and Dean Jolliffe. 2013. Bangladesh—Poverty Assessment: Assessing a Decade of Progress in Reducing Poverty, 2000–2010. Washington, DC: World Bank. Accessed 6 December 2013. http://documents.worldbank.org/curated/en/2013/06/17886000/bangladesh-poverty-assessment-assessing-decade-progress-reducing-poverty-2000-2010.

Giunchi, Elisa. 2010. 'The Reinvention of Sharīʿa under the British Raj: In Search of Authenticity and Certainty'. *Journal of Asian Studies*, 69 4: 1119–42.

Golub, Stephen. 2003. Non-State Justice Systems in Bangladesh and the Philippines: Paper prepared for the United Kingdom Department for International Development. http://www.gsdrc.org/docs/open/DS34.pdf.

Golub, Stephen. 2012. 'The Political Economy of Improving Traditional Justice Systems: A Case Study of NGO Engagement with Shalish in Bangladesh'. In *The World*

Bank Legal Review, edited by Hassane Cisse, Sam Muller, Chantal Thomas, and Wang Chenguang. Washington, DC: World Bank.

Günter, Klaus, and Shalini Randeria. 2001. *Recht, Kultur und Gesellschaft im Prozeß der Globalisierung*. Bad Homburg: Werner Reimers Stiftung.

Gupta, Akhil. 1995. 'Blurred Boundaries: The Discourse of Corruption, the Culture of Politics, and the Imagined State'. *American Ethnologist*, 22 2: 375–402.

Gupta, Akhil. 2012. *Red Tape: Bureaucracy, Structural Violence, and Poverty in India*. Durham, NC: Duke University Press.

Gupta, Akhil. 2013. 'Messy Bureaucracies: Comment on Hull, Matthew. 2012. Government of Paper: The Materiality of Bureaucracy in Urban Pakistan. Berkeley: University of California Press'. *HAU: Journal of Ethnographic Theory*, 3 435–40.

Habermas, Jürgen. 1987. *The Theory of Communicative Action, Vol. II: Lifeworld and System: The Critique of Functionalist Reason*. Cambridge: Polity.

Habermas, Jürgen. 1998. *Faktizität und Geltung: Beiträge zur Diskurstheorie des Rechts und des demokratischen Rechtsstaats*. Frankfurt am Main: Suhrkamp.

Habermas, Jürgen. 2010. 'The Concept of Human Dignity and the Realistic Utopia of Human Rights'. *Metaphilosophy*, 41 4: 464–80.

Hajer, Maarten A. 2009. *Authoritative Governance: Policy-Making in the Age of Mediatization*. Oxford: Oxford University Press.

Hall, Stuart. 1992. 'The West and the Rest. Discourse and Power'. In *Formations of Modernity*, edited by Stuart Hall and Bram Gieben, 185–225. Cambridge: Polity Press in association with the Open University.

Hallaq, Wael B. 2005. *Authority, Continuity, and Change in Islamic Law*. Cambridge: Cambridge University Press.

Hallaq, Wael B. 2009. *An Introduction to Islamic Law*. Cambridge: Cambridge University Press.

Hansen, Hans K., and Tony Porter. 2012. 'What Do Numbers Do in Transnational Governance?' *International Political Sociology*, 6 4: 409–26.

Hertel, Shareen. 2006. *Unexpected Power: Conflict and Change among Transnational Activists*. Ithaca, NY: Cornell University Press.

Hobhouse, Charles E. 1908. Report of the Royal Commission upon Decentralization in India. Volume I: Document type: Command Papers; Reports of Commissioners/ Collection name. London: printed by Darling and Son for His Majesty's Stationery Office.

Hoffman, Eva. 2008. *Lost in Translation: A Life in a New Language*. London: Vintage.

Holzscheiter, Anna. 2005. 'Discourse as Capability: Non-State Actors' Capital in Global Governance'. *Millennium: Journal of International Studies*, 33 3: 723–46.

Hopf, Ted. 2010. 'The Logic of Habit in International Relations'. *European Journal of International Relations*, 16 4: 539–61.

Hossain, Ishtiaq, and Mahmud H. Khan. 2006. 'The Rift within an Imagined Community: Understanding Nationalism(s) in Bangladesh'. *Asian Journal of Social Science*, 34 2: 324–39.

Hossain, Sabbir. 2015. 'Restorative Justice: An Old Mechanism with a New Holistic Approach'. *Bangladesh Law Digest*, August.

Hull, Matthew S. 2012a. 'Documents and Bureaucracy'. *Annual Review of Anthropology*, 41 1: 251–67.

Hull, Matthew S. 2012b. *Government of Paper: The Materiality of Bureaucracy in Urban Pakistan*. Berkeley: University of California Press.

Human Rights Watch. 2012. 'Bangladesh: Discriminatory Family Laws Fuel Female Poverty'. Accessed 8 June 2016. http://www.hrw.org/news/2012/09/16/bangladesh-discriminatory-family-laws-fuel-female-poverty.

Human Rights Watch. 2016. 'Bangladesh: Halt Mass Arbitrary Arrests'. Accessed 14 December 2016. https://www.hrw.org/news/2016/06/17/bangladesh-halt-mass-arbitrary-arrests.

Humphreys, Stephen. 2010. *Theatre of the Rule of Law: Transnational Legal Intervention in Theory and Practice*. Cambridge: Cambridge University Press.

Huntington, Samuel P. 1993. 'The Clash of Civilizations?' Foreign Affairs, Summer.

Hurd, Elizabeth S. 2015. *Beyond Religious Freedom: The New Global Politics of Religion*. Princeton, NJ: Princeton University Press.

Hurd, Ian. 1999. 'Legitimacy and Authority in International Politics'. *International Organization*, 53 2: 379–408.

Hurrell, Andrew. 2003. 'Norms and Ethics in International Relations'. In *Handbook of International Relations*, edited by Walter Carlsnaes, Thomas Risse, and Beth A. Simmons. London: SAGE Publications.

International Crisis Group. 2016. 'Political Conflict, Extremism and Criminal Justice in Bangladesh'. Brussels: ICG.

Islam, Nurul. 2005. *Making of a Nation—Bangladesh: An Economist's Tale*. Dhaka: University Press.

Islam, Zahidul. 2012. 'Gender, Power, and Justice: An Ethnographic Study of a Union Parishad-Led Arbitration Council in Rural Bangladesh'. PhD dissertation submitted at Jawaharlal Nehru University.

Jahan, Ferdous. 2010. Results-Oriented Monitoring Report. On file with the author.

Jahan, Ferdous, and Asif M. Shahan. 2009. 'Access to Justice for the Poor in Bangladesh: Conflict between Western Model and Eastern Culture'. *Journal of Law and Development*, 1 1: 1–29.

Jahan, Ferdous, and Adam Stapleton. 2013. Mid-Term Review Activating the Village Courts in Bangladesh. Accessed 14 November 2013. http://www.undp.org/content/dam/undp/documents/projects/BGD/Final%20AVCB%20MTR%20Report.doc.

Jetschke, Anja, and Andrea Liese. 2013. 'The Power of Human Rights a Decade After: From Euphoria to Contestation'. In *The Persistent Power of Human Rights: From Commitment to Compliance*, edited by Thomas Risse, Stephen C. Ropp, and Kathryn Sikkink. Cambridge: Cambridge University Press.

Kabeer, Naila. 2003. 'Making Rights Work for the Poor: Nijera Kori and the Construction of "Collective Capabilities" in Rural Bangladesh'. IDS Working Paper, no. 200.

Kabeer, Rokeya R. 1965. Administrative Policy of the Government of Bengal (1870–1890). Dacca: National Institute of Public Administration.

Kafka, Ben. 2009. 'Paperwork: The State of the Discipline'. Book History, 12 1: 340–53.

Karim, Lamia. 2011. *Microfinance and Its Discontents: Women in Debt in Bangladesh*. Minneapolis: University of Minnesota Press.

Kaviraj, Sudipta. 2005. 'An Outline of a Revisionist Theory of Modernity'. *European Journal of Sociology*, 46 03: 497–526.

Kaviraj, Sudipta. 2009. 'Marxism in Translation: Critical Reflections on Indian Radical Thought'. In *Political Judgement: Essays for John Dunn*, edited by Richard Bourke, Raymond Geuss, and John Dunn, 172–201. Cambridge: Cambridge University Press.

Keck, Margaret E., and Kathryn Sikkink. 1998. *Activists beyond Borders: Advocacy Networks in International Politics*. Ithaca, NY: Cornell University Press.

Khair, Sumaiya. 2008. *Legal Empowerment for the Poor and Disadvantaged: Strategies Achievements and Challenges: Experiences from Bangladesh*. Dhaka: Colorline.

Khan, Borhan U., and Mahbubur M. Rahman. 2009. 'Local Government Level Restorative Adjudication: An Alternative Model of Justice for Children in Bangladesh'. *Commonwealth Journal of Local Governance*, 4: 26–45.

Khan, Mushtaq. 2013. 'Aid and Governance in Vulnerable States Bangladesh and Pakistan since 1971'. WIDER Working Paper, November, 122: 1–25.

Kötter, Matthias. 2012. 'Non-State Justice Institutions: A Matter of Fact and a Matter of Legislation'. SFB-Governance Working Paper Series, 43.

Krämer, Gudrun, and Sabine Schmidtke. 2006. 'Introduction: Religious Authority and Religious Authorities in Muslim Societies. A Critical Overview'. In *Speaking for Islam: Religious Authorities in Muslim Societies*, edited by Gudrun Krämer and Sabine Schmidtke, 1–14. Leiden: Brill.

Krook, Mona L., and Jacqui True. 2012. 'Rethinking the Life Cycles of International Norms: The United Nations and the Global Promotion of Gender Equality'. *European Journal of International Relations*, 18 1: 103–27.

Laborde, Cécile. 2008. *Critical Republicanism: The Hijab Controversy and Political Philosophy*. Oxford: Oxford University Press.

Latour, Bruno. 1987. *Science in Action: How to Follow Scientists and Engineers through Society*. Cambridge, MA: Harvard University Press.

Latour, Bruno. 2005. *Reassembling the Social: An Introduction to Actor-Network-Theory*. Oxford: Oxford University Press.

Lendvai, Noemi, and Paul Stubbs. 2007. 'Policies as Translation: Situating Trans-National Social Policies'. In *Policy Reconsidered: Meanings, Politics and Practices*, edited by Susan Hodgson and Zoë Irving, 173–89. Bristol: Policy Press.

Levinge, Edward V. 1914. Report of the Bengal District Administration Committee. Calcutta: Bengal Secretariat Press.

Lewis, Bernard. 2003. What Went Wrong? The Clash between Islam and Modernity in the Middle East. New York: Perennial.

Lewis, David. 2004. 'On the Difficulty of Studying Civil Society: Reflections on NGOs, State and Democracy in Bangladesh'. *Contributions to Indian Sociology*, 38 3: 299–322.

Lewis, David. 2011. *Bangladesh: Politics, Economics, and Civil Society*. Cambridge: Cambridge University Press.

Lewis, David, and Abul Hossain. 2008a. 'A Tale of Three Villages'. *Journal of South Asian Development*, 3 1: 33–51.

Lewis, David, and Abul Hossain. 2008b. *Understanding the Local Power Structure in Rural Bangladesh*. Stockholm: Sida.

Lutz, Ellen L., and Kathryn Sikkink. 2000. 'International Human Rights Law and Practice in Latin America'. *International Organization*, 54 3: 633–59.

Madaripur Legal Aid Association. 2011. Annual Activity Report 2009/10. Madaripur: Barnamala Chhpaghar.

Mamdani, Mahmood. 1996. *Citizen and Subject: Contemporary Africa and the Legacy of Late Colonialism*. Princeton, NJ: Princeton University Press.

Mamdani, Mahmood. 2001. 'Beyond Settler and Native as Political Identities: Overcoming the Political Legacy of Colonialism'. *Comparative Studies in Society and History*, 43 4: 651–64.

Marcus, George E. 1995. 'Ethnography in/of the World System: The Emergence of Multi-Sited Ethnography'. *Annual Review of Anthropology*, 24 1: 95–117.

Mathur, Nayanika. 2015. *Paper Tiger: Law, Bureaucracy and the Developmental State in Himalayan India*. Cambridge: Cambridge University Press.

Menski, Werner. 2006. *Comparative Law in a Global Context: The Legal Systems of Asia and Africa*. New York: Cambridge University Press.

Menski, Werner. 2015. 'Bangladesh in 2015'. *Journal of Law and Policy*, 1 1: 9–32.

Mernissi, Fatima. 1996. *The Veil and the Male Elite: A Feminist Interpretation of Women's Rights in Islam*. Reading, MA: Addison-Wesley.

Merry, Sally E. 2006. *Human Rights and Gender Violence: Translating International Law into Local Justice*. Chicago: University of Chicago Press.

Metcalf, Barbara D. 2002. *Islamic Revival in British India: Deoband, 1860–1900*. New Delhi: Oxford University Press.

Meyer, John W., John Boli, George M. Thomas, and Francisco O. Ramirez. 1997. 'World Society and the Nation-State'. *American Journal of Sociology*, 103 1: 144–81.

Mikhail, Ashraf. 2007. 'Legal Aid: Context—Social, Political, Economic Background'. Accessed 20 February 2017. http://dihr.org/legalaid/index.php?option=com_content&task=view&id=16&Itemid=34.

Mitchell, Timothy. 2002. *Rule of Experts: Egypt, Techno-Politics, Modernity*. Berkeley: University of California Press.

Monsoor, Taslima. 1998. 'In Search for Security and Poverty Alleviation: Women's Inheritable Entitlements to Land, the Untapped Resources'. *Bangladesh Journal of International Affairs*, 4 2: 42–56.

Mookherjee, Nayanika. 2015. *The Spectral Wound: Sexual Violence, Public Memories and the Bangladesh War of 1971*. Durham, NC: Duke University Press.

Mosse, David. 2005. *Cultivating Development: An Ethnography of Aid Policy and Practice*. London: Pluto Press.

Mosse, David. 2011. *Adventures in Aidland: The Anthropology of Professionals in International Development*. New York: Berghahn Books.

Mosse, David. 2013. 'The Anthropology of International Development'. *Annual Review of Anthropology*, 42 1: 227–46.

Murshed, Mahboob. 2012. *Review Report on Village Courts Legal Framework*. Dhaka: UNDP.

Mustafa, Sabir. 2013. 'Hefazat-e Islam: Islamist Coalition'. Accessed 9 June 2016. http://www.bbc.co.uk/news/world-asia-22424708.

Nader, Laura. 1990. *Harmony Ideology: Justice and Control in a Zapotec Mountain Village*. Stanford, CA: Stanford University Press.

Nader, Laura. 2002. *The Life of the Law: Anthropological Projects*. Berkeley: University of California Press.

Nandy, Ashis. 2002. *Time Warps: Silent and Evasive Pasts in Indian Politics and Religion*. Delhi: Permanent Black.

Nelson, Matthew J. 2007. 'Who Speaks for Islam? "Authenticity" and the Interpretation of Islamic Law in America's War on Terror'. *Australian Journal of International Affairs*, 61 2: 247–66.

Nelson, Matthew J. 2011. *In the Shadow of Shari'ah: Islam, Islamic Law, and Democracy in Pakistan*. London: C Hurst and Columbia University Press.

Nelson, Matthew J. 2012. 'Inheritance Unbound: The Politics of Personal Law Reform in Pakistan and India'. In *Comparative Constitutionalism in South Asia*, edited by Sunil Khilnani, Vikram Raghavan, and Arun K. Thiruvengadam, 219–46. Delhi: Oxford University Press.

Neumann, Iver B. 2012. *At Home with the Diplomats: Inside a European Foreign Ministry*. Ithaca, NY: Cornell University Press.

Nicolaidis, Kalypso, Berny Sèbe, and Gabrielle Maas, eds. 2014. *Echoes of Empire: Memory, Identity and Colonial Legacies*. London: I.B. Tauris.

Niezen, Ronald, and Maria Sapignoli, eds. 2017. *Palaces of Hope: The Anthropology of International Organizations. Cambridge*: Cambridge University Press.

Onar, Nora F., and Kalypso Nicolaidis. 2013. 'The Decentring Agenda: Europe as a Post-Colonial Power'. *Cooperation and Conflict*, 48 2: 283–303.

Peerenboom, Randall P. 2004. 'Varieties of the Rule of Law: An Introduction and Provisional Conclusion'. In *Asian Discourses of Rule of Law*, edited by Randall P. Peerenboom. London: Routledge Curzon.

Pereira, Faustina. 2013. 'Legal Empowerment and the Rule of Law in Bangladesh'. Accessed 4 December 2016. http://skollworldforum.org/2013/08/13/legal-empowerment-and-the-rule-of-law-in-bangladesh/.

Porter, Theodore M. 1995. *Trust in Numbers: In Pursuit of Objectivity in Science and Public Life*. Princeton, NJ: Princeton University.

Pouliot, Vincent. 2008. 'The Logic of Practicality: A Theory of Practice of Security Communities'. *International Organization*, 62 2.

Raghavan, Srinath. 2013. *1971: A Global History of the Creation of Bangladesh*. Cambridge, MA: Harvard University Press.

Rahamāna, Matiura. 2010. Baseline Survey Report on Village Courts in Bangladesh. [Dhaka]: Activating Village Courts in Bangladesh Project, Local Government Division, Ministry of Local Government, Rural Development and Cooperatives, Government of the People's Republic of Bangladesh.

Rahman, Mahbubar M., and Willem van Schendel. 1997. 'Gender and the Inheritance of Land'. In *Bangladesh in the 1990s: Selected Studies*, edited by Willem van Schendel, and Kirsten Westergaard. Dhaka: University Press.

Randeria, Shalini. 2000. 'Geteilte Geschichte und verwobene Moderne'. In *Zukunftsentwürfe: Ideen für eine Kultur der Veränderung*, edited by Jörn Rüsen, Hanna Leitgeb, Norbert Jegelka, and Chingiz Aĭtmatov. Frankfurt am Main: Campus.

Randeria, Shalini. 2002. 'Entangled Histories of Uneven Modernities: Civil Society, Caste Solidarities and Legal Pluralism in Post-Colonial India'. In *Unraveling Ties: From Social Cohesion to New Practices of Connectedness*, edited by Yehuda Elkana,

Ivan Krastev, Elisio Macamo, and Shalini Randeria, 284–311. Frankfurt am Main: Campus Verlag.

Randeria, Shalini. 2003. 'Cunning States and Unaccountable International Institutions: Legal Plurality, Social Movements and Rights of Local Communities to Common Property Resources'. *European Journal of Sociology/Archives Européennes de Sociologie*, 44 1: 27–60.

Rao, Rahul. 2010. *Third World Protest: Between Home and the World*. Oxford: Oxford University Press.

Rawls, John. 1985. 'Justice as Fairness: Political not Metaphysical'. *Philosophy and Public Affairs*, 14 3: 223–51.

Raz, Joseph. 2009. *The Authority of Law: Essays on Law and Morality*, 2nd ed. Oxford: Oxford University Press.

Reckwitz, A. 2002. 'Toward a Theory of Social Practices: A Development in Culturalist Theorizing'. *European Journal of Social Theory*, 5 2: 243–63.

Riaz, Ali. 2003. '"God Willing": The Politics and Ideology of Islamism in Bangladesh'. *Comparative Studies of South Asia, Africa and the Middle East*, 23 1/2: 301–20.

Riaz, Ali. 2005. 'Traditional Institutions as Tools of Political Islam in Bangladesh'. *Journal of Asian and African Studies*, 40 3: 171–96.

Riaz, Ali. 2008. *Faithful Education: Madrassahs in South Asia*. New Brunswick, NJ: Rutgers University Press.

Ricœur, Paul. 1976. *Interpretation Theory: Discourse and the Surplus of Meaning*. Fort Worth: Texas Christian University Press.

Ricœur, Paul. 2006. *On Translation*. London: Routledge.

Riles, Annelise, ed. 2006. *Documents: Artifacts of Modern Knowledge*. Ann Arbor: University of Michigan Press.

Risse, Thomas. 2000. '"Let's Argue!": Communicative Action in World Politics'. *International Organization*, 54 1: 1–39.

Risse, Thomas, ed. 2013. *Governance without a State? Policies and Politics in Areas of Limited Statehood*. New York: Columbia University Press.

Risse, Thomas, and Stephen C. Ropp. 2013. 'Introduction and Overview'. In *The Persistent Power of Human Rights: From Commitment to Compliance*, edited by Thomas Risse, Stephen C. Ropp, and Kathryn Sikkink. Cambridge: Cambridge University Press.

Risse, Thomas, Stephen C. Ropp, and Kathryn Sikkink, eds. 1999. *The Power of Human Rights: International Norms and Domestic Change*. Cambridge: Cambridge University Press.

Risse, Thomas, Stephen C. Ropp, and Kathryn Sikkink, eds. 2013. *The Persistent Power of Human Rights: From Commitment to Compliance*. Cambridge: Cambridge University Press.

Risse-Kappen, Thomas. 1994. 'Ideas Do Not Float Freely: Transnational Coalitions, Domestic Structures, and the End of the Cold War'. International Organization, 48 2: 185–214.

Rottenburg, Richard. 2014. 'Experimental Engagements and Metacodes'. *Common Knowledge*, 20 3: 540–8.

Said, Edward W. 1978. *Orientalism*. New York: Vintage Books.

Saikia, Yasmin. 2011. Women, War, and the Making of Bangladesh: Remembering 1971. Durham, NC: Duke University Press.

Salomon, Noah. 2011. 'The Ruse of Law: Legal Equality and the Problem of Citizenship in a Multireligious Sudan'. In *After Secular Law*, edited by Winnifred F. Sullivan, Robert A. Yelle, and Mateo Taussig-Rubbo. Stanford, CA: Stanford University Press.

Sarma, P.K., and J.U. Ahmed. 2011. 'An Economic Study of a Small Scale Cattle Fattening Enterprise of Rajbari District'. *Journal of Bangladesh Agricultural University*, 9 1: 141–6.

Schaefer, Saskia. 2015. 'Renegotiating Indonesian Secularism through Debates on Ahmadiyya and Shia'. *Philosophy and Social Criticism*, 41 4–5: 497–508.

Schatz, Edward, ed. 2009. *Political Ethnography: What Immersion Contributes to the Study of Power*. Chicago: University of Chicago Press.

Schensul, Stephen L., Jean J. Schensul, and Margaret D. LeCompte. 1999. *Essential Ethnographic Methods: Observations, Interviews, and Questionnaires*. Walnut Creek, CA: AltaMira Press.

Schuppert, Gunnar F. 2009. 'Zum Umgang mit Unterschiedlichen Konzeptualisierungen der Rule of Law'. In *Normative Pluralität ordnen: Rechtsbegriffe, Normenkollisionen und Rule of Law in Kontexten dies—und jenseits des Staates*, edited by Matthias Kötter and Gunnar F. Schuppert. Baden-Baden: Nomos.

Scott, James C. 1985. *Weapons of the Weak: Everyday Forms of Peasant Resistance*. New Haven, CT: Yale University Press.

Sezgin, Yüksel, and Mirjam Künkler. 2014. 'Regulation of "Religion" and the "Religious": The Politics of Judicialization and Bureaucratization in India and Indonesia'. *Comparative Studies in Society and History*, 56 2: 448–78.

Shehabuddin, Elora. 2008. *Reshaping the Holy: Democracy, Development, and Muslim Women in Bangladesh*. New York: Columbia University Press.

Siddiqi, Dina M. 2003. 'Paving the Way to Justice: The Experience of Nagorik Uddyog'. Accessed 26 March 2017. https://namati.org/resources/paving-the-way-to-justice-the-experience-of-nagorik-uddyog/.

Siddiqi, Dina M. 2011a. 'Crime and Punishment: Laws of Seduction, Consent, and Rape in Bangladesh'. *Social Difference Online*, 1 December 2011: 46–54.

Siddiqi, Dina M. 2011b. 'Islam, Gender, and the Nation: The Social Life of Bangladeshi Fatwas'. In *Communalism and Globalization in South Asia and Its Diaspora*, edited by Deana Heath and Chandana Mathur, 181–203. London: Routledge.

Siddiqi, Dina M. 2011c. 'Sexuality, Rights, and Personhood: Tensions in a Transnational World'. *BMC International Health and Human Rights*, 11 3.

Siddiqi, Dina M. 2011d. 'Transnational Feminism and "Local" Realities: The Imperiled Muslim Woman and the Production of (In)Justice'. *Hawwa*, 9 1: 76–96.

Siddiqi, Dina M. 2013. 'Left behind by the Nation: "Stranded Pakistanis" in Bangladesh'. *SITES: New Series*, 10 2: 150–83.

Simmons, Beth A. 2009. *Mobilizing for Human Rights: International Law in Domestic Politics*. Cambridge: Cambridge University Press.

Tamanaha, Brian Z., Caroline M. Sage, and Woolcock, Michael J.V, eds. 2012. *Legal Pluralism and Development: Scholars and Practitioners in Dialogue*. New York: Cambridge University Press.

Taylor, Charles. 1997. *Philosophical Arguments*. Cambridge, MA: Harvard University Press.

Transparency International. 2012. 'Overview of Corruption within the Justice Sector and Law Enforcement Agencies in Bangladesh'. http://www.transparency.org/whatwedo/answer/overview_of_corruption_within_the_justice_sector_and_law_enforcement_agenci.

Tripp, Charles. 2006. *Islam and the Moral Economy: The Challenge of Capitalism*. Cambridge: Cambridge University Press.

Trubek, David M., and Marc Galanter. 1974. 'Scholars in Self-Estrangement: Some Reflections on the Crisis in Law and Development'. *Wisconsin Law Review*: 1062–101.

Tsing, Anna L. 1997. 'Transitions as Translations'. In Transitions, Environments, Translations: Feminism and International Politics, edited by Joan W. Scott, Cora Kaplan, Debra Keates, 253–72. New York: Routledge.

Tsing, Anna L. 2005. *Friction: An Ethnography of Global Connection*. Princeton, NJ: Princeton University Press.

Turner, Terence. 1993. 'Anthropology and Multiculturalism: What Is Anthropology that Multiculturalists Should Be Mindful of It?' *Cultural Anthropology*, 8 4: 411–29.

UNDP. 2008. *Project Document AVCB*. Dhaka: UNDP.

UNDP. 2013. Millennium Development Goals: Bangladesh Progress Report 2012. Accessed 4 December 2013. http://www.bd.undp.org/content/dam/bangladesh/docs/MDG/MDG%20Report%202012.pdf.

UNDP. 2014. 'Democratic Governance Cluster: Annual Results Reporting 2014'. Accessed 19 October 2016. http://www.undp.org/content/dam/bangladesh/docs/Projects/JUST/JUST%20RR%202014%20final.pdf.

UNDP, UNICEF, and UN Women. 2013. 'Informal Justice Mechanisms: Charting a Course of Human Rights-Based Engagement'. http://www.undp.org/content/dam/undp/library/Democratic%20Governance/Access%20to%20Justice%20and%20Rule%20of%20Law/Informal-Justice-Systems-Charting-a-Course-for-Human-Rights-Based-Engagement.pdf.

van Schendel, Willem. 2009. *A History of Bangladesh*. Cambridge: Cambridge University Press.

Vismann, Cornelia. 2008. *Files: Law and Media Technology*. Stanford, CA: Stanford University Press.

Weber, Max. 1978. *Economy and Society*. Berkeley: University of California Press.

White, Sarah. 1999. 'NGOs, Civil Society, and the State in Bangladesh: The Politics of Representing the Poor'. *Development and Change*, 30: 307–26.

White, Sarah. 2010. 'Domains of Contestation: Women's Empowerment and Islam in Bangladesh'. *Women's Studies International Forum*, 33 4: 334–44.

White, Sarah. 2012. 'Beyond the Paradox: Religion, Family and Modernity in Contemporary Bangladesh'. *Modern Asian Studies*, 46 5: 1429–58.

White, Sarah. 2013. 'Patriarchal Investments: Marriage, Dowry and Economic Change in Rural Bangladesh'. *Bath Papers in International Development*, 9.

Williams, David, and Tom Young. 1994. 'Governance, the World Bank and Liberal Theory'. *Political Studies*, 42 1: 84–100.

Wittgenstein, Ludwig. 1984. *Werkausgabe in acht Bänden—Band 1: Philosophische Untersuchungen*. Frankfurt am Main: Suhrkamp.

Wittgenstein, Ludwig. 1986. *Philosophical Investigations*. Oxford: Basil Blackwell.

Zürn, Michael, Martin Binder, and Matthias Ecker-Ehrhardt. 2012a. 'International Authority and Its Politicization'. *International Theory*, 4 1: 69–106.

Zürn, Michael, Andre Nollkaemper, and Randall P. Peerenboom, eds. 2012b. *Rule of Law Dynamics in an Era of International and Transnational Governance*. Cambridge: Cambridge University Press.

Index

The manufacturer's authorised representative in the EU for product safety is Oxford University Press España S.A. of el Parque Empresarial San Fernando de Henares, Avenida de Castilla, 2 – 28830 Madrid (www.oup.es/en or product.safety@oup.com). OUP España S.A. also acts as importer into Spain of products made by the manufacturer.

www.ingramcontent.com/pod-product-compliance
Lightning Source LLC
LaVergne TN
LVHW011802200926
848484LV00003B/764

* 9 7 8 0 1 9 8 8 0 7 8 6 5 *